STUDY GUIDE

for use with

MACROECONOMICS

Fourth Edition

David N. Hyman

Prepared by

Donald P. Maxwell
University of Central Oklahoma

IRWIN

Chicago • Bogotá • Boston • Buenos Aires • Caracas
London • Madrid • Mexico City • Sydney • Toronto

©Richard D. Irwin, a Times Mirror Higher Education Group, Inc. company, 1989, 1992, 1994, and 1997

Printed in the United States of America.

ISBN 0-256-16158-5

1 2 3 4 5 6 7 8 9 0 P 3 2 1 0 9 8 7 6

TO THE STUDENT

The *Study Guide* to accompany Hyman, *Economics* is designed as a set of interactive modules covering the key concepts developed in the textbook chapters and appendices. These modules will help you understand and apply the concepts you need to know. The *Study Guide* is based on my experiences teaching university economics for two decades.

Changes for the fourth edition of the *Study Guide* include new current events items with questions and answers and revisions consistent with the fourth edition of Hyman's *Economics*. The basic pedagogical organization of the *Study Guide* is unchanged.

Each chapter of the *Study Guide* begins with **Chapter Concepts**, which gives you the important learning objectives of the corresponding textbook chapter. This is followed by **The Chapter in Brief**, which asks you to complete the summary, and in doing so review key concepts. **The Key Terms Review** that follows is a fill-in exercise that will reinforce your understanding of the key terms in David Hyman's *Economics* glossary. Next comes a set of problems and exercises, **Concept Review,** selected to reinforce the main learning objectives of the chapter. These questions are presented in the same order as the concepts appear in the textbook. Each block of questions in the Concept Review section is subtitled and numbered according to the learning concept to which it applies, so that you can concentrate on areas that require extra study. These problems and exercises involve graphing, filling in tables, completing sentences, matching, listing, and discussion. For many chapters, advanced questions are included in the **Advanced Application** section at the end of the Concept Review. These offer additional challenges and the opportunity to apply more advanced analysis, such as algebraic analysis, to certain problems.

After the Concept Review, a mini-test of multiple choice questions, like those you will encounter on exams, is included in Mastery Test. These questions will give you feedback to determine how well you have mastered the important concepts of the chapter. The self-test is followed by Think it Through, a section of discussion questions that ask you to apply the concepts of the chapter to issues and problems. Following this discussion section, selected chapters of the *Study Guide* include **Analyzing the News**. This exercise asks you to read a recent news article or current events item and answer discussion questions. At the end of each chapter or appendix is an answer key. **Chapter Answers** include answers to all sections of the study guide, including discussion questions, so that you can check you progress.

In using the *Study Guide*, I suggest the student first read the textbook chapter, paying particular attention to the introductory statement of learning objectives for the chapter and the concept checks that appear throughout the chapter. Next, complete the fill-in summary section of the *Study Guide*. Go back to the textbook and read and study the section for the parts of the summary that you answered incorrectly. Answer the Key Terms exercise next, after you review the glossary terms in the margins of the text chapter.

The problems and exercises in the Concept Review correspond closely to the examples used by David Hyman in the textbook. Try to answer the questions in the Concept Review and go back to the text for additional study if you have difficulty understanding how to answer a question. You can use the answer key for help, but you will get the most benefit by first studying the text and then working the problems in the *Study Guide*, rather than by going directly to the answer key.

After completing the Concept Review, take the self-test of multiple choice questions and compare your answers to those in the answer key to see where you need to spend additional study time.

Review the concepts in the text and the Study Guide that you have not yet mastered. Now try to answer the discussion questions from the Think it Through and Analyzing the News sections. Read the answers to the discussion questions in the answer section. If there are discussion questions in the answer section that you do not understand, go back to the corresponding sections of the text and Study Guide for additional study.

ACKNOWLEDGMENTS

I would like to thank the editors and staff at Richard D. Irwin, Inc. for providing support throughout the preparation of the fourth edition. I would like to thank David Hyman for making this possible. Finally, thanks to the staff of the Production Department for bringing the *Study Guide* to you.

Don Maxwell
University of Central Oklahoma

CONTENTS

PART I

INTRODUCTION TO ECONOMICS

■ **PART EXERCISE**

Inside Information: *Statistical Abstract of the United States*

In chapters 1 and 2 you will learn about marginal analysis and opportunity cost. Your choice to attend a university involves a comparison of the extra benefits and costs of obtaining a degree. In addition to the cost of tuition and books, a major cost of your education is the income that you sacrifice while being a full-time student.

Suppose the extra benefit (increased future income) from attending your university another year is $50,000. Tuition, books, and other expenses are $10,000 per year. Use the earnings and income data in the *Statistical Abstract of the United States* to get average or median annual earnings which can be used as a measure of the sacrificed income during the year. Be sure to note the demographic and industry characteristics that underlie your data (race, occupation, union, industry, sex, region, etc.). If the cost of an additional year of education is the sum of tuition, books, other expenses, and sacrificed income, would you attend another year of college? Why?

1   ECONOMICS: WHAT IT'S ALL ABOUT

■ CHAPTER CONCEPTS

After studying your text, attending class, and completing this chapter, you should be able to:
1. Describe the mechanism of the economy and the discipline of economics.
2. Understand the concepts of scarcity and opportunity cost.
3. Discuss major branches of economic inquiry: microeconomics, macroeconomics, positive analysis, and normative analysis.
4. Understand the concept of an economic model and its uses.
5. Explain rational behavior and marginal analysis, a method of analyzing the way we make decisions.

■ THE CHAPTER IN BRIEF

Fill in the blanks to summarize chapter content.

Economics is a study concerned with the use society makes of its (1) _Scarce_ (scarce, abundant) resources in attempting to satisfy the (2) _unlimited_ (normal, unlimited) desires of its members. The economy represents the mechanism or structure that organizes scarce resources for the purpose of producing the goods and services desired by society. (3) _Scarcity_ (Inflation, Scarcity) is the fundamental problem facing all economies. It is also the reason decisions or choices involve (4) _opportunity costs_ (opportunity costs, production costs).

The real cost or opportunity cost of any choice is the value of the sacrifice required in making that decision. That sacrifice represents the foregone opportunity to pursue the (5) _best_ (next best, any) decision. A fundamental problem confronting an economy is how to best meet the desires of individuals in a world of scarcity. Economies do this by addressing several basic questions: (a) What will be produced? (b) How will goods and services be produced? (c) To whom will goods and services be distributed? An economy's answers to the first two questions reveal the (6) _efficiency_ (fairness, efficiency) with which resources are used to satisfy the desires of society. The third question requires that society make value judgments regarding the distribution of income.

The two major branches of economic analysis are macroeconomics and microeconomics. (7) _Microeconomics_ (Macroeconomics, Microeconomics) is concerned with the economic behavior of individual decision-making units in the economy. (8) _Macroeconomics_ (Macroeconomics, Microeconomics) is concerned with the effects of the aggregate economic behavior of all individuals, firms, and institutions. Inflation and unemployment are two topics that are studied in (9) _Macroeconomics_ (macroeconomics, microeconomics), whereas the determination of prices and an analysis of markets are subjects dealt with in (10) _Microeconomics_ (macroeconomics, microeconomics).

Positive economic analysis seeks to determine (11) _what is_ ("what ought to be," "what is"). (12) _Normative_ (Positive, Normative) economic analysis emphasizes the "should" or "ought to" approach. Positive analysis tries to uncover cause-and-effect relationships that are subject to empirical observation and verification. In contrast, normative analysis depends upon the analyst's (13) _value judgment_ (value judgment, mathematical skills). Disagreements arise among practitioners in any discipline. With positive analysis, it is possible to resolve disagreements empirically. With normative analysis, disagreements stem from different value systems and must be resolved in ways other than looking at the "facts."

Economic analysis helps us understand the world around us. It helps us understand the functioning of the various sectors in the economy and the choices made by individual decision-making units. (14) _Assumptions_ (Assumptions, Economic theories) simplify reality so that the underlying cause-and-effect relationships among variables can be understood. (15) _Economic variable_ (Economic variables, Data) are quantities or dollar amounts that have more than one value. Theories are necessary in order to better understand the complexities of reality.

(16) _An economic model_ (A bar graph, An economic model) is a simplified way of expressing a theory. It can be expressed verbally, graphically, in tables, or mathematically. Assumptions underlie a theory because theories are (17) _abstractions from_ (depictions of, abstractions from) reality, and it is necessary to establish the environment and motivation of people for which the theory holds. Economic models can be used to develop hypotheses. A hypothesis is a statement of relationship between two variables that can be tested by empirical verification. A good model is one that can generate accurate predictions. But even a model that does not predict perfectly can still be useful in helping us understand the causal relationships among variables and the consequence of the assumptions underlying the model. The causal relationships that we want to understand are difficult to isolate unless we make the assumption of (18) _Ceteris paribus_ (*ceteris paribus*, the invisible hand). Otherwise, we cannot be sure that we have identified the exact relationship between the two variables of interest.

Economic analysis makes the assumption of rationality. Rationality means that most people behave as if they are comparing the additional gains or benefits from a choice or decision to the sacrifices or opportunity costs associated with that decision. The opportunity cost of a decision is known as its marginal (19) _benefit_ (benefit, cost). If the marginal benefits of a decision exceed the marginal costs, the individual's net gain or benefit (20) _increases_ (increases, decreases). If the marginal cost of a decision exceeds the marginal benefits, the decision would not be undertaken because the individual would experience a net (21) _loss_ (loss, gain). If a choice or decision is pursued to the point where marginal benefits and marginal costs are equal, the individual achieves the (22) _minimum_ (maximum, minimum) net gain.

■ KEY TERMS REVIEW

Write the key term from the list below next to its definition.

Key Terms

~~Economy~~
~~Economics~~
~~Opportunity cost~~
~~Microeconomics~~
~~Marginal analysis~~
~~Theory~~
~~Variable~~
~~Economic model~~
~~Marginal cost~~

~~Macroeconomics~~
~~Scarcity~~
~~Positive analysis~~
~~Normative analysis~~
~~Ceteris Paribus~~
~~Behavioral assumption~~
~~Rational behavior~~
~~Marginal benefit~~

Definitions

opportunity costs

1. **marginal cost** : the cost of choosing to use resources for one purpose measured by the sacrifice of the next best alternative for using those resources.

2. **microeconomics** : economic analysis concerned with the individual choices made by participants in the economy—also called *price theory.*

3. **positive analysis** : analysis of the effects of changes in conditions or policies on observable economic variables.

4. **economy** : the mechanism through which the use of labor, land, structures, vehicles, equipment, and natural resources is organized to satisfy the desires of people who live in a society.

5. **scarcity** : the imbalance between the desires of people in a society and the means of satisfying those desires.

6. **normative analysis** : evaluates the desirability of alternative outcomes according to underlying value judgments.

7. **economics** : a study of society's use of scarce resources in the satisfaction of the unlimited desires of its members.

8. **macroeconomics** : economic analysis that considers the overall performance of the economy with respect to total national production, consumption, average prices, and employment levels.

9. **variable** : a quantity or dollar amount that can have more than one value.

10. **Ceteris paribus** : "other things being equal"—used to acknowledge that other influences aside from the one whose effect is being analyzed must be controlled for in testing a hypothesis.

behavioral assumption

11. **Theory** : establishes people's motivation for the purpose of understanding cause-and-effect relationships among economic variables.

12. **marginal analysis** : a decision-making technique involving a systematic comparison of benefits and costs of actions.

13. **marginal benefit** : the additional benefit obtained when one extra unit of an item is obtained.

5

marginal cost theory

14. ___Opportunity cost___ : the sacrifice made to obtain an additional unit of an item.

15. ___economic model___ : an abstraction or simplification of actual relationships; establishes cause-and-effect relationships.

economic model

16. ___rational behavior___ : seeking to gain by choosing actions for which the benefit exceeds the cost.

17. ___behavioral assumption___ : a simplified way of expressing economic behavior or how some sector of the economy functions.

■ CONCEPT REVIEW

Concept 1: *Describe the mechanism of the economy*

1. List the three basic questions that all economies must answer:
   a. ___What to produce___
   b. ___How to produce it___
   c. ___To whom will the products be given___

Concept 2: *Opportunity cost*

2. Identify the likely opportunity costs associated with the following decisions.

   Hint: Think in terms of what would likely be sacrificed in pursuing a decision. In other words, what would have been the next best use of your time, money, or resources?

   a. You decide to attend a university full time.
   b. Your decision to purchase a new home results in a larger portion of your income committed to mortgage payments.
   c. You are having such a good time in the Caribbean, that you decide to extend your vacation by taking an additional week of vacation at no pay.
   d. As a manager, you decide to commit some of the corporation's resources to a plant expansion project.

Concept 3: *Positive and normative analysis*

3. In the blanks provided, indicate whether the following statements involve positive (P) or normative (N) analysis:

   a. _N_ Fred ought to get his act together.
   b. _P_ My professor arrives for class late every morning.
   c. _P_ The drought in the Midwest is increasing corn prices.
   d. _N_ Government is too obtrusive and therefore its power should be reduced.
   e. _N_ Lower state income tax rates are always preferable to higher rates.
   f. _P_ Poverty is a serious problem in the United States. *N*

4. Monitor your own statements as you interact with friends, family members, or fellow students and try to determine if your statements are based upon fact or observation or value judgments. For one day, carry a sheet of paper divided into two columns—label one column "fact" and the other "value judgment." Record your interactions with others and think about whether positive or normative statements are being made.

Concept 4: *Economic models and uses*

5. Develop a hypothesis regarding the level of family spending on goods and services and the level of family income. Describe that hypothesized relationship by setting up two columns of data reflecting the variables in your hypothesis. Is the hypothesized relationship a positive or negative relationship? Suppose that you gathered actual data on your variables and for some families your hypothesized relationship did not hold. Of what use is the *ceteris paribus* assumption in trying to isolate the relationship between family spending and income?

> Family Spending on Goods   Family Income ($)
> and Services ($)

6. Suppose that you want to investigate the relationship between prices of restaurant meals and the quantity of meals demanded by local area households. Economic theory implies that there is a negative relationship between price and quantity demanded but that income, tastes, preferences, and other variables also influence quantity demanded. Clearly state your hypothesis and its underlying assumptions.

Concept 5: *Marginal analysis*

7. Suppose child care legislation is enacted providing for child care payments of up to $1,000 to low-income working families and tax credits for other families with children under age 4 in which at least one parent works. Assume that you are a single parent with young children. Using marginal analysis, assess the impact of such a program on your decision to work or to work additional hours.

8. Assume that the price you are willing to pay for an additional unit of a good measures the marginal benefit received. How could you measure the marginal cost of the decision to consume that extra unit?

9. A rational decision maker comparing the extra gains and losses of a decision will maximize ~~minimize~~ net gains if the decision or choice is pursued to the point where marginal cost equals marginal benefit. Explain the logic of this statement.

7

Advanced application: opportunity costs

10. Suppose that you are a farmer capable of producing corn or soybeans. Over the years you have maintained records regarding your total production of both crops. Assume that you have made full and efficient use of your resources throughout this period. Furthermore, assume that the only reason corn relative to soy production has changed is because of your desire to grow the combination of crops that produce the highest net farm income. Referring to your production data below, determine the opportunity cost of producing an additional bushel of soybeans. If the current price of a bushel of corn is $7, what is the dollar value of that opportunity cost?

Production Data (000s of bushels)

	Soy	Corn
1981	100	20
1982	50	40
1983	25	50
1984	0	60
1985	75	30
1986	150	0
1987	125	10

a.   Opportunity cost measured in bushels of corn: ___2/25___ bushels

b.   Opportunity cost measured in dollars: $ ___0.56___

Advanced application: marginal analysis

11. You are an administrator of the Environmental Protection Agency concerned with allocating cleanup funds from the agency's Superfund for the removal of toxic wastes. The following data represent the marginal benefits and costs associated with removing units of pollution from a polluted river. Your task is to decide if there is a net gain to society from cleaning the river and what level of pollution reduction would maximize that net gain.

Units of Pollution Reduction	Marginal Benefits	Marginal Costs
	(millions of dollars)	
0	$ -	$ -
1	10	2
2	8	4
3	6	6
4	4	8
5	2	10

a.   Is there a net gain to society from cleaning the river? Discuss.

b.   Nets gains are maximized at a level of pollution reduction of ___3___, where marginal benefits and marginal costs are ___equal___.

8

Select the best answer.

1. Which of the following best describes the study of economics?
   a. A study concerned with how to make money
   b. A fuzzy combination of Wall Street and insurance
   c. A study of how society uses its goods and services in determining the proper distribution of income
   d. A study of how society uses its scarce economic resources in satisfying the unlimited desires of society

2. The mechanism through which resources are organized in order to satisfy the desires of society is known as:
   a. a corporation.
   b. government.
   c. an economy.
   d. a factory.

3. Scarcity means that:
   a. resources are in finite supply.
   b. poverty takes its toll on those with limited means.
   c. choices are unnecessary.
   d. an imbalance exists between desires and the means by which those desires are satisfied.

4. The real cost of a choice or decision is its opportunity cost. Which of the following best defines opportunity cost?
   a. The actual dollar outlay required to produce a good or service
   b. The value of the forgone next best alternative
   c. The value to the resources required to implement the decision
   d. The value of the loss that occurs when a speculative investment does not meet profit expectations

5. If a state government had a limited amount of tax and other revenue but decided to substantially increase the amount of appropriations to public education, appropriations to other functions such as corrections, health, and welfare would diminish. What concept is represented by this statement?
   a. Opportunity costs
   b. Normative analysis
   c. Efficiency
   d. None of the above

6. Microeconomics is a branch of economics that:
   a. studies the impact of inflation on the unemployment rate.
   b. studies the behavior of individual decision-making units in the economy.
   c. studies the effects and consequences of the aggregate behavior of all decision-making units.
   d. is only concerned with the determination of income.

7. Macroeconomics is a branch of economics that:
   a. studies the effects and consequences of the aggregate behavior of all decision-making units in the economy.
   b. is only concerned with the determination of individual market prices.
   c. studies the behavior of individual decision-making units in the economy.
   d. studies neither inflation nor unemployment.

8. Topics such as business cycles, unemployment, and inflation are studied in _____, whereas the determination of prices and the study of individual markets are studied in _____.
   a. positive analysis/normative analysis
   b. normative analysis/positive analysis
   c. microeconomics/macroeconomics
   d. macroeconomics/microeconomics

9. Which of the following involves value judgments?
   a. Normative analysis
   b. Positive analysis
   c. The search for a superconducting material operable at room temperature
   d. The decision to install lifeline (discount) electric utility rates for the elderly
   e. A and d

10. _____ makes "ought to" or "should" statements, whereas _____ makes statements based upon observable events and therefore can be subjected to empirical verification.
    a. positive analysis/normative analysis
    b. normative analysis/positive analysis
    c. macroeconomics/microeconomics
    d. microeconomics/macroeconomics

11. The decision-making technique involving a systematic comparison of the benefits and costs of actions is known as:
    a. deductive reasoning.
    b. total gains analysis.
    c. marginal analysis.
    d. ceteris paribus.

12. A/An _____ is a simplification of reality seeking to uncover the underlying cause-and-effect relationships among economic _____.
    a. assumptions/variables
    b. economic theory/assumptions
    c. hypothesis/theories
    d. economic theory/variables

13. Which of the following is true regarding economic variables?
    a. Economic variables have more than one value.
    b. Economic variables are quantities or dollar amounts.
    c. Economic variables are necessary to economic theories and models.
    d. All of the above.

14. A/An _____ is a simplified way of expressing an economic theory.
    a. economic model
    b. assumption
    c. abstraction
    d. economic principle

15. Which of the following assumptions is necessary in order to isolate the relationship between two variables?
    a. "All things allowed to vary"
    b. "All things held constant"
    c. "*Ceteris paribus*"
    d. B and c

16. If gasoline prices rise, the quantity of gasoline demanded will fall. This statement is a/an:
    a. assumption.
    b. theory.
    c. abstraction.
    d. hypothesis.

17. If household purchases of automobiles are determined by both the level of household income and the interest rate and you want to isolate the relationship between interest rates and auto sales, you must assume:
    a. that the interest rate remains unchanged.
    b. that auto sales remain unchanged.
    c. that household income remains unchanged.
    d. none of the above because you would want to know both the effect of interest rates and income on auto sales.

18. Which of the following best defines rational behavior?
    a. Seeking to gain by choosing to undertake actions for which the marginal benefits exceed the associated marginal costs
    b. A comparison of the total gains and losses from a decision
    c. Decisions that avoid habit or impulse purchases
    d. Improving net gain by pursuing decisions in which the marginal costs of a decision exceed the marginal benefits

19. _____ can be defined as the extra benefit received from undertaking some action.
    a. Total benefit
    b. Total gain
    c. Marginal benefit
    d. Total net gain

20. _____ can be defined as the extra cost associated with some action.
    a. Total cost
    b. Marginal cost
    c. Total loss
    d. Total net loss

11

21. The total net gain from a decision or action reaches a _____ when a decision or action is pursued to the point where _____ equals _____.
    a. maximum, total cost, total benefit
    b. minimum, marginal benefit, marginal cost
    c. minimum, total benefit, marginal benefit
    d. maximum, marginal benefit, marginal cost

22. The sacrifice made to obtain an additional unit of an item is known as:
    a. opportunity cost.
    b. the maximum tradeoff.
    c. marginal cost.
    d. a and c.
    e. b and c.

23. You are an executive earning an annual income of $50,000. You are considering quitting your job and returning to college to complete a degree. You estimate that the cost of tuition and books will be $8,000 for the year. The total cost of completing your education:
    a. is the cost of tuition and books only.
    b. is the opportunity cost and is less than $8000.
    c. is the opportunity cost which is slightly larger than the cost of tuition and books because transportation costs need to be considered.
    d. is several times larger than your outlay on books and tuition and consists mainly of your forgone income during the year.

24. Suppose you are considering voting for a politician, in part, because the politician says that higher taxes are bad. His political opponent argues that higher taxes may or may not cause serious work disincentives.
    a. The preferred politician's position is based upon positive analysis.
    b. The political opponent's argument is based upon normative analysis.
    c. The political opponent's argument is heavily influenced by personal value judgments and is thus an example of positive analysis.
    d. Neither politician is employing normative analysis because both individuals are basing their comments on "facts."
    e. The preferred politician is expressing a value judgement and is using normative analysis.

25. As a manager for a local retailer, you collect product price and sales data to determine how sales are influenced by price changes. You expect to find that when prices rise, quantities purchased decrease and vice versa. Instead, you find the following result: higher prices are associated with more goods purchased. Which one of the following statements is correct?
    a. The manager has shown that intuition serves as an unreliable guide in analysis.
    b. The unexpected result is an indication that it is necessary to collect and analyze data before predicting outcomes.
    c. The manager did not isolate the relationship between product price and quantities purchased. He did not make the *ceteris paribus* assumption. Thus, it is uncertain whether observed changes in quantities purchased are the result of price changes or other influences.
    d. Observation should precede theory. Explanations should always be made to fit the facts.

26. Fred chooses to go on a date with Sarah, but by doing so sacrifices the opportunity to take Mary. Fred's choice reveals:
    a. that Fred is not maximizing his net gains (net benefits) because he could date both ladies.
    b. that Fred's perceived marginal benefits from his choice are greater than the opportunity costs.
    c. that Fred's sacrifice (opportunity cost) is greater than the marginal benefits realized from the date with Sarah.
    d. None of the above—People do not use marginal analysis when making personal choices.

27. The perceived value or benefit to you from a pizza is $9. The pizza's price is $11. Will you purchase the pizza?
    a. Yes, because I am a billionaire and price is no consideration.
    b. No, as a billionaire, I still nevertheless maximize my net gains or benefits by purchasing up to the point where marginal benefits no longer exceed marginal costs.
    c. No, because the price of the pizza exceeds my opportunity cost.
    d. No, the marginal benefit associated with consuming the pizza exceeds the marginal cost.

■ THINK IT THROUGH

1. Define economics, including its branches, microeconomics and macroeconomics. What are some topics typically addressed by each of these branches?

2. Explain why scarcity and opportunity costs are related. Give an example from your personal or business experiences of the opportunity cost of a decision.

3. As you will discover later in the text, a perfectly competitive economy produces a distribution of income where labor income is based upon the productivity of labor. This is consistent with the protestant ethic which states that hard work and reward should go hand in hand. These statements involve both positive and normative analysis. Discuss.

4. Define the concepts of economic theory and economic models. Discuss the importance of assumptions underlying models and theories.

5. Pollution is harmful to society, and the reduction of pollution levels increase society's total benefits. But if a 50% reduction in the pollution level resulted in an equality between the marginal benefits and marginal costs associated with pollution reduction, society would be better off if pollution were not eliminated completely. Reconcile the two statements.

6. A rational person would never engage in habit or impulse buying. Discuss.

7. A hypothesis requires the use of the *ceteris paribus* assumption. Why? Give an example.

8. A theory must depict reality. Do you agree? Explain.

■ CHAPTER ANSWERS

The Chapter in Brief

1. Scarce 2. Unlimited 3. Scarcity 4. Opportunity cost 5. Next best 6. Efficiency 7. Microeconomics 8. Macroeconomics 9. Macroeconomics 10. Microeconomics 11. "What is" 12. Normative 13. Value judgments 14. Economic theories 15. Economic variables 16. Economic model 7. Abstractions from 18. *Ceteris paribus* 19. Cost 20. Increase 21. Loss 22. Maximum

Key Terms Review

1. Opportunity costs 2. Microeconomics 3. Positive analysis 4. Economy 5. Scarcity 6. Normative analysis 7. Economics 8. Macroeconomics 9. Variable 10. *Ceteris paribus* 11. Behavioral assumptions 12. Marginal analysis 13. Marginal benefit 14. Marginal cost 15. Theory 16. Rational behavior 17. Economic model

Concept Review

1. a. What will be produced?
   b. How will goods and services be produced?
   c. To whom will goods and services be distributed?

2. a. If you attend a university full time, there are a number of potential sacrifices all of which have value. The most obvious sacrifice is the potential income you could have earned had you been employed full time. You may have less time to spend with your family and friends, as well as less leisure time. Direct outlays on tuition, room, and board could have been invested or saved.

   b. As recently as the early 1970s it was not uncommon for homeowners to allocate only 15% of their incomes to mortgage payments. Today it is more common for families to spend as much as 25% to 35% of their incomes for housing. If you commit a much larger share of your income to housing, given scarcity (or a limited income), you must cut your spending elsewhere. The reduction in the value of goods and services consumed as a result of purchasing a more expensive home represents the opportunity cost of your decision.

   c. If you choose to take a week of vacation without pay, you obviously sacrifice the income you would have earned otherwise. That extra week, as a result, is much more costly to you than the previous week of vacation.

   d. If corporate funds are to be used for a specific project, they cannot be used for alternative investment projects. Depending on the needs of the firm, the funds could be invested in financial assets generating an interest income. The funds could be used for other investment projects yielding income. Businesses interested in achieving the highest level of profit will usually allocate funds to the projects yielding the highest return because to do otherwise would mean that the firm would be sacrificing opportunities to earn profit.

3. a. N b. P c. P d. N e. N f. N

5. *Hypothesis*: Other things held constant, family spending on goods and services is expected to be positively related to family income.

   If upon gathering data on family spending and income it is found that the relationship between spending and income is not positive, that does not mean that your hypothesis is invalid. To determine the validity of your hypothesis, you must isolate the relationship you are interested in from all other variables that might influence family spending. If you do not, you cannot be

14

sure that an increase in family spending is the result of increases in income or some third variable.

6. *Hypothesis*: Other things being the same, the price of restaurant meals and the quantity of restaurant meals demanded are expected to be inversely (negatively) related.

   The *ceteris paribus* assumption is necessary to control for other factors that influence quantity demanded, such as income and tastes and preferences. For instance, prices could be falling but incomes could fall as well. A family might dine out less often even at lower prices if their income has fallen.

7. As a working parent and particularly a single working parent, one of the major costs associated with work is child care. If you worked full time at a minimum wage of $4.25 per hour and paid $450 per month for child care for two children, you would have $230 dollars left over to support you and your family. There is little incentive to work full time for a month just to bring home $230. But suppose that as a result of new legislation, $100 of that monthly child care bill is paid for by the government. You are now left with $330 per month. This amount, although insufficient to meet the minimum needs of a family of three, is nevertheless still very important. If you were deterred from working before the new law, publicly subsidized child care payments increase the net gain to you from work and might induce you to seek employment. If you are already working, these payments might induce you to work additional hours because now the net gains from work are higher.

   The marginal benefits from working an additional hour include among other things the value of goods and services that can be purchased with the income earned from that hour of work. The marginal cost of work involves the sacrifices incurred in order to work. These sacrifices include the loss of leisure time, the loss of time spent with family and friends, and the resources spent on such things as child care and transportation that could have otherwise been spent on goods and services.

   Child care subsidies can be viewed as reducing the marginal cost of an hour of work or as increasing the marginal benefits realized from work. A reduction in day care costs increases the amount of the hourly wage available for non-day care expenditures. In this sense, the marginal benefit of an hour of work increases. Regardless of how the problem is viewed, total net gains from work increase. This will likely increase employment among single parents.

8. The marginal cost of a decision to consume a unit of a good is the sacrificed next-preferred goods that could have been consumed. The dollar value of this forgone consumption is a measure of marginal cost.

9. Maximize, marginal costs, marginal benefits

   If marginal benefits exceed marginal costs from some action, a person can add more to his or her total benefits than total costs by undertaking the action. In other words, net benefit or gain increases. As long as marginal benefits exceed marginal costs, total net gains can be increased by pursuing an activity. When an activity has been pursued to the point where marginal benefits and costs are equal, no further increases to net benefits can be realized because the addition to total benefits would just be offset by the addition to total costs of the action.

10. a. Two fifths of a bushel of corn. Historical production data reveal that for every 10,000-bushel increase in corn production, there is a 25,000-bushel decrease in soy output. Because the farmer is fully using his or her resources and employing these resources

efficiently, the only way soy production can be increased is by withdrawing resources from corn production and employing those resources in soy production. Consequently, for every bushel increase in corn production, there is a 2.5-bushel decrease in soy production. In other words, for every additional bushel of soy produced, corn production must be reduced by two fifths of a bushel.

b. Two fifths of a bushel times $7 per bushel = $2.80. The opportunity cost of producing a bushel of soy measured in dollars represents the dollar value of that sacrificed output of corn.

11. a. Yes, because marginal benefits from pollution reduction up to a point exceed the sacrifice incurred in reducing pollution.

b. 3, equal at $6 million. At this point, society's total benefits and costs equal $24 million and $12 million, respectively. Society's net gain is therefore $12 million. No other level of pollution reduction will result in as large of a net gain.

Mastery Test

1. d 2. c 3. d 4. b 5. a 6. b 7. a 8. d 9. e 10. b 11. c 12. d 13. d 14. a 15. c 16. d 17. c 18. a 19. c 20. b 21. d 22. d 23. d 24. e 25. c 26. b 27. b

Think it Through

1. Economics is a study of how society uses its scarce resources to satisfy the unlimited wants of its members. Macroeconomics is a study of the effects of the aggregate economic behavior of all decision-making units in the economy, whereas microeconomics is concerned with an analysis of the decision making of individual firms, households, or other decision-making units. Business cycles, inflation, and unemployment are topics covered in macroeconomics. Microeconomics, also known as *price theory*, analyzes among other things individual markets and the determination of prices.

2. If there were no scarcity, the opportunity costs of decisions requiring the use of resources would be zero. There would be such a thing as a "free lunch." If resources were available everywhere and in unlimited supply, the farmer in the above example could at any time produce more soy or corn without having to sacrifice the output of the other.

3. The first statement regarding a competitive economy's ability to reward labor on the basis of labor's productive contribution is deduced from economic theory, which itself is a collection of postulates based upon empirically verifiable observations. In this sense, this statement involves positive analysis. The second statement declares that this method of income distribution is "good." But this is based upon a value system consistent with the protestant ethic, which is only one of many possible value systems. It is therefore a normative statement.

4. Economic theory is a simplification of reality seeking to establish and explain important cause-and-effect relationships in the economy. An economic model is a simplified way of expressing a theory. A model can be presented verbally, in tables, in graphs, or mathematically. Assumptions are necessary for both theories and models because they outline the environment or motivation of people for which the theory and model hold.

5. If pollution reduction were undertaken to the point where marginal benefit and marginal cost were equal and that happened to be at a 50% level of pollution reduction, then no further net gains to society could be realized by additional reductions in pollution. In fact, if additional

pollution reduction beyond the 50% level resulted in marginal costs exceeding marginal benefits, society would experience a net loss and be worse off than when there was more pollution.

6. In fact it might be quite rational for a person to engage in habit or impulse buying if that person experiences psychic loss, dissatisfaction, or stress associated with certain actions or choices. A person may buy the first used car he or she sees but may be doing so in part because of a distaste for bargaining and haggling. A person may shop only locally because of an aversion to driving in traffic.

7. A hypothesis is a statement of relationship between two economic variables. To be certain that you have isolated the cause-and-effect relationship between the two variables, it is necessary to hold the effect of other influencing variables constant. Otherwise, you cannot be sure that the relationship you have hypothesized is valid or instead results from some third variable that you have not considered.

8. A good theory yields accurate predictions, but even a theory that predicts inaccurately is of value in establishing cause-and-effect relationships and determining the significance of assumptions.

CHAPTER SUPPLEMENT
GRAPHS: A BASIC TOOL FOR ANALYZING ECONOMIC RELATIONSHIPS

■ THE SUPPLEMENT SUMMARY IN BRIEF

Fill in the blanks to summarize appendix content.

Describing data graphically requires a number of considerations. Does the variable take on positive values only or does it also take on negative values? What is the unit of measurement? For what purpose are the data to be plotted? If you want to present a cause-and-effect relationship between two variables, a plot of the variables on a (1) _bargraphs_ (set of axes, bar graph) would be appropriate. If you are interested in the cause-and-effect relationship of a third variable, a (2) _bargraph_ (bar graph, set of axes) cannot be used. If you are only interested in presenting the fluctuation in a variable over time, a plot on a set of axes is usually all that is required, although a bar graph can be employed.

Because most economic variables take on positive values, a set of axes having an origin in the extreme (3) _southwest_ (northeast, southwest) corner is required. As you read vertically upward or horizontally rightward from the origin, units of measurement become increasingly positive. Each axis is defined in terms of a unit of measurement. Units of measurement can be discrete or continuous. A (4) _discrete_ (discrete, continuous) variable is expressed in units that are indivisible. A (5) _discrete_ (discrete, (continuous)) variable is divisible into fractions of a whole.

A plot of a specific set of values or (6) _coordinates_ (coordinates, intersections) of two variables on a set of axes produces a curve when the points are connected by a line. The curve can reveal important information regarding the association among the two variables plotted. If the variable on the vertical axis increases when the variable plotted on the horizontal axis increases, there is a (7) _positive_ (positive, negative) relationship between the two variables. If the variable on the vertical axis decreases when the variable plotted on the horizontal axis increases, the relationship is a (8) _negative_ (positive, negative) one. If there is no change in the variable plotted on the vertical axis when the variable on the horizontal axis changes, there is no relationship between the variables.

The (9) _slope_ (intersection, slope) of a curve describes the rate of change in the variable on the vertical axis given a change in the variable on the horizontal axis. A curve describing a positive relationship between variables has a (10) _positive_ (positive, negative) slope. A curve describing a negative relationship has a (11) _negative_ (positive, negative) slope, and a curve indicating no relationship between the two variables has a slope of zero. On a bowl-shaped or inverted bowl-shaped curve, a slope of zero represents the point at which the curve (or the value of the variable plotted on the vertical axis) reaches a maximum or minimum value. Two curves that just touch each other but do not intersect have (12) _equal_ (unequal, equal) slopes at that point of tangency. If two curves (13) _intersect_ (intersect, are tangent), the two slopes at that point can both be positive or negative or one can be positive and the other negative, but they cannot be equal to each other as is the case with (14) _a tangency_ (an intersection, a tangency).

■ KEY TERMS REVIEW

Write the key term from the list below next to its definition.

Key Terms

Origin   Coordinate
Curve   Positive (direct) relationship
Slope   Negative (inverse) relationship
Bar graph   Discrete variable
Intersection   Continuous variable
Tangency   Time series data

Definitions

1. _slope_ : Measures the rate at which the Y variable, on the vertical axis, rises or falls along a curve as the X variable, on the horizontal axis, increases.

2. _time series data_ : Data that show fluctuations in a variable over time.

3. _origin_ : On a set of axes, the point designated by *0*, at which variables *X* and *Y* both take on values of zero.

4. _bar graph_ : A graph that shows that value of a *Y* variable as the height of a bar for each corresponding value of the *X* variable.

5. _intersection_ : The point at which two curves cross on a set of axes.

6. _inverse relationship_ : Depicted by a downward-sloping curve on a set of axes; it indicates that variable *Y* decreases whenever variable *X* increases.

7. _direct relationship_ : Depicted by an upward-sloping curve on a set of axes; it indicates that variable *Y* increases whenever variable *X* increases.

8. _continuous variable_ : A variable that can realistically and meaningfully take on minute fractions of values.

9. _tangency_ : A point at which two curves just touch each other but do not intersect.

10. _coordinate_ : A pair of numbers that corresponds to values for variables *X* and *Y* when plotted on a set of axes.

11. _discrete variable_ : A variable that cannot vary by fractions of units.

12. _curve_ : A straight or curved line drawn to connect points plotted on a set of axes.

20

■ CONCEPT REVIEW

1. a. Using the production data from question 10 in the Concept Review section in Chapter 1, construct the following bar charts:

Production Data

	Soybeans (000s of bushels)	Corn (000s of bushels)
1981	100	20
1982	50	40
1983	25	50
1984	0	60
1985	75	30
1986	150	0
1987	125	10

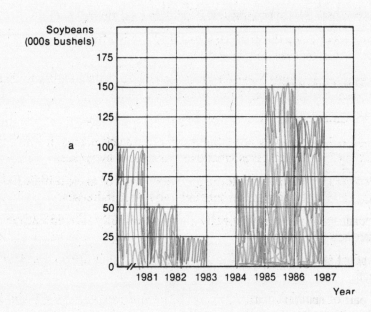

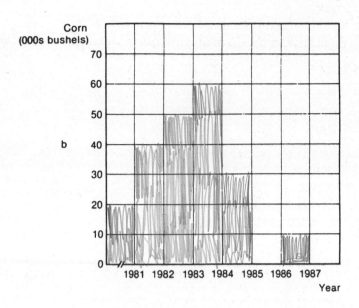

Corn
(000s bushels)

b

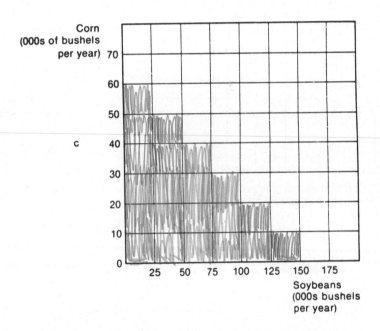

Corn
(000s of bushels
per year)

c

Soybeans
(000s bushels
per year)

b. Which of the above bar charts depict time series data and which depict a functional relationship representing the concept of opportunity costs?

1. Figure A Time

2. Figure B Time

3. Figure C functional

22

2. The following data represent quantities of tennis racquets demanded by consumers and supplied by producers at various prices:

Tennis Racquets

Price per Racquet	Quantity Demanded	Quantity Supplied
	(000s per month)	
$10	75	15
20	65	20
30	55	25
40	45	30
50	35	35
60	25	40
70	15	45

a. In the figure below, plot a curve showing the relationship between price and quantity demanded by consumers. The relationship is a _negative_ relationship and has a _negative_ slope.

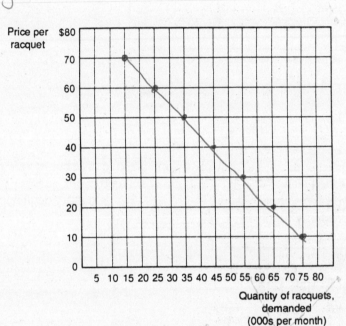

Price per racquet

Quantity of racquets, demanded
(000s per month)

23

b. In the figure below, plot a curve showing the relationship between price and quantity supplied by producers. The relationship is a _positive_ relationship and has a _positive_ slope.

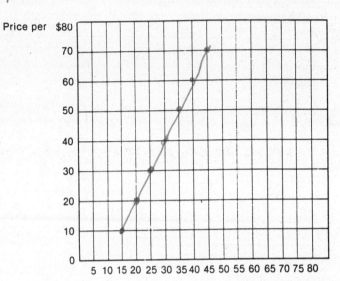

Price per $80

Quantity of supplied
(000s per month)

c. In the figure below, plot both curves from parts a and b above. The coordinate at which the two curves cross is called a/an _intersection_. At what price and quantity supplied and demanded do the two curves cross? Price _$50_, quantity demanded _35_, quantity supplied _35_.

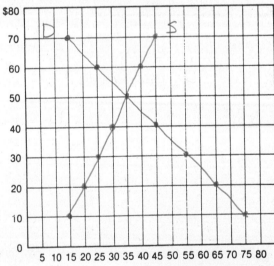

Price per $80
racquet

Quantity of racquets supplied
and demanded
(000s per month)

24

3. Suppose that you are a manager for a producer of business forms and you have noticed that over time your sales of business forms appear to increase as the rate of growth in the nation's output or GDP increases. That observed relationship is depicted in the table below:

	Rate of Growth in GDP (%)	Sales of Business Forms (cases)
Year 1	3.0	15,000
2	3.5	17,000
3	2.0	11,000
4	5.5	25,000
5	6.0	27,000

a. In the figure below, plot a time series curve describing the behavior of the rate of growth in GDP.

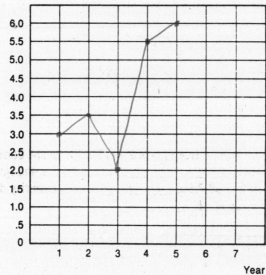

b. In the figure below, plot a time series curve describing the behavior of business forms sales.

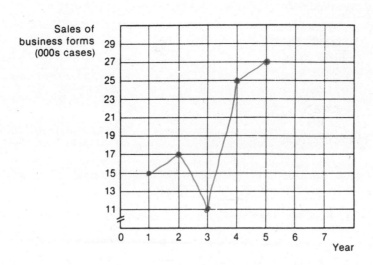

c. In the figure below, plot the functional relationship between the rate of growth in GDP and sales of business forms.

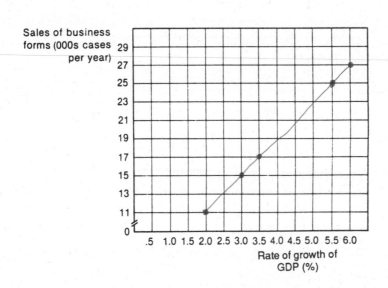

4. a. For the figures below, indicate whether a tangency exists or an intersection occurs at:

        Point A in left figure: _Tangency_

        Point B in right figure: _Intersection_

   b. For the figures below, indicate whether the curves at the point of tangency or intersection have a positive or negative slope.

        Curve 1 in left figure: _negative_

        Curve 2 in left figure: _negative_

        Curve 1 in right figure: _negative_

        Curve 2 in right figure: _positive_

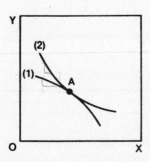 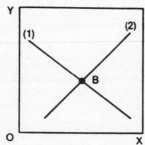

5. Referring to the figures below, indicate on the numbered spaces below whether the slope at the designated points are positive, negative, or zero.

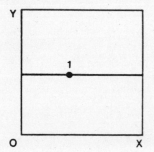 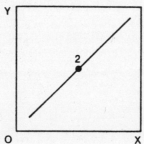

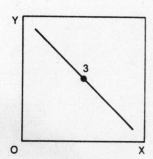

27

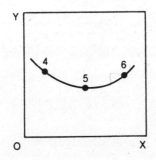

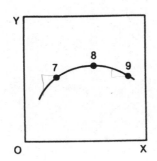

1. _Zero_
2. _positive_
3. _negative_
4. _positive   negative_
5. _Zero_
6. _negative   positive_
7. _positive_
8. _Zero_
9. _negative_

Advanced applications

6. Using the data shown in question 3, what would you predict to happen to business form sales if the rate of growth in GDP is expected to be 4.5% in year 6?

_21,000_

7. Suppose two variables are related to each other by the following equation:

$Y = a+bX$, where $a = 10$ and $b = 1/2$

a. Complete the table. (Use the Y1 column for the case where $a = 10$.)

X	Y1	Y2
100	60	110
200	110	160
300	160	210
400	210	260
500	260	310
600	310	360
700	360	410
800	410	460

b. Plot the relationship between X and Y1 in the figure below.

(1) The slope = _____ ½ _____

(2) The intercept (value of Y1 at X = 0) = _____ 10 _____

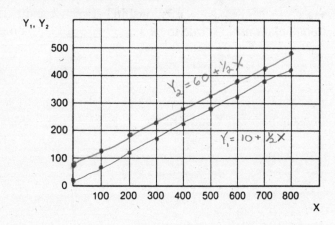

c. Assume that the constant term a in the above equation increases from 10 to 60. Complete column Y2 above and plot the new relationship in the figure in part b. The curve has shifted _____ upward _____. The slope = _____ ½ _____ and the intercept = _____ 60 _____.

29

■ MASTERY TEST

Select the best answer.

1. Which of the following does not indicate a functional relationship between variables X and Y?
    a. As X increases, Y increases
    b. As X decreases, Y increases
    c. As X increases, Y remains unchanged
    d. As X decreases, Y decreases

2. When a value for X is paired with a value for Y on a set of axes, this combination of values is known as:
    a. a tangency.
    b. an intersection.
    c. a coordinate.
    d. the origin, if at least one value is zero.

3. A curve represents a set of coordinates that are connected by a line. Which of the following statements is true?
    a. A curve by definition cannot be a straight line.
    b. A curve must have either a positive or negative slope.
    c. A line of zero slope is not a function and therefore is not a curve.
    d. A curve may be a straight or a curved line. If it is a curved line, it is possible to have a positive, negative, or zero slope at different points on that curve.

4. If Y increases as X is increased, there is a _____ relationship between X and Y. If Y decreases as X is increased, the functional relationship is said to be a _____ one.
    a. adverse, positive
    b. negative, positive
    c. obtuse, negative
    d. positive, negative

5. A function exhibiting a positive relationship between X and Y has a _____ slope and a curve that is _____.
    a. positive, upsloping
    b. negative, downsloping
    c. positive, downsloping
    d. negative, upsloping

6. A function exhibiting a negative relationship between X and Y has a _____ slope and a curve which is _____.
    a. positive, upsloping
    b. negative, downsloping
    c. positive, downsloping
    d. negative, upsloping

7. Which of the following defines the origin?
    a. The origin is the beginning of a set of time series data.
    b. The origin is the coordinate on a set of axes where the value of variables X and Y are both zero.
    c. The origin is the coordinate on a set of axes where the values of variables X and Y represent the initial values of the data plotted.
    d. The origin is that point on the northeast corner of a set of positive axes.

30

8. The slope can be defined as the:
   a. change in *Y*/change in *X*.
   b. rate of change in *Y* over time.
   c. rate of change in *X* over time.
   d. None of the above.

9. A _____ variable is indivisible into fractions of a unit, whereas a _____ variable is divisible into fractions of a whole.
   a. continuous, discrete
   b. discrete, continuous
   c. positive, negative
   d. time series, constant

10. Which of the following variables have discrete units of measurement?
    a. Automobiles
    b. Gasoline
    c. Coffee beans
    d. The nation's money supply

11. Of the following variables, which one is a continuous variable?
    a. Computer
    b. House
    c. Basketball
    d. Natural gas

12. When two curves just touch each other, they have _____ slopes.
    a. equal
    b. unequal
    c. positive and negative
    d. only zero

13. The point at which two curves just touch each other is called:
    a. a tangency.
    b. the origin.
    c. a data point.
    d. an intersection.

14. The point at which two curve cross is called:
    a. a tangency.
    b. the origin.
    c. a data point.
    d. an intersection.

15. The values of *X* and *Y* at an intersection:
    a. will be the same on both curves.
    b. will be the same on both curves for the *X* variable only.
    c. will not be the same on both curves.
    d. depend upon the placement of the origin.

■ THINK IT THROUGH

1. Referring to the data below, plot the price and quantity demanded data on the axes below. On the same set of axes, plot the price and quantity supplied data and interpret the meaning of the intersection. Suppose a third variable changes, such as the introduction of VCRs, and as a result the quantity of movie tickets demanded at each price level declines by 20,000 tickets per week. What happens to the curve representing the demand data? What happens to the intersection?

Moves to left
Moves to $4 +40,000 per week

Price per Ticket Demanded		Quantity Supplied	Quantity
	(000s per week)		
$2	80 *60*	20	
3	70 *50*	30	
4	60 *40*	40	
5	50 *30*	50	
6	40 *20*	60	
7	30 *10*	70	

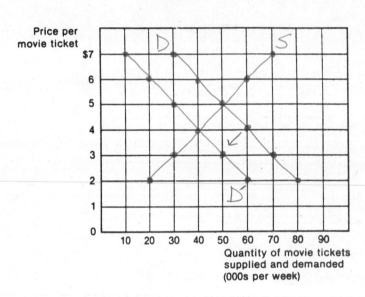

Price per movie ticket

Quantity of movie tickets supplied and demanded (000s per week)

2. The following data represent the relationship between interest rates and building permits issued for new residential construction in a local housing market. Plot the relationship on the axes below and determine if a positive or negative relationship exists. Because of a regional recession, assume that local incomes decline and outmigration of people reduce the demand for new housing and thus reduce building permits issued by 100 permits per month at each mortgage rate. Plot the new relationship on the same set of axes and compare the position and slope of the new curve to the one that you previously plotted.

32

Mortgage Rate %	Permits Issued per month	
8.5	1050	950
9.0	1000	700
9.5	950	850
10.0	900	800
10.5	850	750
11.0	800	700
11.5	750	650

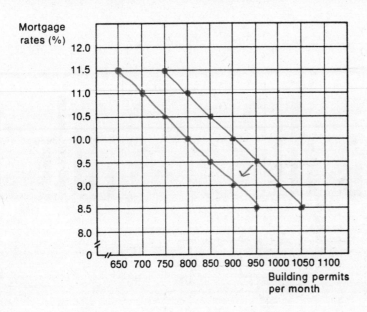

negative

Slope same
Moved to left

33

■ ANSWERS TO CHAPTER SUPPLEMENT

The Supplement Summary in Brief

1. A set of axes or a bar graph 2. Bar graph 3. Southwest 4. Discrete 5. Continuous 6. Coordinates
7. Positive 8. Negative 9. Slope 10. Positive 11. Negative 12. Equal 13. Intersect 14. Tangency

Key Terms Review

1. Slope 2. Time series data 3. Origin 4. Bar graph 5. Intersection 6. Negative relationship
7. Positive relationship 8. Continuous variable 9. Tangency 10. Coordinate 11. Discrete variable
12. Curve

Concept Review

1. a.

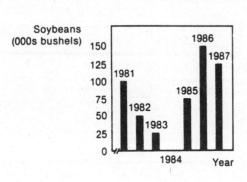

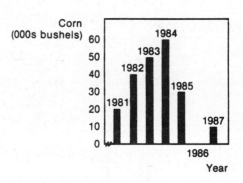

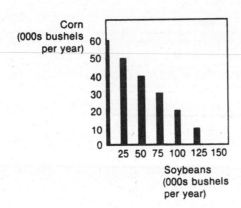

    b. (1) Time series

       (2) Time series

       (3) Functional relationship

2. a.

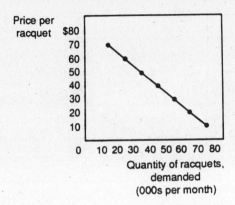

Negative, negative

b.

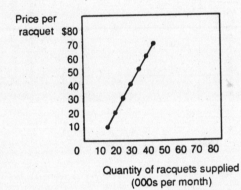

Positive, positive

c.

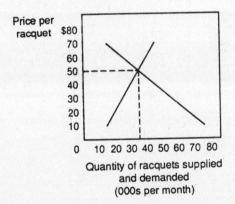

Intersection, $50, 35, 35

35

3. a.

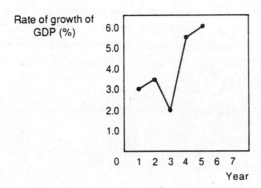

b.

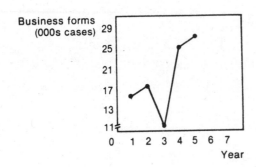

c.

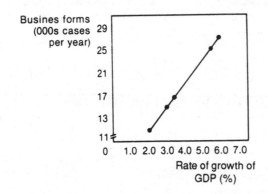

4. a.   Tangency, intersection
   b.   Negative, negative, negative, positive

5. 1. Zero 2. Positive 3. Negative 4. Negative 5. Zero 6. Positive 7. Positive 8. Zero 9. Negative

6. From the functional relationship shown in part c of question 3, it can be seen that a positive relationship exists between the rate of growth in GDP and sales of business forms. The slope of the curve is the change in business form sales for each percentage change in the rate of growth of GDP. Business form sales increase by 4,000 cases for each 1% increase in the GDP growth rate. If you expect that the growth rate of GDP will be 4.5% in year 6, then sales of business forms can be predicted to fall from 27,000 to 21,000 cases.

7. a.

Y1	c. Y2	Upward, 1/2, 60
60	110	
110	160	
160	210	
210	260	
260	310	
310	360	
360	410	
410	460	

b.

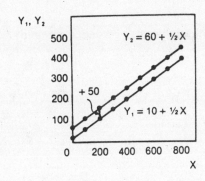

(1) 1/2 (2) 10

Mastery Test

1. c 2. c 3. d 4. d 5. a 6. b 7. b 8. a 9. b 10. a 11. d 12. a 13. a 14. d 15. a

37

Think It Through

1. The two curves intersect at point A in the figure below. At that point, the values for price and quantity are the same on both curves. At a price per movie ticket of $5, the quantity demanded and quantity supplied both equal 50,000 tickets per week. A reduction of 20,000 tickets demanded at each price shifts the demand curve leftward. The new intersection shows that a price of $4 is now required to equate quantity demanded and quantity supplied at a level of 40,000 tickets per week.

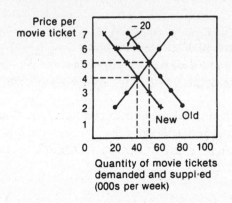

2. The relationship between mortgage rates and new building permits issued is a negative one. If building permits issued decline at each mortgage rate by 100 permits per month, the new curve lies to the left of the old curve but has the same slope.

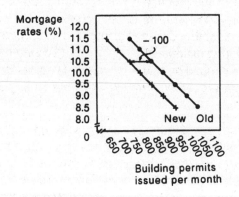

38

2   PRODUCTION POSSIBILITIES AND OPPORTUNITY COST

■ CHAPTER CONCEPTS

After studying your text, attending class, and completing this chapter, you should be able to:

1. Explain how limited available technology and scarce resources imply limited production possibilities over a period of time.
2. Show how the use of productive capacity to make more of one good or service available involves sacrificing the opportunity to make more of other items available.
3. Understand the concept of productive efficiency and discuss its significance.
4. Discuss the basic determinants of a nation's production possibilities and how these can expand over time.
5. Demonstrate that when you use income over a period to buy more of one item, you sacrifice the opportunity to buy more of some other item over the period.
6. Explain how international trade can allow citizens to enjoy consumption possibilities that exceed their nation's domestic production possibilities.

■ THE CHAPTER IN BRIEF

Fill in the blanks to summarize chapter content.

(1) *Production* (Economy, Production) is the process of using economic resources or inputs in order to produce output. Economic resources consist of labor, (2) *Capital* (capital, money), natural resources, and entrepreneurship. The quantity and productivity of economic resources and the extent and efficiency with which they are employed determine the output potential of a nation during a given period of time. Constraints in the availability or use of resources represent the (3) *scarcity* (opportunity costs, scarcity) confronting nations. (4) *Technology* (Technology, A larger labor force) allows us to delay the sacrifices implied by scarce resources by increasing the productivity of resources. Improvements in resource productivity mean that a nation can produce more output with a given endowment of resources.

A (5) *production possibilities* (marginal benefit, production possibilities) curve is a convenient tool for showing the implications of scarce resources. Assuming (a) a given quantity and productivity of resources, as well as a given state of the art with respect to technology and (b) full and efficient employment of resources, it can be shown that a nation can produce more of one class of goods, such as environmental improvement services, only by (6) *sacrificing* (sacrificing, increasing) the production of other goods. That sacrifice is a nation's (7) *opportunity cost* (dollar outlay, opportunity cost) of producing more of a given good. As a nation produces more of a good, the opportunity cost (8) *rises* (rises, falls) because resources that are increasingly (9) *less* (less, more) productive must be transferred from the production of other goods. This implies that a given increase in the production of one good will require ever (10) *larger* (smaller, larger) reductions in output of other goods. The law of increasing costs exists because resources (11) *are not* (are, are not) equally adaptable to all employments.

A point on the production possibilities curve represents a combination of the two classes of goods in question where output is at a maximum. A point inside the curve implies either

(12) _unemployed_ (unemployed, fully employed) resources or (13) _inefficiently_ (efficiently, inefficiently) employed resources. A point outside the curve represents a combination of goods that is (14) _unattainable_ (attainable, unattainable) in the short run. But with an increase over time in the quantity and productivity of resources, together with improvements in technology, a point outside the curve is attainable in the long run.

Maximum production is attainable in the short run when resources are employed fully and efficiently. Productive efficiency means that a nation (15) _can_ (can, cannot) reallocate resources among the production of goods and services and achieve a gain in the output of one good only by causing a reduction in the output of another. Specialization and the division of labor are critical for the attainment of maximum productive efficiency.

The process of economic growth can be shown as (16) _outward_ (inward, outward) shifts over time in the production possibilities curve. A nation can generally produce more of all goods over time as long as it experiences resource growth and an improvement in the quality of resources and technology. A nation's growth is influenced by its willingness to forgo some (17) _current_ (future, current) production of consumable output so that resources can be used for the production of (18) _capital_ (consumable outputs, capital). Production of capital today increases the production possibilities in the future not only by increasing the quantity of capital but also by increasing the productivity of other resources.

The problem of scarcity confronting nations also confronts the individual. An individual has a limited amount of income per time period with which to consume and save. Given the prices of goods and services, that limited income can purchase, at a maximum, those combinations of goods and services which require the full expenditure of income. A curve representing these various combinations of goods and services is known as a (19) _budget line_ (budget line, production possibilities curve). An increase in income over time allows the individual to consume more of all goods. This is shown by an (20) _outward_ (inward, outward) shift of the budget line. Holding income constant but allowing prices to fall likewise (21) _increases_ (increases, decreases) the quantities that can be purchased. This too shifts the budget line (22) _outward_ (inward, outward). Rising prices or inflation will shift the budget line (23) _inward_ (inward, outward) if income remains constant. Finally, given a limited income and constant prices, the only way an individual can consume more of one good is by reducing consumption of other goods. The opportunity cost of consuming more of one good is the (24) _reduction_ (increase, reduction) in consumption of quantities of other goods.

■ KEY TERMS REVIEW

Write the key term from the list below next to its definition.

Key Terms

Economic resources

Labor

Capital

Natural resources

Entrepreneurship

Technology

Production possibilities curve

Law of increasing costs

Productive efficiency

Division of labor

Economic growth

Definitions

1. _economic resources_: the inputs used in the process of production.

2. _division of labor_ : the specialization of workers in particular tasks that are part of a larger undertaking to accomplish a given objective.

3. _capital_ : the equipment, tools, structures, machinery, vehicles, materials, and skills created to help produce goods and services.

4. _production possibilities_ curve: a curve that show feasible combinations of two goods (or broad classes of goods) that can be produced with available resources and current technology.

5. _Entrepreneurship_ : the talent to develop products and processes and to organize production of goods and services.

6. _Economic growth_ : the expansion in production possibilities that results from increased availability and increased productivity of economic resources.

7. _Technology_ : the knowledge of how to produce goods and services.

8. _labor_ : the physical and mental efforts of human beings in the production of goods and services.

9. _productive efficiency_: attained when the maximum possible output of any one good is produced given the output of the other goods. At this point it is not possible to reallocate economic resources to increase the output of any single good or service without decreasing the output of some other good or service.

10. _natural resources_: acreage and the physical terrain used to locate structures, ports, and other facilities; also, climate and natural resources that are used in crude form in production.

11. _law of increasing costs_: states that the opportunity cost of each additional unit of output of a good over a period increases as more of that good is produced.

■ CONCEPT REVIEW

Concept 1: *Scarce resources and limited production possibilities*

1. List four economic resources:
   a. _labor_
   b. _capital_
   c. _natural resources_
   d. _entrepreneurship_

2. Which of the following uses of resources will likely increase labor productivity? (+, Increase; 0, No change.)
   + a. _0_ Expenditures on capital
   b. _0_ Expenditures on more fashionable clothes
   c. _+_ Expenditures on health care
   d. _+_ Expenditures on education and training
   e. _0_ Expenditures on military goods

41

Concept 2: *Production possibilities and opportunity cost*

3. The data in the table below represent the production possibilities for a nation producing two classes of goods.

Production Possibilities	Consumer Goods	Capital Goods
	(millions of units)	
A	0	90
B	20	80
C	40	65
D	60	47
E	80	26
F	100	0

a. On the axes below, plot a production possibilities curve from the data in the table above.

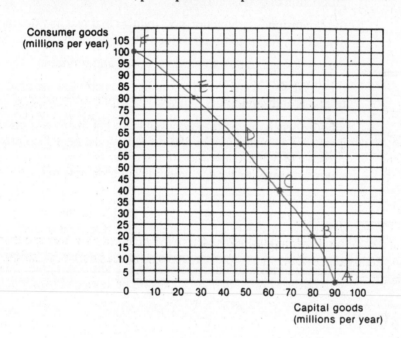

b. What is the meaning of a point <u>on</u> the production possibilities curve? *maximum production*

c. What is the opportunity cost associated with an increase in the production of consumer goods by 20 million units?

    (1) From point B to C? ____15____ units of capital

    (2) From point C to D? ____18____ units of capital

    (3) From point D to E? ____21____ units of capital

    (4) From point E to F? ____26____ units of capital

d. Do opportunity costs rise or fall as additional units of consumer goods are produced? Explain.

    Rises

42

4. Referring to the figure below:
   a. Interpret the meaning of point A. *inefficient*
   b. Interpret the meaning of point B. *unattainable*

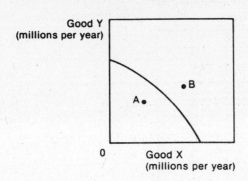

Concept 4: *Determinants of a nation's production possibilities*

5. Indicate whether the following events would cause the production possibilities curve to shift outward (O) or would leave it unchanged (U):
   a. __U__ Increased production of houses at full employment
   b. __O__ Increases in the quantity of resources
   c. __O__ Improvements in the quality and productivity of economic resources
   d. __O__ A reduction in prices
   e. __O__ Increases in income
   f. __O__ Improvements in technology

6. a. On the axes below, draw a production possibilities curve for a nation. Now assume that economic growth is taking place. Draw a new production possibilities curve on the same axes reflecting this growth.

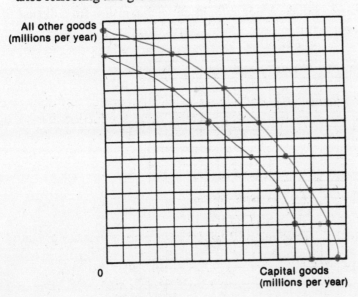

43

b. On the axes below, draw a production possibilities curve for a nation. Assume as above that the nation is experiencing growth, but also assume that the economy is investing more heavily in capital and technology than the economy shown above in part a. Draw a new production possibilities curve reflecting this.

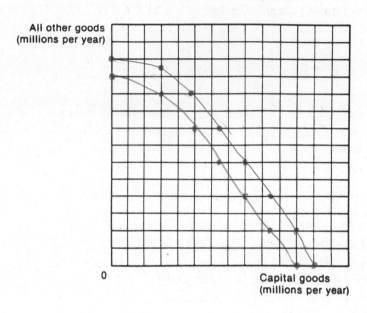

7. a. If a nation used resources for capital or technological improvements for a specific industry, such as the aircraft industry, what are the implications regarding future levels of production not only in the aircraft industry but for other industries as well? *increase production*

b. Show the shift in a nation's production possibilities curve that results from the use of resources discussed above.

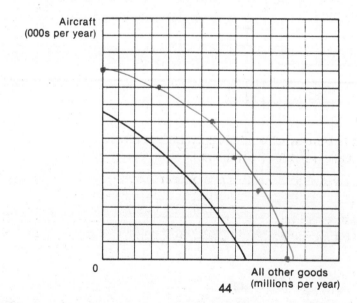

44

Concept 5: *Limited income and opportunity cost*

8. Suppose that as a university student you receive $50 per month from your parents to be used as spending money. You spend all of your money each month on beer or compact discs (CDs). Assume that the price per six-pack of beer is $2.50 and the price of a CD is $10.

   a. Determine six combinations of beer and CDs that cost a total of $50. List the combinations in the table below.

100

Combination	Beer (six packs)	CDs (units)		
A	0	5	0	10
B	4	4	8	8
C	8	3	16	6
D	12	2	24	4
E	16	1	32	2
F	20	0	40	0

   b. Plot these combinations below. The curve that you have plotted is called a
   <u>budget line</u> .

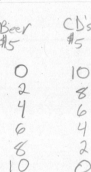

Beer $5	CD's $5
0	10
2	8
4	6
6	4
8	2
10	0

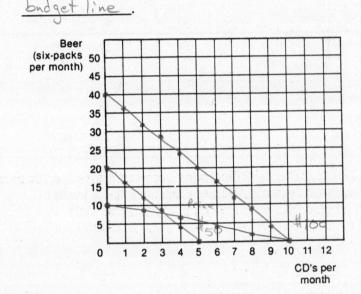

Beer (six-packs per month)

CD's per month

   c. On the figure in part b, show what would happen to the curve if:
   (1) your parents began to send $100 per month
   (2) your total funds are still $50, but the price of beer increases to $5 and the price of CDs decreases to $5.

9. **Advanced application: budget line**
   a. Derive the equation for the budget line in Question 8, part b.

Beer CD
8   3

45

b. In question 8, part c1 alters the equation for the budget line in what way? Part c2 alters the equation in what way?

10. **Insights on Issues**
(Billions of dollars)

Output (Gross Domestic Product)	$4,922.7
Consumption	3,314.0
Government Spending	937.8
Trade (Exports - Imports)	-41.7

a. According to Jane Gravelle, national saving can be measured by subtracting _Output_, _Trade_, and _Consumption_ from _Spending_.

b. Referring to the data above, national saving equals $ _629.2_.

c. An 1% percent overestimate of consumption produces a _10_ % error in the level of national saving.

(handwritten calculations in left margin:)

8
4922.7
- 41.7
4881.0
-3314.0
1567.0
- 937.8
629.2

46

■ MASTERY TEST

Select the best answer.

1. Which of the following can be defined as the process of using economic resources to produce outputs?
   a. Economics
   b. Production
   c. Economy
   d. Technology

2. Economic resources consist of:
   a. money, credit, and capital
   b. labor, capital, and money
   c. labor, capital, natural resources, and money
   d. labor, capital, natural resources, and entrepreneurship

3. Which of the following best defines capital?
   a. Money
   b. Socks and bonds
   c. Investment funds available for speculative financial outlays
   d. Goods or skills that are produced in order to produce goods and services

4. Scarcity exists in the short run because:
   a. at a given point in time technological growth increases at a constant rate.
   b. at a given point in time the quantity and quality of resources and the state of technology are fixed.
   c. resources are usually employed inefficiently.
   d. the world's resources are in finite supply.

5. A nation must sacrifice the output of some goods in order to produce other goods during a given period of time if:
   a. there is less than full employment of resources.
   b. resources are inefficiently employed.
   c. there is both full and efficient use of economic resources.
   d. a nation relies on capital goods production.

6. If a nation is currently operating at a point on its production possibilities curve, in order to increase production of one good, the production of other goods must be:
   a. held constant.
   b. increased.
   c. decreased.
   d. None of the above.

7. If a nation is currently operating at a point inside its production possibilities curve, it:
   a. has full employment.
   b. has unemployed and/or inefficiently employed resources.
   c. is operating at full potential.
   d. must reduce the output of one good in order to produce more of another good.

47

8. The law of increasing costs states that:
   a. opportunity costs rise as more of a good is produced.
   b. opportunity costs fall as more of a good is produced.
   c. rising resource prices are inevitable because of scarcity.
   d. economic growth is always associated with inflation.

9. The law of increasing costs is the result of the fact that:
   a. resources can be easily adapted to the production of any good.
   b. scarcity reduces supply and increases costs.
   c. resources are not equally adaptable to all employments.
   d. people reach a point of satiation at which they no longer purchase goods.

10. Economic growth is the process whereby the production possibilities curve shifts:
    a. inward.
    b. outward.
    c. either inward or outward.
    d. outward, then inward.

11. Points outside of the production possibilities curve are _____ in the _____.
    a. attainable/short run
    b. unattainable/short run
    c. attainable/long run
    d. unattainable/long run
    e. b and c

12. Production efficiency is achieved:
    a. if resources are reallocated among the production of goods and services and the output of one good can be increased without decreasing the output of other goods.
    b. if there is no waste in the production process.
    c. if resources are reallocated among the production of goods and services and the output of one good can be increased only by reducing the output of other goods.
    d. at a point within the production possibilities curve.

13. If nation A commits a larger share of its resources to capital and technological improvements than nation B, then over time _____ will realize _____ outward shifts in its production possibilities curve.
    a. nation B/larger
    b. nation A/smaller
    c. nations A and B/the same
    d. nation B/smaller

14. An individual's ability to consume goods and services depends upon:
    a. income only.
    b. the rate of inflation.
    c. the individual's income and the prices of the goods and services consumed.
    d. tastes.

15. A/An _____ is a curve indicating an individual's ability to consume various combinations of two goods or services over a period of time.
   a. production possibilities curve
   b. income curve
   c. price line
   d. budget line

16. The budget line shifts _____ when there is a/an _____ in income.
   a. inward/increase
   b. outward/decrease
   c. inward/decrease
   d. outward/decrease or increase

17. An individual's ability to increase the consumption of goods and services is _____ when the price of one or both goods _____.
   a. increased/decrease
   b. decreased/decrease
   c. increased/increase
   d. unchanged/increase unless income decreases

18. The sacrifice or opportunity cost associated with an individual's consumption of an additional good :
   a. is the reduction in other goods consumed when the individual does not spend all of his or her income.
   b. is the increase in other goods consumed when unused income is spent.
   c. is the reduction in other goods consumed when an individual has no additional income.
   d. None of the above

19. How is a nation's production possibilities curve affected in the long run by a boom in both new and existing housing sales in the present?
   a. Since housing is not productive capital, there is no impact on the nation's production possibilities curve.
   b. Housing consumption increases worker productivity, causing a move up along the production possibilities curve.
   c. Increased housing production in the present means that fewer other goods and services, including capital, are produced. The rate of economic growth will not be as great at it would have otherwise been, causing the production possibilities curve to shift outward by a smaller amount.
   d. The production possibilities curve will initially shift inward, but will eventually shift outward as labor productivity increases.

20. You received a monthly income of $1,000 which is spent on food and automobile payments. The cost per month for food is $400 and the monthly auto payment is $200. Let F represent the monthly food cost and A represent the monthly auto payment. Which of the following expressions represents your income constraint (or budget line)? Assume F is placed on the vertical axis and A on the horizontal axis.
   a. $1000 = $200 A + $400 A
   b. $400 = $400 F - $200 A
   c. $1000 = $400 F + $200 A
   d. F = 2.5 - .5 A

49

21. Which of the following statements best explains why a nation's consumption possibilities line lies outside of its production possibilities line?
    a. International trade requires nations to give up more than they receive, adversely affecting production and causing the production possibilities curve to shift inward away from the production possibilities curve.
    b. If nations specialize in and export goods for which they have an comparative advantage and import goods for which they have a comparative disadvantage, more goods can be obtained through domestic production and trade than from domestic production alone.
    c. The consumption possibilities line lies outside the production possibilities line because consumers are able to borrow and spend more than their domestically earned income.
    d. In order for the consumption possibilities line to lie outside of the production possibilities line, a nation must always export more than it imports.

22. Which of the following best explains a linear production possibilities curve?
    a. Beyond some level of production, worker productivity increases at an increasing rate.
    b. As more of a given class of goods is produced in a period, proportionately more of the other class of goods must be sacrificed.
    c. The opportunity cost of producing a given class of goods over a period remains constant.
    d. The opportunity cost of producing a given class of goods over a period decreases.

23. Suppose a nation produces two types of goods, capital and food. However, assume that in the capital goods industry firm A produces 2 units of capital per worker per week whereas firm B produces 5 units of capital per worker per week. If resources are fully employed, is this nation at a point on its production possibilities curve?
    a. No, a worker can be reallocated from firm B to firm A for a net gain of 4 units of capital.
    b. Yes, full employment guarantees that a economy is on its production possibilities curve.
    c. Yes, full employment means full production and allocative efficiency.
    d. No, a worker can be reallocated from firm A to firm B for a net gain of 3 units of capital. Thus, the economy must be inside of its production possibilities curve.

■ THINK IT THROUGH

1. Explain why a nation's endowment of economic resources necessitates choices between current and future uses of resources.

2. Explain under what conditions a nation incurs an opportunity cost as it produces more of a good. How does the law of increasing cost fit into your discussion?

3. How do technology and capital expenditures improve the quality or productivity of "other" economic resources?

4. Assume that the United States contributes disproportionately more resources to the defense of Western Europe than do the other NATO allies, and as a consequence these other countries can invest a larger share of their resources in capital and other goods and services. Use production possibility curves to show both the short- and long-run consequences regarding the economies of the United States and Western Europe.

■ CHAPTER ANSWERS

The Chapter in Brief

1. Production 2. Capital 3. Scarcity 4. Technology 5. Production possibilities curve 6. Sacrificing
7. Opportunity cost 8. Rises 9. Less 10. Larger 11. Are not 12. Unemployed 13. Inefficiently
14. Unattainable 15. Can 16. Outward 17. Current 18. Capital 19. Budget line 20. Outward
21. Increases 22. Outward 23. Inward 24. Reduction

Key Terms Review

1. Economic resources 2. Division of labor 3. Capital 4. Production possibilities curve
5. Entrepreneurship 6. Economic growth 7. Technology 8. Labor 9. Productive efficiency
10. Natural resources 11. Law of increasing costs

Concept Review

1. a. Labor b. Capital c. Natural resources d. Entrepreneurship
2. a. + b. 0 c. + d. + e. 0
3. a.

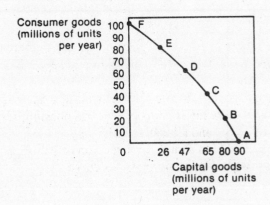

b. A point on the production possibilities curve represents a maximum level of production over a period of time for consumer and capital goods. At this level of production, resources are fully and efficiently employed.
c. (1) 15 (2) 18 (3) 21 (4) 26
d. Rise. Opportunity costs rise because in order to produce more and more consumer goods, increasing quantities of resources have to be reallocated from the capital goods industry to the consumer goods industry, and these resources are increasingly less adaptable to consumer goods production.
4. a. A point inside the curve represents a level of production involving unemployed resources or inefficient production or both.
b. A point outside the curve is unattainable in the short run because of resource constraints. In the long run, however, it is possible to reach point B if the productivity and quantity of resources increase.

51

5. a.   U b. O c. O d. U e. U f. O
6. a.

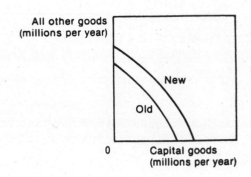

b.

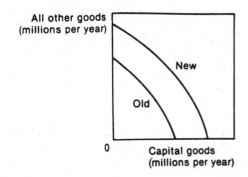

7. a.   Even if capital or technological improvements were made only in the aircraft industry, the levels of production in other industries would likely increase. The capacity to produce in the aircraft industry has increased, which means that more aircraft <u>can</u> be produced than before. Since capital increases the productivity of other resources, more aircraft could be produced with the same quantity of resources previously employed in the aircraft industry, or the same number of aircraft could be produced as before but now with fewer resources. These resources, therefore, could be used elsewhere in producing other goods and services.

   b.

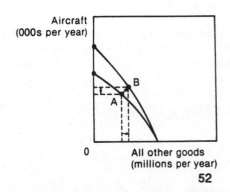

8. a.

Combination	Beer	CDs
A	20	0
B	16	1
C	12	2
D	8	3
E	4	4
F	0	5

b. Budget line

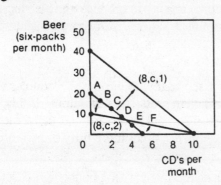

c. (1) (on figure above)

(2) (on figure above)

9. a. Assume that the student's income (I) is spent in its entirety on beer(B) and compact discs (CDs). Furthermore, assume the price of beer(PB) and the price of a CD (PCD) are \$2.50 and \$10, respectively.

$$I = (PB)(B) + (PCD)(CD)$$

Solve the above equation for (B).

$$B = I/PB - (PCD/PB)(CD)$$

Notice that the vertical intercept of the budget line is the level of income divided by the price of beer. Also notice that the slope of the budget line is negative and equals the ratio of prices of the two goods.

b. (1) An increase in income will increase the intercept term or constant term in the above equation. The budget line will shift upward.

(2) A decrease in the price of CDs and an increase in the price of beer will make the slope less negative and will decrease the intercept term. The budget line becomes flatter, with the vertical intercept decreasing.

10. a. Consumption, government spending, and trade from output

b. \$712.6

c. -4.65%

53

■ Mastery Test

1. b 2. d 3. d 4. b 5. c 6. c 7. b 8. a 9. c 10. b 11. e 12. c 13. d 14. c 15. d 16. c 17. a 18. c 19. c 20. d
21. b 22. c 23. d

Think it Through

1. A nation's endowment of resources, whether plentiful or limited, is a constraint to future growth. With full and efficient use of resources, a nation can produce only so much over a given period of time. Using resources today for capital means giving up the consumption of other goods today. But capital increases the future capacity to produce and also increases the productivity of economic resources. Because of this, a nation that forgoes consumption today and invests in capital will be able to consume more tomorrow.

2. A nation incurs a sacrifice or opportunity cost associated with the use of resources when (a) there is full employment of resources and (b) efficient production of output. If this were not the case, a nation could produce more of one good without necessarily reducing the consumption of other goods by either employing its resources more fully or by more efficiently producing its output.

   At full employment and efficient production, a nation incurs rising opportunity costs if it produces more and more of a given good because of the law of increasing costs. Because resources are not completely adaptable to all uses, they must be withdrawn in increasing amounts from other industries in order to produce given quantities of the good.

3. Both capital and technology increase the productivity of the production process. More output can be produced with the same amount of resources. A farmer with a tractor is far more productive than one with a digging stick. This is the story of American agriculture. The enormous productivity increases in the U.S. farm sector have been made possible by the mechanization of agriculture.

4. The United States not only sacrifices output of consumer goods and services in the short run but also sacrifices a higher rate of future economic growth and living standards.

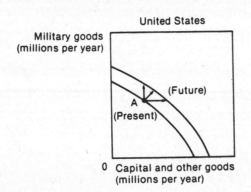

54

Western Europe, in contrast, is able to consume both more capital and other goods in the short run and because of greater capital investments will realize a faster rate of GDP growth in the future.

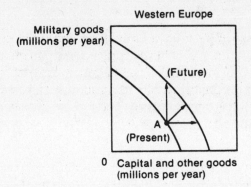

PART II

SUPPLY AND DEMAND
MARKETS AND THE PRICE SYSTEM

■ **Part Exercise**   *Getting Information on Financial and Commodity Markets*

In Part II, you will learn about supply and demand and the price system. You will also learn about the loanable funds market and the determination of interest rates. Use *The Wall Street Journal* over a two week period and record changes in interest rates. Be sure to identify the specific interest rates that you use. What possible changes in the supply of and demand for loanable funds could cause these observed changes? Explain.

3   MARKET TRANSACTIONS: BASIC SUPPLY AND DEMAND ANALYSIS

■ CHAPTER CONCEPTS

After studying your text, attending class, and completing this chapter, you should be able to:

1. Discuss the purposes and functions of markets.
2. Explain how a demand curve shows the law of demand and distinguish between a change in demand and a change in quantity demanded.
3. Show how a supply curve illustrates the law of supply and distinguish between a change in supply and a change in quantity supplied.
4. Describe the conditions required for market equilibrium and locate the equilibrium point on a supply and demand diagram.
5. Explain the consequences of shortages and surpluses in markets and how prices adjust in a free and unregulated competitive market to eliminate shortages or surpluses.
6. Show how changes in supply and demand affect market equilibrium.

■ THE CHAPTER IN BRIEF

Fill in the blanks to summarize chapter content.

Understanding the concept of a market and the role it plays in the allocation of resources and the distribution of output is critical to an understanding of how economies function. (1)_Markets_ (Markets, Trade publications) communicate information to buyers and sellers alike. The forces of supply and demand, which are basic to every market, interact to produce a (2)_quantity_ (market quantity, market price) that acts as a vehicle for communicating the wants of buyers to sellers. (3)_Supply + Demand_ (Cost-benefit analysis, Supply and demand analysis) is a method of isolating the forces of supply and demand so that the factors determining market prices can be understood. This allows us to better understand the communication and rationing functions of the price system.

Quantity demanded constitutes amounts of goods and services that buyers are willing and able to buy at a given price during a given period. A (4)_schedule_ (demand schedule, demand curve) is a table of data showing the relationship between the prices of a good and the associated quantities demanded, holding all other influencing factors unchanged. A (5)_curve_ (demand curve, demand schedule) is a plot of the price-quantity demanded coordinates. The demand schedule and its demand curve show that price and quantity demanded are negatively related. This relationship is known as the law of (6)_demand_ (increasing returns, demand). When there is a change in price, quantity demanded changes. This is called a (7)_change in quantity_ (change in demand, change in quantity demanded). A change in demand determinants other than the price of the good will shift the demand curve. A shift in the demand curve means that, at a given price, quantity demanded will either increase or decrease. This is called a (8)_change in demand_ (change in demand, change in quantity demanded). Changes in demand are caused by changes in (a) income, (b) wealth, (c) the prices of related goods, (d) price expectations, (e) tastes, and (f) the number of buyers in the market.

Quantity supplied represents the quantities that sellers are willing and able to produce and make available to the market at a given price during a given period. A (9)_schedule_ (supply schedule, supply curve) is a table of data showing the relationship between the prices of a good and the associated quantities supplied by sellers, all other influences on supply remaining the same. A (10) _Curve_ (supply curve, supply schedule) is a plot of the price-quantity supplied coordinates. The relationship between price and quantity supplied is a positive one and is called the law of (11) _supply_ (monetary incentives, supply). A (12) _change in quant_ (change in quantity supplied, change in supply) is caused by a price change. This is shown by a movement along a given supply curve. A (13) _supply_ (change in quantity supplied, change in supply) is the result of influences other than price, such as (a) the price of inputs, (b) prices of other goods, (c) technology, (d) price expectations, and (e) the number of sellers in a market. These nonprice influences shift the supply curve.

The forces of supply and demand interact to produce a market (14) _equilibrium_ (outcome, equilibrium), or state of balance, where the quantities demanded by buyers are just equal to the quantities supplied by sellers. In a state of equilibrium, buyers and sellers have no incentive to alter levels of consumption or production. It is the market (15) _price_ (price, quantity) that equates the quantities supplied and demanded.

A price above a market equilibrium price results in a (16) _surplus_ (shortage, surplus) because the quantity supplied at this price exceeds the quantity demanded. A price below the equilibrium price causes a (17) _shortage_ (shortage, surplus) because the quantity demanded exceeds the quantity supplied. In a competitive market, a seller tries to get rid of surpluses by (18) _cutting prices_ (increasing inventories, cutting prices). Falling prices will reduce surpluses. When the price falls enough to equal the market equilibrium price, the (19) _surplus_ (shortage, surplus) is eliminated completely.

Shortages require some form of rationing. Sellers ration the limited supply of goods among competing buyers by (20) _increasing_ (increasing, decreasing) prices. But price increases reduce the quantities demanded and increase the quantities supplied, which in turn reduce the shortage. Shortages are completely eliminated when the price has risen (21) _equal to_ (above, equal to) the market equilibrium price. Market prices remain unchanged in a competitive market unless the underlying forces of supply or demand change. A change in demand, a change in supply, or a change in both supply and demand (22) _can_ (can, cannot) alter the market equilibrium price and quantity.

■ KEY TERMS REVIEW

Write the key term from the list below next to its definition.

Key Terms

Market
Change in quantity
  demanded
Supply and demand
  analysis
Quantity demanded
Demand schedule
Law of demand
Complements
Demand curve
Surplus
Change in relative
  price
Change in demand
Normal good

Market equilibrium
Quantity supplied
Demand
Supply
Law of supply
Supply schedule
Supply curve
Change in quantity
  supplied
Substitutes
Change in supply
Shortage
Equilibrium
Inferior good

Definitions

1. _Change in rel. price_ : an increase or decrease in the price of a good relative to an average of the prices of all goods.

2. _demand curve_ : a graph that shows how quantity demanded varies with the price of a good.

3. _Supply schedule_ : a table that shows how the quantity supplied of a good is related to the price.

4. _quantity supplied_ : the quantity of a good sellers are willing and able to make available in the market over a given period at a certain price, other things being equal.

5. _Supply_ : a relationship between the price of an item and the quantity supplied by sellers.

6. _law of supply_ : other things being equal, the higher the price of a good, the greater the quantity of that good sellers are willing and able to make available over a given period.

7. _market_ : an arrangement through which buyers and sellers meet or communicate in order to trade goods or services.

8. _Supply + demand analysis_ : explains how prices are established in markets through competition among many buyers and sellers, and how those prices affect the quantities traded.

9. _Market equilibrium_ : attained when the price of a good adjusts so that the quantity buyers are willing and able to buy at that price is just equal to the quantity sellers are willing and able to supply.

10. _shortage_ : exists if the quantity demanded exceeds the quantity supplied of a good over a period of time.

61

11. ~~market~~ equilib : prevails when economic forces balance so that economic variables neither increase nor decrease.

12. surplus : exists if the quantity supplied exceeds the quantity demanded of a good over a period of time.

13. Change in Supply : a change in the relationship between a good's price and the quantity supplied in response to a change in a supply determinant other than the good's price.

14. Change in quant demand : a change in the amount of a good buyers are willing and able to buy in response to a change in the price of the good.

15. Change in demand : a change in the relationship between the price of a good and the quantity demanded caused by a change in a demand determinant other than the price of the good.

16. Complement : goods whose use together enhances the satisfaction a consumer obtains from each.

17. Substitute : goods that serve a purpose similar to that of a given good.

18. Supply curve : a graph that shows how the quantity supplied varies with the price of a good.

19. law of demand : in general, other things being equal, the lower the price of a good, the greater the quantity of that good buyers are willing and able to purchase over a given period.

20. Change in quant supplied : a change in the amount of a good sellers are willing to sell in response to a change in the price of the good.

21. demand : a relationship between an item's price and the quantity demanded.

22. demand sched : a table that shows how the quantity demanded of a good would vary with price, given all other demand determinants.

23. quantity demand : the amount of an item that buyers are willing and able to purchase over a period at a certain price, given all other influences on their decision to buy.

24. inferior good : good whose demand declines as income increases.

25. normal good : good whose demand increases as income increases.

■ CONCEPT REVIEW

Concept 2: *Demand, law of demand, changes in demand and quantity demanded*

1. The following is a demand schedule for corn:

Price per Bushel	Quantity Demanded (000s bushels per week)	
	(a)	(b)
$4.00	850	800
3.75	900	850
3.50	950	900
3.25	1,000	950
3.00	1,050	1000
2.75	1,100	1050
2.50	1,150	1100

a. Put the demand curve on the diagram below.

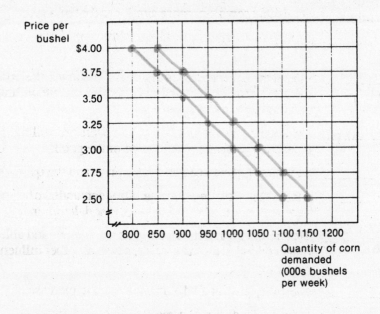

b. What kind of relationship exists between the price per bushel of corn and the quantity of corn demanded? inverse

c. Assume that the prices of other vegetables are falling relative to the price of corn. Will this cause the demand curve to shift? Why? yes demand for corn decrease

d. Assume that the quantity of corn demanded decreases by 50,000 bushels at every price level. Show the impact of this by completing column b above.

e. Show the impact from part d on the demand curve that you plotted in part a.

2. List six nonprice determinants of demand:
   a. income
   b. Wealth
   c. price subs + comps
   d. expectation price
   e. Tastes
   f. # of buyers

3. Indicate for each of the following if a demand curve for automobiles will shift to the right (R), left (L), or remain unchanged (U):

   a. ___R___ Auto prices fall
   b. ___L___ Price of gasoline triples
   c. ___R___ Incomes decrease
   d. ___U___ Stock market gains increase wealth
   e. ___L___ Public transit fares fall to zero
   f. ___R___ Auto price increase expected

Concept 3: *Supply, law of supply, changes in supply and quantity supplied*

4. The following is a supply schedule for corn:

Price per Bushel	Quantity Supplied (000s of bushels per week)	
	(a)	(b)
$4.00	1600	1500
3.75	1400	1300
3.50	1200	1100
3.25	1000	900
3.00	800	700
2.75	600	500
2.50	400	300

a. Plot the supply curve on the diagram below.

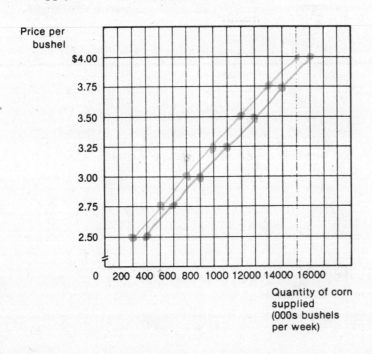

b. Is there a positive or negative relationship between the price of corn and the quantity of corn supplied? Explain. *Positive*

c. Suppose a serious drought reduces corn output at each price by 100,000 bushels. Show the impact in column b above by completing the table.

d. Plot the new supply curve from column b on the diagram from part a.

5. List five nonprice determinants of supply:

a. *# suppliers*

b. *price components*

c. *technology*

d. *price other goods*

65

e. <u>price expectations</u>

6. Which of the following will cause the supply curve for hamburgers to shift to the right (R), left (L), or remain unchanged (U)?

L decrease
a. ___L___ Increase in the price of hamburger meat
b. ___U___ Increase in the price of hamburgers
L
c. ___R___ Increase in the price of chicken nuggets
d. ___R___ Introduction of new cost-saving technology in the hamburger industry

Concepts 4 and 5:   *Market equilibrium price and quantity; shortages and surpluses*

7. The table below contains the price, quantity supplied, and quantity demanded data from column a of questions 1 and 4.

Price per Bushel	Quantity Demanded		Quantity Supplied	
	(000s of bushels per year)			
	(a)	(b)	(c)	(d)
$4.00	850	1160	1600	2100
3.75	900	1150	1400	1900
3.50	950	1200	1200	1700
3.25	1000	1250	1000	1500
3.00	1050	1300	800	1300
2.75	1100	1350	600	1100
2.50	1150	1400	400	900

3.25
1000 000

a. From the table above, determine the market equilibrium price and quantity in bushels.
b. On the diagram below, plot both the demand and supply curves. Identify the equilibrium price and quantity.

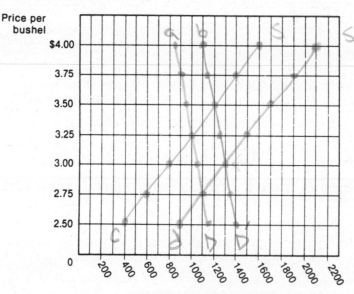

Quantity of corn demanded and supplied
(000s of bushels per week)

66

c. At a price of $3.75, a _surplus_ exists in the amount of _500000_ because quantity demanded is _less_ than quantity supplied.
d. At a price of $2.75, a _shortage_ exists in the amount of _500000_ because quantity demanded is _more_ than quantity supplied.
e. What is meant by the statement that competitive markets are self-equilibrating?

Concept 6: *Changes in supply and demand and market equilibrium*

8. Referring to the supply and demand schedules in question 7 above:
   a. Suppose that an increase in income causes the demand for corn to increase by 250,000 bushels at each price. Show the change in question 7, column b. Plot the new demand curve on the diagram in question 7.
   b. The market equilibrium price has _increased_ from $ _3.25_ to $ _3.50_. Market equilibrium output has _increased_ from _1000_ bushels to _1200_ bushels.
   c. Suppose that because of excellent weather, corn production increases at every price by 500,000 bushels. Show the change by completing column d from question 7. Plot the new supply curve on the diagram in question 7.
   d. Comparing the original equilibrium—demand curve a and supply curve c—to the new equilibrium with supply curve d, market equilibrium price has _decreased_ from $ _3.25_ to $ _2.75_. Market quantity has _increased_ from _1000_ bushels to _1100_ bushels.
   e. Comparing the original equilibrium—demand curve a and supply curve c—to a new equilibrium with demand curve b and supply curve d, market equilibrium price has _decreased_ from $ _3.25_ to $ _3.00_ and market quantity has _increased_ from _1000_ to _1300_ bushels.

9. Indicate below if the market price and quantity of concert tickets increases (+), decreases (-), or is indeterminate (0):

	Price	Quantity
a. Stock market losses reduce wealth	-	-
b. Income increases	+	+
c. Season ticket prices are expected to rise	+	+
d. Musicians' union wins large pay increase	+	-
e. Price of movie tickets falls	-	-
f. Population increases	+	+

Advanced Application: Changes in supply and demand and market equilibrium

10. Let the following equations represent demand and supply curves for some good:

   Demand curve: $Qd = a - bP$
   Supply curve: $Qs = c + dP$
      where   a, b, c, and d are positive constants
                     Qd = quantity demanded
                     Qs = quantity supplied
                     P = price

   a. Solve the above equations for the market equilibrium price. $P = (a-c)/(d+b)$
   b. Solve for the equilibrium quantity. $Q = (ad+bc)/(d+b)$
   c. Interpret the equations for price and quantity. What causes price or quantity to rise or fall?

Select the best answer.

1. In a free and unregulated competitive economy:
   a. wants are communicated to producers by the purchase orders of wholesalers.
   b. wants of buyers are communicated to sellers through the determination of prices in markets.
   c. sellers use market survey instruments to determine what and how much to produce.
   d. markets play an insignificant role.

2. The quantities of goods that buyers are willing and able to purchase at a specific price over a period of time, other influences held unchanged, is a definition for:
   a. quantity demanded.
   b. supply.
   c. total sales.
   d. demand.

3. The demand _____ is a table of price and quantity demanded data in which the *ceteris paribus* assumption is employed. The _____ is a plot of that data.
   a. table/scatter diagram
   b. schedule/marginal cost curve
   c. curve/schedule
   d. schedule/demand curve

4. The law of demand states that, other things being the same:
   a. price and income are positively related.
   b. income and sales are positively related.
   c. price and quantity demanded are positively related.
   d. price and quantity demanded are inversely related.

5. Which of the following will not cause a change in demand?
   a. Change in income
   b. Change in the price of the good in question
   c. Change in the prices of related goods, such as complements or substitutes
   d. Expectation of higher prices

6. If two goods are substitutes and the price of one good increases, the demand for the other good will:
   a. not change.
   b. increase.
   c. not be related.
   d. decrease.

7. If two goods are complementary goods and the price of one good increases, the demand for the other will:
   a. not change.
   b. increase.
   c. not be related.
   d. decrease.

8. If a good is a normal good, an increase in income will:
   a. increase supply.
   b. decrease demand.
   c. increase demand.
   d. decrease supply.

9. The quantities of a good that sellers are willing and able to produce and make available to the market at a specific price over a given period, other things being constant, is a definition of:
   a. demand.
   b. equilibrium.
   c. demand curve.
   d. quantity supplied.

10. The law of supply states that, other influences being unchanged:
    a. price and quantity demanded are inversely related.
    b. price and quantity supplied are inversely related.
    c. income and quantity supplied are unrelated.
    d. price and quantity supplied are positively related.

11. A change in quantity supplied can be caused by a change in
    a. price.
    b. income.
    c. technology.
    d. price of inputs.

12. A shift in a supply curve is known as a:
    a. supply shift.
    b. change in quantity supplied.
    c. rotation.
    d. change in supply.

13. Which of the following will not cause a leftward shift in the supply curve?
    a. Decrease in input prices
    b. Increase in the prices of other goods that could be produced with the same resources and technology —
    c. Expectation of lower product prices
    d. Decrease in the number of sellers —

decrease

14. Market equilibrium occurs when:
    a. the forces of supply and demand oppose each other.
    b. the forces of price and quantity oppose each other.
    c. a market price just equates quantity demanded and quantity supplied.
    d. a market quantity just equates quantity supplied and quantity demanded.

15. A price above the market equilibrium price results in:
    a. a shortage.
    b. inflation.
    c. excess demand.
    d. a surplus.

16. A price below the market equilibrium price results in:
    a. a shortage.
    b. inflation.
    c. insufficient demand.
    d. a surplus.

17. An increase in the demand for a good will _____ price and _____ quantity.
    a. decrease/decrease
    b. increase/decrease
    c. increase/increase
    d. decrease/increase

18. A decrease in supply of a good will _____ price and _____ quantity.
    a. decrease/decrease
    b. increase/decrease
    c. increase/increase
    d. decrease/increase

19. An increase in both demand and supply will _____ price and _____ quantity.
    a. decrease/ decrease
    b. have an indeterminate effect on/increase
    c. increase/increase
    d. increase/have an indeterminate effect on

20. If the price of movie tickets increases significantly, then the price of VCRs will probably _____ and the market quantity of VCRs will _____.
    a. increase/decrease
    b. increase/increase
    c. decrease/decrease
    d. decrease/increase

21. Assume that consumer incomes increase as a result of increases in wage rates. Using supply and demand analysis, which of the following best explains the impact on market price? Assume that the good in question is an inferior good.
    a. Market price increases because the demand for the good increases relative to supply.
    b. Market price increases because supply increases and demand decreases.
    c. Market price is indeterminate because the supply decreases as demand increases.
    d. Market price is indeterminate because supply and demand both decrease.

22. What will likely happen to market price and market quantity of a good if technological improvements occur simultaneously with decreases in the price of a substitute good?
    a. Market price will rise and market quantity will fall.
    b. Market price will fall and market quantity will rise.
    c. Both market price and quantity will rise.
    d. Both market price and quantity will fall.
    e. Market price will fall, but market quantity is indeterminate.

70

23. Suppose farms produce both wheat and barley. What will happen to the market price and quantity of wheat if the price of barley increases?
    a. Market price falls and market quantity rises.
    b. Both market price and quantity increase.
    c. Both market price and quantity decrease. —
    d. Market price increases and market quantity decreases. —

24. Which answer best explains the following statement? "An increase in income increases quantity supplied."
    a. Producers behave according to the law of supply which says that income and supply are positively related.
    b. As income increases, demand increases if the good is a normal good, causing market price and quantity supplied to rise.
    c. If the good is an inferior good and income increases, spending on the good will increase, inducing firms to increase quantity supplied.
    d. This statement is incorrect because changes in income change demand, not quantity supplied.

25. Which of the following best explains the cause and effect process associated with an increase in demand?
    a. An increase in demand increases price and causes a surplus at the existing level of output. Producers respond by apportioning that surplus among consumers.
    b. An increase in demand causes price to increase, producing shortages and the need to increase supply.
    c. An increase in demand increases price and causes a shortage at the existing level of output. Producers respond to the shortage by discounting prices so quantity supplied will increase.
    d. An increase in demand initially will cause a shortage as quantity demanded exceeds quantity supplied at the existing price. Firms respond by increasing price, producing an incentive to increase quantity supplied.

■ THINK IT THROUGH

1. A market economy is a type of economy that relies on the market to .... (Complete the statement as thoroughly as you can.)

2. Use supply and demand analysis to assess the impact of a drought.
    a. Discuss the impact of the drought on the market for corn.
    b. Discuss the probable impact on feedlots that use corn as feed.

3. If a market is currently in equilibrium and an increase in demand occurs, what happens to the market price? *Explain*.

4. Using supply and demand analysis, discuss the impact on the market for golf balls if golf course green fees increase.

5. Suppose that you operate a dry cleaning firm in a small city and you and the other dry cleaners are earning handsome profits. Because of the profit potential, a national dry cleaning firm enters the area and opens several new dry cleaners. Assess the impact on the market for dry cleaning in this city.

CHAPTER ANSWERS

The Chapter In Brief

1. Markets 2. Market price 3. Supply and demand analysis 4. Demand schedule 5. Demand curve 6. Demand 7. Change in quantity demanded 8. Change in demand 9. Supply schedule 10. Supply curve 11. Supply 12. Change in quantity supplied 13. Change in supply 14. Equilibrium 15. Price 16. Surplus 17. Shortage 18. Cutting prices 19. Surplus 20. Increasing 21. Equal to 22. Can

Key Terms Review

1. Change in relative price 2. Demand curve 3. Supply schedule 4. Quantity supplied 5. Supply 6. Law of Supply 7. Market 8. Supply and demand analysis 9. Market equilibrium 10. Shortage 11. Equilibrium 12. Surplus 13. Change in supply 14. Change in quantity demanded 15. Change in demand 16. Complements 17. Substitutes 18. Supply curve 19. Law of demand 20. Change in quantity supplied 21. Demand 22. Demand schedule 23. Quantity demanded 24. Inferior good 25. Normal good

Concept Review

1. a.

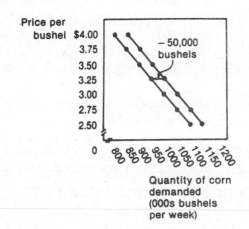

b. Negative or inverse
c. If other vegetables are considered substitutes for corn, the demand for corn falls and the demand curve shifts leftward as the prices of other vegetables are falling.
d.   (b)

```
            800
            850
            900
            950
           1000
           1050
           1100
```

e. The demand curve shifts leftward as shown in the diagram above in part a.

2. a. Income b. Wealth c. Prices of substitutes and complements d. Price expectations e. Tastes f. Number of buyers

3. a. U b. L c. L d. R e. L f. R

72

4. a.

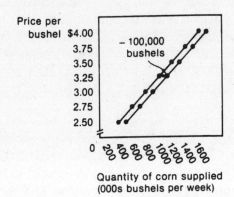

Price per
bushel $4.00
3.75
3.50
3.25
3.00
2.75
2.50

− 100,000
bushels

0 200 400 600 800 1000 1200 1400 1600

Quantity of corn supplied
(000s bushels per week)

b. Positive, higher prices increase the willingness and ability of suppliers to increase production.

c.   (b)

1500
1300
1100
900
700
500
300

d. The supply curve shifts leftward as shown in the diagram above in part a.

5. a. Prices of other goods b. Prices of inputs c. Technology d. Price expectations e. Number of sellers

6. a. L b. U c. L d. R

7. a. $3.25, 1,000,000

b.

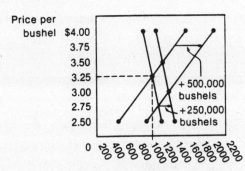

Price per
bushel $4.00
3.75
3.50
3.25
3.00
2.75
2.50

+ 500,000
bushels
+ 250,000
bushels

0 200 400 600 800 1000 1200 1400 1600 1800 2000 2200

Quantity of corn demanded
and supplied (000s of bushels)

c. Surplus, 500,000 bushels, less

d. Shortage, 500,000 bushels, greater

e. Competitive markets are self-equilibrating because market forces will eliminate shortages and surpluses. Shortages are eliminated as market prices rise and surpluses are eliminated as suppliers lower prices to sell excess inventory.

8. a.   (b)
       1100
       1150
       1200
       1250
       1300
       1350
       1400

b. Increased, $3.25, $3.50, increased, 1,000,000, 1,200,000

c.   (d)
       2100
       1900
       1700
       1500
       1300
       1100
        900

d. Decreased, $3.25, $2.75, increased, 1,000,000, 1,100,000

e. Decreased, $3.25, $3, increased, 1,000,000, 1,300,000

9.

	Price	Quantity
a.	—	—
b.	+	+
c.	+	+
d.	+	—
e.	—	—
f.	+	+

10. Market equilibrium requires that Qd = Qs. Setting the supply and demand curves equal to each other:

$$a - bP = c + dP$$

and solving for P, the market equilibrium price, gives:

a. $P = (a - c)/(d + b)$

Substituting this expression for P into either the demand or supply equation and solving for Q, the market equilibrium quantity, yields:

b. $Q = (ad + bc)/(d + b)$

c. Q is positive and P must be positive. P is positive if the intercept of the demand curve a exceeds the intercept of the supply curve c. This always is expected to be the case. Changes in the nonprice determinants of supply and demand influence the supply and demand equations by changing the value of the intercept terms, a or c. For instance, an increase in income would increase a assuming the good is a normal good. If it is an inferior good, the increase in income will reduce a. As can be seen from the equations above, an increase in a will increase P and Q. A decrease in a will decrease P and Q. An increase in c caused by a nonprice determinant of supply causes P to decrease and Q to increase.

74

Mastery Test

1. b 2. a 3. d 4. d 5. b 6. b 7. d 8. c 9. d 10. d 11. a 12. d 13. a 14. c 15. d 16. a 17. c 18. b 19. b 20. b 21. d 22. e 23. d 24. b 25. d

Think it Through

1. A market economy is a type of economy that relies on the market to allocate resources and distribute output. The impersonal interaction of the forces of supply and demand communicate the wishes of consumers to sellers via the market price. Changes in demand alter the price, and it is the change in price that causes a supplier to respond by altering production. As producers alter levels of production, they alter their levels of employment of resources. Thus markets determine what is to be produced and in what quantities. Resources flow to markets experiencing increases in quantity and away from markets experiencing decreases in production. Output is distributed based upon a buyer's ability to pay. Other things being constant, rising market prices reduce the ability to pay, whereas decreases in market prices increase the ability to pay.

2. a. As is shown in the diagram below, the drought reduces the supply of corn increasing the price per bushel of corn and reducing the market quantity of corn.

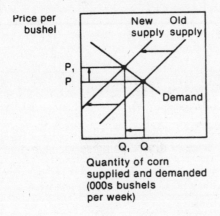

b. If corn is an input to feedlot operations and the price of corn is increasing, the supply of feedlot services will decrease, causing the price of those services to increase and the quantity of feedlot services to fall.

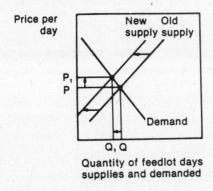

75

3. If demand increases, then at the current market price there is a shortage because quantity demanded exceeds quantity supplied.In order to ration the limited number of goods or services among many buyers, the price of the good or service is increased. Increases in price reduce quantity demanded but increase quantity supplied. This in turn reduces the shortage. As long as a shortage exists, the rationing function of prices implies that prices will continue to rise. Prices will no longer increase when the shortage is eliminated.The shortage no longer exists at the new market equilibrium.

4. Greens fees and golf balls are complementary goods. If the price of greens fees increases, the demand for golf balls will decrease. As can be seen in the figure below, a decrease in the demand for golf balls reduces the market price and quantity.

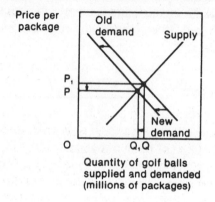

Quantity of golf balls supplied and demanded (millions of packages)

5. If several new dry cleaners open for business, the local market supply of dry cleaning services will increase. This causes a decrease in the price of dry cleaning services, but an increase in total market quantity.

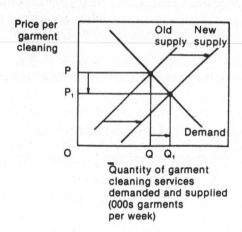

Quantity of garment cleaning services demanded and supplied (000s garments per week)

76

4   USING SUPPLY AND DEMAND ANALYSIS

■ CHAPTER CONCEPTS

After studying your text, attending class, and completing this chapter, you should be able to:

1. Demonstrate how market equilibrium prices deal with the problem of scarcity by rationing goods and services and explain why prices would be zero for nonscarce goods.
2. Explain how supply and demand conditions affect the price and sales potential for new products.
3. Show how wages and interest rates are determined in competitive markets.
4. Use supply and demand analysis to show how government control of prices in competitive markets can result in shortages or surpluses.

■ THE CHAPTER IN BRIEF

Fill in the blanks to summarize chapter content.

Supply and demand analysis is a useful tool for analyzing personal, business, and social problems and issues. It shows the importance of prices in the allocation of resources. Prices help us deal with the problem of scarcity in both the allocation of resources and the distribution of output. Do prices have a role when scarcity does not exist? Goods in abundant supply such as air are called (1)_nonscarce goods_(essential commodities, nonscarce goods) because there is no positive price for which quantity demanded exceeds quantity supplied. If a positive price is not possible, markets do not develop. Markets develop only when positive prices are possible.

But even at positive prices, a market may not develop if the minimum price required by sellers exceeds the maximum price that buyers are willing and able to pay for the first unit of output. A market for new products can only develop when demand and supply have reached a point where the (2)_maximum_(maximum, minimum) price buyers are willing and able to pay for the first unit of output exceeds the (3)_minimum_(maximum, minimum) price sellers are willing to take for that unit.

In addition to the markets for goods and services, supply and demand analysis can be used to assess changes in competitive labor and credit markets. The price per unit of labor is called the (4)_wage_(labor cost, wage). When the supply of labor equals the demand, there is a market wage and quantity of labor employed. Everyone who wants to work at that wage is employed. If the demand for the product produced by that labor increases, the demand for labor by employers will likewise increase. This causes the wage to (5)_rise_(rise, fall) and the quantity of labor employed to (6)_increase_(decrease, increase). In a recession, as the demand for goods and services falls, the demand for labor declines, causing both wages and employment to also (7)_fall_(rise, fall).

Changes in the demand and supply of loanable funds determine interest rate movements. In an economic expansion, individuals, businesses, and government as a group borrow more. Interest rates (8)_rise_(rise, fall) as the demand for loanable funds increases. If the supply of loanable funds increases, say as a result of an increase in savings by both businesses and individuals, interest rates will (9)_rise_(rise, fall) and (10)_more_(more, less) credit will be extended by lenders.

Prices are not always allowed to perform the rationing function. Society will often sanction government price controls as an attempt to aid certain interest groups, such as farmers, unskilled workers, and low-income renters and borrowers. (11)_ceilings_ (Price ceilings, Price floors) are government-mandated prices that are set below market equilibrium prices. A price below the market price causes (12)_shortage_(surpluses, shortages). Rent controls, while helping those fortunate enough to pay controlled rents, cause (13)_shortage_(surpluses, shortages) of low-income housing and reduce the incentive of landlords to maintain properties.

When shortages develop there must be a way to allocate the limited goods and services among the buyers. A market system relies on prices to do this. But with price ceilings, prices are not allowed to perform that function. Waiting in line, eligibility criteria, and ration stamps are three methods of nonprice rationing. All three are less efficient than prices in responding to shortages. There will still be those people willing and able to pay prices above the controlled price. In response to this potential market, illegal or (14)_black_ (new markets, black markets) develop.

(15)_floors_(Price ceilings, Price floors) are controlled prices that are set above the market price. Prices above market equilibrium prices cause (16)_surpluses_(surpluses, shortages). Whereas prices fall to eliminate the surplus, other means have to be used to deal with surpluses, such as with agricultural price-support programs. Farmers either have to be rewarded to reduce plantings or the surpluses have to be purchased, stored, and distributed by government. Resources that could have been used elsewhere in the economy are being used to eliminate or deal with surpluses that would have been efficiently eliminated by a functioning price system. Although farmers as a special interest group benefit, consumers lose in that they pay (17)_higher_(lower, higher) prices, and the allocation of resources in the economy is (18)_less_(less, more) efficient.

Minimum wage laws set minimum wages at a level above the market wage in most labor markets. The intent of such legislation is to increase the income of the poorest members of society, those individuals who also happen to have the lowest skill levels. But as was the case with agricultural price supports, (19)_surpluses_(surpluses, shortages) develop. The unemployment rate among the unskilled is (20)_higher_(lower, higher). The minimum wage benefits those lucky enough to find employment at that wage, but causes (21)_more_(more, less) unemployment in that segment of society that can least afford to be unemployed.

Price controls distort the economy. They benefit some at the expense of others and prohibit a competitive economy from efficiently rationing resources. If the motives underlying price controls are socially desirable, society would gain if methods other than price controls could be employed to make certain interest groups better off without impairing the functioning of a competitive economy.

KEY TERMS REVIEW

Write the key term from the list below next to its definition.

Key Terms

Nonscarce good   Price ceiling
Wages   Nonprice rationing
Credit   Black market
Interest   Price floor

Definitions

1. *nonscarce good*: a good for which the quantity demanded does not exceed the quantity supplied at a zero price.

2. *price ceiling*: establishes a maximum price that can legally be charged for a good or service.

3. *wages*: the price paid for labor services.

4. *interest*: the price for the use of funds, expressed as a percentage per dollar of funds borrowed.

5. *price floor*: a minimum price established by law.

6. *black market*: a market in which sellers sell goods to buyers for more than the legal prices.

7. *credit*: the use of loanable funds supplied by lenders to borrowers, who agree to pay back the funds borrowed, according to an agreed-upon schedule.

8. *nonprice rationing*: a device that distributes available goods and services on a basis other than willingness to pay.

CONCEPT REVIEW

Concept 3: *The determination of wages and interest rates in competitive markets*

1. You are a manager of a business and you are trying to decide if you should borrow funds for plant expansion today at the current interest rate of 12%. The morning newspaper reports that the Federal Reserve System has announced that within the next month it will begin to expand the funds that banks have on hand to extend credit.

   a. Show the impact on the supply of loanable funds curve in the diagram below.

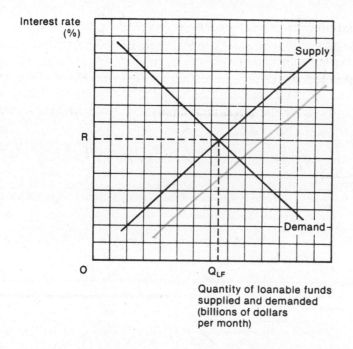

Interest rate (%)

Supply

R

Demand

O Q_LF

Quantity of loanable funds
supplied and demanded
(billions of dollars
per month)

b. How will your analysis of future interest rates influence your decision to borrow today?

2. You are a college sophomore trying to decide if you should major in mechanical engineering. Employability and income prospects are important considerations in your choice. As shown in the diagram below, the market for engineers is currently producing entry wages of $35,000.

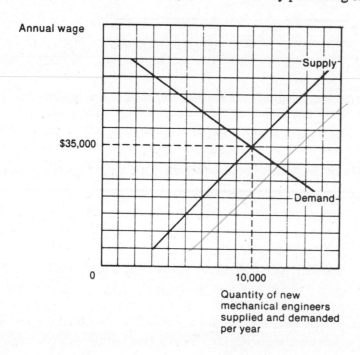

Annual wage

Supply

$35,000

Demand

0 10,000

Quantity of new
mechanical engineers
supplied and demanded
per year

a. If you and thousands of other college students are induced by these wages to become majors in engineering, in time the supply of engineers will ___increase___. Show the future supply curve on the diagram above.

b. Entry wages in the future would ___decrease___, and the total employment of engineers would ___increase___.

c. How might these expected future wages and employment levels influence your decision today to major in engineering?

Concept 4: *Government price controls—shortages and surpluses*

3. The diagram below represents the market for good X.

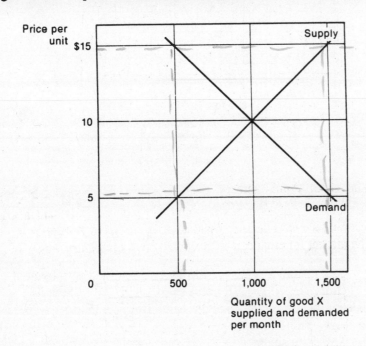

Price per unit

Quantity of good X supplied and demanded per month

a. The market price is $___10___, and the market quantity equals ___1000___ units of X.

b. If a price ceiling is established at $5, a ___shortage___ would exist in the amount of ___1000___ units. Show on the diagram above the impact of this price ceiling.

c. If a price floor is set at $15, a ___surplus___ would exist in the amount of ___1000___ units. Show this on the graph above.

81

4. Given the market for unskilled labor in the diagram below:

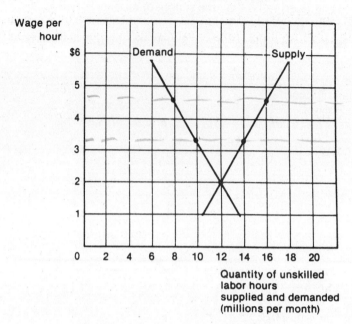

Wage per hour

Quantity of unskilled labor hours supplied and demanded (millions per month)

a. The market wage and level of employment equals $__2__ and __12__ hours, respectively.

b. A minimum wage is now established at $3.35 per hour.
   (1) Show on the graph above.
   (2) Wages _increase_ from $__2__ to $_3.35_ and employment _decreases_ from __12__ hours to __10__ hours.

c. What would happen if the minimum wage increased from $3.35 to $4.70 per hour?
   (1) Show on the above graph.
   (2) Wages _increase_ from $_3.35_ to $_4.70_ and employment _decreases_ from __10__ hours to __8__ hours.

5. List three forms of nonprice rationing:
   a. _standing in line_
   b. _ration stamps_
   c. _eligibility_

Advanced Application: Determination of interest rates

6. As a portfolio manager you must react to anticipated changes in interest rates with respect to your company's holding of financial assets such as stocks, cash, and bonds. Based on the current interest rate of 10%, your research shows that for each one percentage point change in the interest rate, the quantity of loanable funds supplied changes by $2 billion and the quantity of loanable funds demanded changes by $3 billion. If you anticipate that the demand for loanable funds will increase by $5 billion, what would you predict regarding the future rate of interest?

7. Insights on Issues

According to Abram Bergson, identify three ways the "... disintegration of Soviet and Eastern European communism and their resulting shifts toward a western-type market economy..." affect the average American.

a._____

b._____

c._____

Select the best answer.

1. Markets for new products would not develop if:
   a. the price required by producers to produce the first unit of output exceeded the price that buyers are willing and able to pay for that first unit.
   b. profits exceeded that which could be earned on financial assets.
   c. the price required by producers to produce the first unit of output was less than the price buyers are willing and able to pay for the first unit.
   d. None of the above

2. Goods for which there is no positive price in which quantity demanded does not exceed quantity supplied, are known as:
   a. scarce goods.
   b. normal goods.
   c. inferior goods.
   d. nonscarce goods.

3. An important function of prices in competitive markets is:
   a. the rationing function.
   b. to ensure that producers make profits.
   c. to eliminate any unemployment.
   d. to communicate to buyers the wishes of sellers.

4. In a competitive labor market, wages are determined:
   a. by buyers.
   b. by unions.
   c. by sellers.
   d. by the forces of supply and demand.

5. An increase in the demand for labor by businesses _____ wages and _____ employment.
   a. increases/decreases
   b. decreases/decreases
   c. increases/increases
   d. decreases/increases

6. If because of a recession the demand for loanable funds decreases, what would happen to market interest rates and the quantity of credit extended?
   a. Interest rates would increase and the quantity of credit would decrease.
   b. Interest rates would decrease and the quantity of credit would not change.
   c. Interest rates would not change but the quantity of credit would fall.
   d. Both interest rates and the quantity of credit would decline.

7. Rents controls:
   a. are price ceilings.
   b. cause shortages of low-income housing.
   c. result in the deterioration of low-income housing through the lack of maintenance.
   d. All of the above.

8. The minimum wage law is an example of:
   a. an employment enhancement strategy.
   b. a price ceiling.
   c. a price floor.
   d. a well-designed policy intended to reduce teenage unemployment.

9. Price ceilings cause:
   a. no change in market quantities.
   b. shortages.
   c. quantity supplied to increase.
   d. surpluses.

10. Price floors cause:
    a. no change in market quantities.
    b. shortages.
    c. quantity demanded to increase.
    d. surpluses.

11. Agricultural price supports:
    a. benefit farmers.
    b. harm consumers.
    c. require the use of scarce resources to deal with surpluses.
    d. All of the above

12. If in some labor markets the market wage for unskilled labor exceeds the minimum wage:
    a. unemployment would result.
    b. wages would rise.
    c. the minimum wage law would not have an adverse impact on unemployment.
    d. wages would fall.

13. Which of the following cannot be considered true regarding price controls?
    a. Some people within special interest groups gain.
    b. Some people within the targeted special interest groups may actually lose.
    c. Resources are more efficiently used in the economy.
    d. Resources are less efficiently used in the economy.

14. Which of the following is not a nonprice form of rationing?
    a. Grouped staging
    b. Waiting in line
    c. Ration stamps
    d. Eligibility criteria

15. Price ceilings create an environment conducive to the development of:
    a. new products.
    b. black markets.
    c. higher employment.
    d. a saving ethic.

16. Suppose a firm introduces a radically-advanced stereo speaker system to the market, but finds that the system is not selling. What might be a likely cause for the apparent lack of consumer interest?
    a. The market demand and supply curves intersect at too high of a price.
    b. The market demand and supply curves intersect at a low price, but product quality is poor.
    c. The market demand curve's intercept on the horizontal axis is at a lower level of output than the market supply curve's intercept.
    d. The market demand curve's intercept on the vertical axis is at a lower price that the market supply curve's intercept.

17. Which of the following statements best explains the existence of black markets?
    a. There will always be a depraved segment of the population engaged in illegal activities.
    b. Black markets only exist in centralized socialist nations where people are not free to exercise their will.
    c. Black markets arise where prices are kept below market equilibrium prices, suggesting that some consumers would be willing and able to pay higher prices for these goods rather than to go without.
    d. Government price floors cause shortages and provide incentives for black market entrepreneurs to violate government price controls.

18. What might happen to market interest rates if households increase saving while federal government borrowing is increasing?
    a. The interest rate increases because the demand for loanable funds increases.
    b. The supply of loanable funds increases and the demand for loanable funds decreases, causing the market rate of interest to rise.
    c. Both the supply of and demand for loanable funds decrease, causing the market rate of interest to fall.
    d. The supply of and demand for loanable funds increase, resulting in an indeterminate change in the market rate of interest.

19. Suppose you work in an area where the market wage rate for unskilled labor is $5.00. New federal legislation is passed, increasing the minimum wage to $4.25. What happens to the level of unemployment?
    a. Unemployment increases because price floors always produce surpluses.
    b. Unemployment increases because there are some labor force participants that are willing and able to work at the minimum wage, but cannot find employment.
    c. Unemployment decreases because a minimum wage above the market wage causes labor shortages.
    d. Unemployment does not change because a below-market minimum wage has no impact on business employment decisions.

20. The air we breathe is essential for life, yet it does not command a price in the market. Why?
    a. The supply curve for air intercepts the horizontal axis at a level of output greater than the level of output at which the demand for air intercepts the horizontal axis.
    b. The demand curve for air intercepts the vertical axis at a price greater than the price at which the supply of air intercepts the vertical axis.
    c. The demand curve for air intercepts the horizontal axis at a level of output greater than the level of output at which the supply of air intercepts the horizontal axis.
    d. The supply curve of air intercepts the vertical axis at a price greater than the price at which the demand for air intercepts the vertical axis.

THINK IT THROUGH

1. Discuss the importance of the price system in a market-based economy.

2. Discuss how interest rates are determined in a competitive market for loanable funds. Identify the gainers and losers from usury laws. Under what conditions would the usury laws be ineffective? If it is socially desirable to make credit available at below-market interest rates, what are other ways to benefit the targeted interest group without resulting in as much economic inefficiency as usury laws.

3. The minimum wage increased to $4.25 in 1991. Identify the likely gainers and losers. If it is socially desirable to increase the incomes of the unskilled beyond the levels that would prevail in a competitive labor market, what are other ways of doing this so that unskilled workers can be better off without causing as much inefficiency as would be the case with price controls?

4. In the early 1970s, President Nixon installed a series of wage and price controls. Prices were temporarily frozen on all goods and services. The supply of and demand for gasoline put upward pressure on gasoline prices, but these prices were temporarily controlled. In effect, the price freeze acted as a price ceiling. What do you think occurred in the gasoline market? Explain.

ANALYZING THE NEWS

Using the skills derived from studying this chapter, analyze the economic facts that make up the following article and answer the questions below.

1. Why are the prices of "first growth" Bordeaux wines expected to increase for the 1995 vintage?

2. If wine buyers "...look in the shadow of the great years if they want to turn up good value," explain what might happen to the price of the 1994 vintage?

Thirsty Wine Collectors
Awaiting the 1995 Bordeaux

By Charles Fleming
Staff Reporter of The Wall Street Journal.

Good cheer and bad tidings for Bordeaux drinkers. First the good news: 1995 looks like it will be a very good vintage for Bordeaux wines, probably the best since 1990.

Now the bad news. Starting prices for this year's Bordeaux wines from the top few vineyards—known in the trade as "first growth" wines—will likely be up sharply from last year once merchants start taking orders for wine-futures contracts in the spring. Many professionals estimate that this year's vintage will sell for 10% to 30% above last year's.

"At this stage, we think that it will be a very good vintage. They are wines which express a lot of fruitiness and a lot of charm," says Christian Moueix, chairman of Etablissements Jean-Pierre Moueix and producer of some of Bordeaux's most famous wines, including the near-legendary Chateau Petrus in Pomerol.

The main reason everyone is so upbeat about this year's vintage is that weather conditions were nearly perfect when the grapes were harvested in September.

There's pent-up excitement and demand for the 1995 because 1993 and 1994 were looking to be as great as the 1990 vintage "right up until the last minute of the harvest, when it rained," says Michael Aaron, head of the New York wine shop Sherry-Lehmann. But the late downpour skipped 1995, and "the anticipation and excitement is building."

Expect an "extreme" price increase that might bring a case to the $1,000 mark, he warns. And the wine won't even be drinkable until after New Year's 2000.

Some more-cautious observers note that there may be some element of wishful thinking in all the hype. After all, most Bordeaux wine producers need another great year, on the scale of the memorable 1989 vintage, after suffering a mostly disappointing run since the end of the 1980s. "The ingredients are certainly exciting. But [at present] the great vintage of 1995 remains desire rather than fact," says Adam Brett-Smith of Corney & Barrow wine merchants in London.

If 1995 does deliver on its early promise, some wine professionals suggest that enthusiasts should take a careful look at 1994. As things stand, 1994 ranks as a good—but not great—year, which in terms of quality will likely be outdone by 1995. However, if producers raise their prices too sharply for 1995, the previous vintage will suddenly begin to look like a very good value.

In fact, a number of wine professionals say that Bordeaux bargain hunters should always look in the shadow of the great years if they want to turn up good value. "It happened in 1983, and again in 1988, which was overshadowed by the turbo-charged, up-front quality of 1989 and 1990," says Mr. Brett-Smith.

"Buy all the 1988 Bordeaux that you can," Serena Sutcliffe, who heads Sotheby's international wine department in London and is herself a Master of Wine. "It's a real keeper."

Although the 1995 wine won't be released from the chateaux' cellars for almost two years, and won't be at its best for a decade or so, wine enthusiasts and investors won't have to wait that long to start building up their cellars. By May, once the chateaux have announced their prices and have put their blended wines up for tasting, merchants in Bordeaux and London will start signing up orders for wine futures, an informal arrangement often referred to as buying wine *en primeur*.

The wine-futures market focuses primarily on top Bordeaux wines, notably the first-growth and some of the better second-growth vineyards. By paying a set price today for delivery of an agreed number of cases at a future date, investors avoid price fluctuations and guarantee delivery.

The French International Financial Futures Market, or Matif, has considered setting up a wine contract, but that remains little more than an idea at present, says Matif Chairman Gerard Pfauwadel in Paris.

Many wine professionals express some skepticism about the idea of a fully fledged wine-futures market and recoil from the idea of buying wine for purely speculative reasons.

"It's not a quick investment and no one should put all their money into wine. But buying more than you need and selling some of it off later is one way to finance your drinking," says Ms. Sutcliffe of Sotheby's.

Buying futures is also a means of keeping costs down, wine merchants argue. For example, if you bought a case of 1993 Chateau Margaux en primeur when it was first offered in May 1994, you would have paid about $38 a bottle before tax, says Annie Lotte of Bordeaux Primeurs in southwestern France. Today, the same wine is selling 32% higher.

Like other merchants, Ms. Lotte also reports an early awakening of interest in the 1995 vintage among her clients.

"People are asking for pre-reservations, but we aren't taking any orders yet," she says. Bordeaux Primeurs will publish its first price list in May next year, to be followed by a second list three months later, adjusting prices to reflect supply and demand.

In the meantime, Mr. Aaron, the New York wine merchant, suggests trying, Chateau Lafite 1982. It's drinkable now, he says, and is "superb" and available for about $275 a case. "It's rich but elegant, and perfect with your Christmas dinner."

Fleming, Charles. "Thirsty Wine Collectors Awaiting the 1995 Bordeaux," Wall Street Journal, Sec.B, Friday, December 22, 1995, p.8.

CHAPTER ANSWERS

The Chapter in Brief

1. Nonscarce goods 2. Maximum 3. Minimum 4. Wage 5. Rise 6. Increase 7. Fall 8. Rise 9. Fall 10. More 11. Price ceilings 12. Shortages 13. Shortages 14. Black markets 15. Price floors 16. Surpluses 17. Higher 18. Less 19. Surpluses 20. Higher 21. More

Key Terms Review

1. Nonscarce good 2. Price ceiling 3. Wages 4. Interest 5. Price floor 6. Black market 7. Credit 8. Nonprice rationing

Concept Review

1. a.
   b. If you expect interest rates to fall, then other things being equal, you could lower borrowing costs by delaying borrowing until interest rates have fallen.

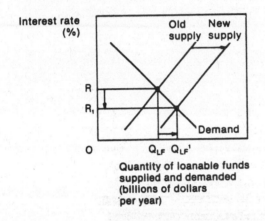

2. a. Increase

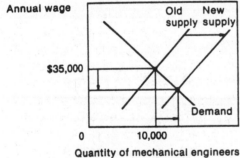

b. Decease, increase

c. You might be deterred from becoming an engineering major in anticipation of lower market wages that might prevail at the time you graduate and enter the labor force. This, of course, assumes that nothing else is expected to influence wages in the future and that you are placing a very high priority on entry level wages relative to other benefits received from an occupation or course of study.

3. a. $10, 1000

   b. Shortage, 1000

   c. Surplus, 1000

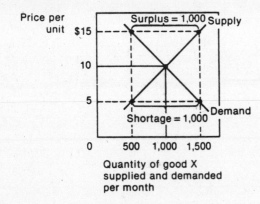

4. a. $2, 12 million

   b. (1)

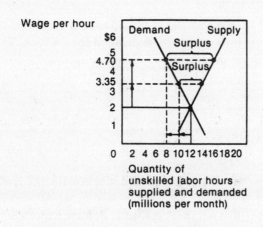

   (2) Increase, $2, $3.35, decreases, 12 million, 10 million

   c. (1) Answer on the above diagram

   (2) Increase, $3.35, $4.70, decreases, 10 million, 8 million

5. a. Waiting in line

   b. Ration stamps

   c. Eligibility criteria

6. This question can be solved graphically or algebraically with just the information given. Assume that the demand and supply curves for loanable funds are linear. This means that the

91

slopes of both curves are constant. Assume also that no other influences are shifting the supply or demand curves other than the increase in demand of $5 billion. We are told that the current interest rate is 10%. This is the rate at which the supply and demand curves intersect. Increasing or decreasing the interest rate by one percentage point increases or decreases the quantity of loanable funds supplied by $2 billion and decreases or increases the quantity of loanable funds demanded by $3 billion. As can be seen in the figure below, this produces supply and demand curves that intersect at a market interest rate of 10%. Shifting the demand curve rightward by $5 billion increases the market interest rate to 11%.

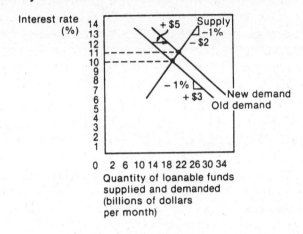

Another way to solve the problem would be to use the equilibrium price equation derived in question 10 from Chapter 5. Except in this case let's call the price the interest rate.

Let $R = (a - c)/(d + b)$, where R = the interest rate
A change in $R = 1/(d + b)$ x the change in $(a - c)$

Recall that we are assuming constant slopes. Therefore d and b remain unchanged. The a term is the constant term that reflects noninterest rate influences on the demand for loanable funds—that shifts the demand curve. Since we are making the *ceteris paribus* assumption, the c term is held constant.

A change in $R = 1/(2 + 3)$ x $5 billion
= 1%

Interest rates are expected to rise from 10% to 11%

7. a. U.S. economic activity will slow because of U.S. defense cuts.
   b. A decline in global oil exports from the former Soviet Union will increase the price of oil in the United States.
   c. Grain deficits in the former Soviet Union will result in increased U.S. farm exports.

Mastery Test

1. a 2. d 3. a 4. d 5. c 6. d 7. d 8. c 9. b 10. d 11. d 12. c 13. c 14. a 15. b 16. d 17. c 18. d 19. d 20. a

Think it Through

1. Your answer needs to emphasize the rationing function of prices. Price changes will in time eliminate shortages or surpluses. The price system allocates resources efficiently. Prices repre-

sent the vehicle by which the wishes of buyers are communicated to sellers. In short, prices coordinate the purchase plans of buyers with the production plans of sellers.

2. In a competitive market for loanable funds, the forces of supply and demand determine the market rate of interest and the market quantity of credit. Usury laws impose an interest rate ceiling and benefit those lucky enough to obtain loans at the controlled rate (those people with higher incomes and credit ratings), but impose costs on those who must go without credit (those people with lower incomes and poorer credit ratings). One alternative to regulated interest rates might be subsidies to low-income borrowers or those with poor credit ratings to be used to defer the cost of borrowing at the market rate of interest. Lenders could be encouraged to make loans to these people if lenders were protected from loan defaults by some form of government guarantee. This alternative would still require the use of scarce resources that would not have been required in a market involving no intervention. But at least the price system can perform its rationing function.

3. An increase in the minimum wage will increase the incomes of those able to find employment at that wage. But the level of unemployment will increase among those least able to afford the loss of a job—the poor and unskilled. Incomes and employability can be increased a number of ways without having to resort to price controls. Job training programs that increase the productivity of the unskilled will increase their prospects for employment and better wages. Income transfers (such as Aid to Families with Dependent Children) can be used to supplement the incomes of the poor and unskilled. Again, these alternatives require the use of scarce resources but at least do not prevent the price system from functioning.

4. Severe gasoline shortages developed at the frozen price. Because prices could not perform their rationing function, people waited endlessly in line at service stations all across the nation. The problem continued to be serious until the price controls were removed.

Analyzing the News

1. Prices are expected to rise 10% to 30% because of expectations of substantial increases in demand. Weather was "perfect" in 1995 for a great vintage. The previous two years were not as good because of last-minute rains. Because of pent-up demand and expectations of a great vintage, demand for the 1995 wine will likely drive price much higher.

2. If wine hunters view the previous year's wine as a close substitute to the 1995 vintage, an increase in the price of the 1995 wine will increase the demand for the 1994 wine, increasing its market price.

5 THE PRICE SYSTEM AND THE MIXED ECONOMY

■ CHAPTER CONCEPTS

After studying your text, attending class, and completing this chapter, you should be able to:

1. Examine the framework of a pure market economy and show how the circular flow of income and expenditure in a capitalistic economy keeps it functioning.

2. Explain the price system as a means to allocate resources in terms of what is produced, how it is produced, and how it is distributed.

3. Identify the defects of a pure market system.

4. Briefly outline the functioning of the modern mixed and open economy, including the role of government and principles of taxation.

■ THE CHAPTER IN BRIEF

Fill in the blanks to summarize chapter content.

(1)_____ (Capitalism, Socialism) is an economic system characterized by private owner-ship, freedom of choice and enterprise, and a limited economic role for government. A capitalistic economy relies on the (2)_____ (benevolence of sellers, price system) to answer the "what, how, and to whom" questions basic to all economies. (3)_____ (Profit, Money) is the guiding force in capitalistic systems. It is what induces sellers to acquire resources to produce goods that are profitable to produce and to withdraw resources from other uses that are less profitable or involve no profit. (4)_____ (Economic dominance, Economic rivalry) is also an essential characteristic in which there are large numbers of both buyers and sellers in markets and in which economic power is dispersed among many sellers and buyers such that no one seller or buyer dominates market outcomes.

For a market system to operate efficiently, it must not only produce output efficiently, but buyers and sellers must also be allowed to engage in mutually gainful trades or transactions. Transactions in a (5)_____(money, barter) economy do not involve the exchange of money for goods, but the exchange of goods for goods. It is an inefficient form of exchange because of the high transac-tion costs involved in finding "producers-consumers" with which to trade. Barter requires a (6)_____ (single coincidence of wants, double coincidence of wants). Money great-ly facilitates the exchange process because it allows individuals to specialize in the production of a single good, to convert any surplus into money by selling it in the market, and to spend the money on goods and services produced by other sellers. With money, a double coincidence of wants (7)_____(is, is not) required.

A (8)_____(supply and demand diagram, circular flow diagram) is a useful way of identifying the major sectors in a pure market economy and the relationships among those sectors. Businesses purchase resources from households in order to produce the output of goods and ser-vices consumed by households. Households derive their income from the sale of resources to the business sector. It is in this market for resources that supply and demand conditions determine the market prices that businesses must pay for resources and therefore the market wages, rents, and interest plus profits received by households. A household's income is the result of the quantities of resources sold in the resource market and the market prices at which those resources sell.

Households use their income, in part, to purchase the output of business. Household expenditures become the firm's sale revenue. The revenue from sales is used by businesses to purchase the resources necessary to produce output. In the markets for goods and services, supply and demand determine prices, which in turn influence the quantities of goods and services demanded and supplied.

In a pure market economy, the price system answers the three basic questions: What is produced? How are goods produced? To whom are goods distributed? Goods are produced if they are profitable to produce. Resources are used first to produce the most (9)_____(profitable, desirable) goods and services. Profitability depends, in part, upon the prices prevailing in both product and resource markets. Because of economic rivalry, successful producers are those that are able to earn enough income over time to continue in business. Sellers who introduce new technology can realize lower costs and, as a result, higher profits. But increased production resulting from higher profits increases market supply and reduces prices. This requires other sellers to adopt the new technology just to maintain profits. The (10)_____(newest, least costly) methods of production are adopted and quickly disseminated among other sellers. The market distributes goods based upon a buyer's willingness and ability to pay. Ability to pay is determined by household income and the prices of goods and services purchased.

The market system has several common defects. Private firms will not produce some goods that benefit society because prices cannot be used to exclude those unwilling to pay. These goods are known as (11)_____(private goods, public goods). Markets may overproduce or underproduce if market prices do not reflect all benefits and costs associated with the production or consumption of output. (12)_____(Negative, Positive) externalities occur when costs accrue to parties other than sellers and buyers. Sellers in this case make decisions based upon marginal costs that do not reflect these external or "third-party" costs. Their costs are lower than if all costs were considered and that induces them to produce (13)_____(less, more) than they would otherwise. In contrast, the production or consumption of goods may confer benefits on third parties, implying that market demand curves do not reflect all benefits associated with goods, but just those benefits received by the buyer of the good. (14)_____(Negative, Positive) externalities result in too (15)_____(much, little) output in that persons other than direct consumers benefit from the good. Sellers respond only to the effective demands registered by buyers, not third parties.

Other problems of a market system involve the absence of competition in markets and the ability of sellers to control market outcomes to the disbenefit of society. A market system can produce a skewed distribution of income in which a small percentage of families receive a much larger percentage of income and own an even larger percentage of the nation's wealth. A market system does not guarantee the absence of unemployment or poverty. Because of market shortcomings, modern economies rely on (16)_____(significant, no) government intervention in the economy to improve upon the allocation of resources or to correct other market problems. These modern market economies are known as (17)_____(mixed economies, pure market economies) because decisions regarding resource use are made by both the private and public sectors of the economy.

Modern market economies also engage in international trade. Exports of goods and services result in inflows of business revenue and income, whereas imports require payments to foreigners. Foreign income-producing assets purchased and owned by citizens of the United States and foreign-owned assets in the United States produce similar income flows and payments.

The (18)_____(democratic, federal government) system consists of various levels of government, each with its own powers to provide services and to regulate the private sector. The basic functions of government include (a) the establishment of rights to use productive resources and the regulation of private actions, (b) provision of goods and services, (c) redistribution of income, and (d) (19)_____ (stabilization of the economy, provision of armed forces). Government-provided goods and services can be categorized in two basic ways. Some publicly provided goods are made available free of charge to all members of society, and the cost is financed with taxes or through borrowing. National defense, public health, and (20)_____(national parks, welfare benefits) are some examples of this type of good. Some tax-financed government goods and services are made available only to some individuals meeting certain eligibility criteria. Examples include education, Social Security pensions, and (21)_____(national parks, welfare benefits).

Taxes are evaluated on the basis of efficiency and equity. Taxes can be levied on the basis of the taxpayer's ability to pay or the benefits received from the government good or service. A person with a higher income may pay more taxes than an individual with a lower income, and yet the tax can still be a (22)_____ (progressive, regressive) tax in which individuals with higher incomes pay a smaller percentage of their incomes in taxes than lower-income persons. A (23)_____ (progressive, regressive) tax, such as the personal income tax, requires individuals with higher incomes to pay a larger percentage of their incomes in taxes. A flat-rate tax is an example of a (24)_____(regressive, proportional) tax in which persons with different incomes pay the same percentage of their income in taxes.

Economic decisions are based on (25)_____ (marginal, average) tax rates rather than (26)_____ (marginal, average) tax rates. Whether or not an individual engages in an activity or a change in some activity depends in part on the after-tax net gains. The decision to work an extra hour depends on the net take-home wage. What is important is not the worker's average tax per dollar earned, but the increase in tax associated with an additional hour of work. Taxes can result in efficiency losses from less employment, less productivity, and less saving and capital growth. This efficiency loss or (27)_____ (excess burden, tax loss) of a tax is the loss in net benefits from resource use caused by the distortion in choices resulting from taxation.

Write the key term from the list below next to its definition.

Key Terms

Capitalism
Mixed economy
Price system
Taxes
Federal system
  of government
Government transfers
Progressive tax
Average tax rate
Barter

Free market
Public goods
Externalities
Marginal tax rate
Excess burden

Regressive tax
Proportional tax
Government failure

Definitions

1. _____: goods that are consumed equally by everyone whether they pay or not.

2. _____: a mechanism by which resource use in an economy is guided by market prices.

3. _____: characterized by private ownership of economic resources and freedom of enterprise in which owners of factories and other capital hire workers to produce goods and services.

4. _____: the process of exchanging goods (or services) for goods (or services).

5. _____: costs or benefits of market transactions that are not reflected in the prices buyers and sellers use to make their decisions.

6. _____: an economy in which governments as well as business firms provide goods and services.

7. _____: exist when there are no restrictions that prevent buyers and sellers from entering or exiting a market.

8. _____: numerous levels of government, each with its own powers, exist to provide services and regulate private affairs.

9. _____: payments made directly to certain people or organizations for which no good or service is received in return at that time.

10. _____: exists when voters approve programs for which marginal costs exceed marginal benefits.

11. _____: compulsory payments associated with income, consumption, or holding of property that persons and corporations are required to make each year to governments.

12. _____: a tax for which the fraction of income used to pay it decreases as income increases.

13. _____: a tax for which the fraction of income used to pay it increases as income increases.

14. _____: a tax for which the percentage of income paid in taxes is the same no matter what the taxpayer's income.

15. _____: the amount of taxes paid divided by the dollar value of the item taxed.

16. _____: the extra tax paid on extra income or the extra dollar value of any other taxed item.

17. _____: the loss in net benefits from resource use caused by the distortion in choices resulting from taxation.

■ CONCEPT REVIEW

Concepts 1 and 4:   *Framework of a pure market economy; circular flow of income and expenditure; mixed economy*

1. List six characteristics of a pure market economy:

    a. _____

    b. _____

    c. _____

    d. _____

    e. _____

    f. _____

2. In the diagram below, match the flow or box with one of the following:

    a. ____ 1. Market for goods and services (product markets)

    b. ____ 2. Resource markets (input markets)

    c. ____ 3. Rents, interest, wages, and profits

    d. ____ 4. Economic resources

    e. ____ 5. Goods and services

    f. ____ 6. Expenditures on goods and services

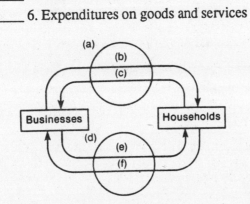

3. Referring to the following diagram, identify the flows between government and business firms, households, product markets, and input markets:

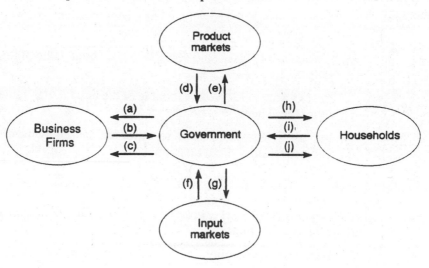

a. _____

b. _____

c. _____

d. _____

e. _____

f. _____

g. _____

h. _____

i. _____

j. _____

Concept 3:   *Defects of a pure market economy*

4. List four common defects of a market economy:

   a. _____

   b. _____

   c. _____

   d. _____

5. The diagram below represents the market for electricity. Electric power companies are burning bituminous coal and emitting sulfur into the atmosphere, creating acid rain that destroys forests and kills lakes.

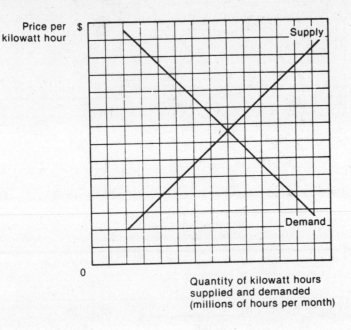

Price per $
kilowatt hour

Supply

Demand

0

Quantity of kilowatt hours
supplied and demanded
(millions of hours per month)

a. This is an example of a good involving _____ externalities.
b. On the diagram, show what would happen if these electric power companies were required to install scrubbers to remove sulfur from their emissions?
c. Market price of electricity _____ and market quantity _____.

6. Suppose the following diagram represents the market for AIDS therapy. Private pharmaceutical companies and health suppliers are in a race to discover and market a successful treatment. The demand for AIDS therapy reflects only the private demand of those infected with the virus and willing and able to pay for the treatment. Society as a whole, however, benefits from successful AIDS therapy because individuals who would have otherwise been infected are not infected because of the treatment that persons with AIDS are receiving.

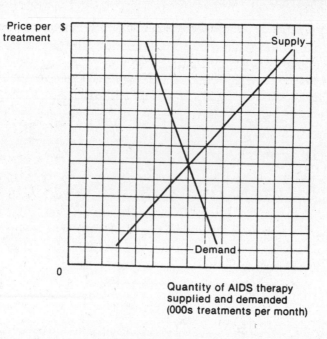

Price per $ treatment

Supply

Demand

0

Quantity of AIDS therapy
supplied and demanded
(000s treatments per month)

a. This is an example of a good involving _____ externalities.
b. According to the diagram above, there are too _____ resources allocated to AIDS therapy.
c. If government subsidizes AIDS research and the development of successful treatments, show on the diagram the likely impact on the market for AIDS therapy.
d. Market price of AIDS treatment _____ and market quantity _____.
e. Why must government be involved?

Concept 4: Roles of Government and Principles of Taxation

7. Taxes are generally considered equitable if taxpayers pay taxes on the basis of their _____ or the_____ from the public good or service consumed.

8. Indicate for the taxes below whether they are progressive, regressive, or proportional taxes.
   a. _____ Federal personal income tax
   b. _____ Sales tax
   c. _____ Payroll tax (FICA)
   d. _____ Flat-rate tax
   e. _____ Cigarette excise tax

9. List four functions of government and give an example of each.
   a. _____
   b. _____
   c. _____
   d. _____

10. Government goods and services can be classified as (1) goods that are made available to all citizens free of charge and (2) goods and services that are available only to certain citizens based on specific eligibility criteria. For each of the goods or services below, indicate whether

102

the good or service is of the first or second category. Use (1) for the first category and (2) for the second category.

a. _____ National defense   b._____ Medicaid
c. _____ Roads   d._____ Fire protection
e. _____ Food stamps   f._____ National parks
g. _____ Police   h._____ Social security
i. _____ Education

Advanced Application: Externalities

11. The Sleaze E Chemical Company is presently dumping untreated effluent into a river. Downstream residents and other users of the river suffer from pollution. You are a policy maker in charge of determining the socially desirable level of pollution for the river and the appropriate effluent tax or charge per gallon of untreated effluent to impose on Sleaze E. You want to impose a tax high enough to induce Sleaze E to treat its discharge up to the point at which the proper level of pollution is reached.

Sleaze E Treated Discharge (000s gallons)	Units of Pollution Reduction	Marginal Benefits	Marginal Costs
0	0	$0	$0
10	1	10	2
20	2	8	4
30	3	6	6
40	4	4	8
50	5	2	10

a. Using the marginal benefits and marginal costs columns, determine the units of pollution reduction that maximize the net gain to society. Assume that the marginal benefit and cost data include external costs and benefits. How many gallons of discharge will Sleaze E have to treat in order to reach that level of pollution reduction?

b. The diagram below represents the relationship between Sleaze E's marginal cost of treating discharge and the quantity of discharge treated. What tax per unit of untreated effluent would be sufficient to induce Sleaze E to treat its effluent up to the level desired by society?

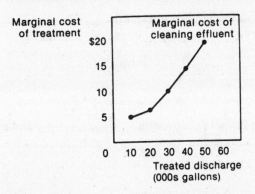

Insights on Issues

12. Briefly describe Robert Solow's views regarding stabilization policy and economic regulation.

103

■ MASTERY TEST

Select the best answer.

1. Which of the following is not true of a pure market system?
   a. Private ownership
   b. Freedom of enterprise and choice
   c. Significant government income redistribution programs
   d. Presence of economic rivalry

2. A pure market economy relies on which of the following to answer the three basic questions: (1) What is produced? (2) How are goods produced? (3) To whom are goods distributed?
   a. Barter
   b. Money
   c. Property rights
   d. Price system

3. The catalyst or driving force in a market system that induces sellers to acquire resources to produce products is:
   a. money.
   b. profit.
   c. price.
   d. benevolence.

4. Economic rivalry means:
   a. that there are large numbers of consumers, but not sellers in markets.
   b. that the survival of the fittest criterion of business behavior is operative in the economy.
   c. there are large numbers of buyers and sellers in markets such that no one buyer or seller dominates market outcomes.
   d. that competitive firms produce profitable goods.

5. The advantage of a money economy as compared to a barter economy is :
   a. the avoidance of a double coincidence of wants.
   b. that money allows economic specialization and the division of labor.
   c. that money greatly facilitates the process of exchange.
   d. All of the above

6. In a circular flow diagram of the economy, households represent the _____ side of the input market, whereas business represents the _____ of the product market.
   a. demand/demand
   b. supply/supply
   c. demand/supply
   d. supply/demand

7. In a circular flow diagram of the economy, households provide _____ and receive _____, which when _____ become the _____ of businesses.
   a. goods/money/saved/capital
   b. money/bonds/employed/capital
   c. economic resources/money income/expended/sales revenue
   d. money income/employment/used/property

8. Economic rivalry in a pure market economy ensures that:
   a. only the healthiest firms use the most advanced technology.
   b. new cost-saving technology is rapidly disseminated among sellers in the economy.
   c. firms will adopt the least-cost combination of resources.
   d. b and c
   e. a and c

9. Goods are distributed in a pure market economy:
   a. by government.
   b. by both the private and public sectors.
   c. on the basis of the buyer's willingness and ability to pay for goods and services.
   d. to those with the highest wages.

10. Private businesses will not allocate resources to the production of goods when prices cannot be used to exclude those unwilling to pay. These goods are known as:
   a. inferior goods.
   b. public goods.
   c. loss goods.
   d. external goods.

11. Goods that when consumed or produced impose costs on third parties involve:
   a. public external effects.
   b. positive externalities.
   c. marginal costs.
   d. negative externalities.

12. Goods that when consumed or produced confer benefits on third parties involve:
   a. public external effects.
   b. positive externalities.
   c. marginal benefits.
   d. negative externalities.

13. Goods involving positive externalities result in :
   a. an efficient allocation of resources.
   b. productive efficiency, but not allocative efficiency.
   c. an overallocation of resources to the production of the good.
   d. an underallocation of resources to the production of the good.

14. Actual market economies give rise to all but one of the following:
   a. a skewed distribution of income
   b. poverty among plenty
   c. full employment
   d. less than competitive markets

15. In a market economy subject to market failures, society's well-being can be improved:
   a. by no government intervention.
   b. by government intervention that corrects resource misallocation and modifies other market outcomes consistent with the desires of society.
   c. by the price system.
   d. if decisions regarding public goods production are left to the private sector.

16. Modern market economies that rely on both the private and public sectors of the economy to answer the three basic questions are known as:
    a. modern market economies.
    b. pure market systems.
    c. pure capitalistic economies.
    d. mixed economies.

17. Which of the following is true regarding the three basic economic questions?
    a. A pure market economy answers the what, how, and to whom questions with a combination of private and public planning.
    b. The "to whom" question in any economic system must be answered by the public sector, whereas the other two questions are answered by self-interested government bureaucrats.
    c. In a mixed market economy, both private and government decision makers ultimately answer the three basic questions.
    d. In a pure market economy, the price system (or system of markets) coordinates the decisions of private producers, consumers, and suppliers of inputs, but government planning is required to answer the "to whom" question.

18. "Markets fail when resources are overallocated to the production of certain goods." Which of the following best explains this statement?
    a. As markets mature, firms grow large and unresponsive to consumers, often producing more output than is desired.
    b. Producers do not face the full costs of production if negative externalities exist. Firms produce more than they would if they were forced to realize all costs of production.
    c. When prices rise above market equilibrium prices, markets fail because surpluses grow, resulting in an overallocation of resources.
    d. It is impossible for markets to overallocate resources because prices will fall, eliminating surplus production.

19. Which of the following is an example of market failure?
    a. Monopolistic pricing
    b. The production of a good with external benefits
    c. A skewed distribution of income
    d. Periodic episodes of rising unemployment
    e. All of the above

20. What are key features associated with public goods?
    a. Public goods are desired by citizens and must be priced low enough for median-income households to purchase.
    b. Public goods are rival in consumption, but cannot be priced.
    c. Public goods are nonrival in consumption and once provided, entail a zero marginal cost of provision.
    d. Public goods can be provided by either the private or public sector, but because of tradition, most public goods are produced and provided by government.

21. Two concepts of equity in taxation are the _____ and _____ concepts.
    a. egalitarian, utopian
    b. ability-to-pay, benefits received
    c. democratic, republican
    d. progressive, regressive

22. A tax for which the fraction of income used to pay it decreases as income increases is called a:
    a. progressive tax.
    b. regressive tax.
    c. proportional tax.
    d. flat-rate tax.

23. A tax for which the fraction of income used to pay it increases as income increases is called a:
    a. progressive tax.
    b. regressive tax.
    c. proportional tax.
    d. value-added tax.

24. A flat-rate tax is an example of :
    a. a progressive tax.
    b. a regressive tax.
    c. a proportional tax.
    d. the U.S. income tax.

25. The appropriate tax concept to be used in marginal analysis is the:
    a. total tax liability from the full extent of an activity.
    b. marginal tax rate.
    c. average tax rate.
    d. ability-to-pay concept.

26. Welfare payments fall under which of the following government functions?
    a. Establishment of rights to use resources and the regulation of private actions
    b. Provision of goods and services
    c. Redistribution of income
    d. Stabilization of the economy

27. Education expenditures fall under which of the following government functions?
    a. Establishment of rights to use resources and the regulation of private actions
    b. Provision of goods and services
    c. Redistribution of income
    d. Stabilization of income

28. Payments made by government to certain persons or organizations for which no good or service is currently received in return are called:
    a. government spending
    b. welfare benefits
    c. government off-budget expenditures
    d. government transfer payments

29. The benefits-received principle of taxation applies to which of the following taxes?
    a. Sales taxes
    b. Income taxes
    c. Gasoline excise taxes
    d. Property taxes
    e. None of the above

30. The excess burden of a tax:
    a. rises when tax rates increase.
    b. exists because taxes alter economic choices from what they would have been in the absence of the tax.
    c. falls as tax rates decrease.
    d. a and b
    e. b and c

31. As income rises from $20,000 to $30,000 to $40,000, tax revenue from a certain tax rises from $400 to $500 to $600. The tax in question is a:
    a. proportional tax.
    b. benefits-received tax.
    c. progressive tax.
    d. regressive tax.

■ THINK IT THROUGH

1. During inflationary periods of the 1970s, a number of barter services were established as a means of combatting inflation. These barter arrangements made use of computers to register the goods and services that the users were willing to supply and the goods that would be acceptable in exchange. Would such a barter system be as efficient as one with money? Explain.

2. A basic function of government in a pure market economy is to facilitate the functioning of the economy, but not to modify market outcomes. Discuss.

3. For a pure market economy, explain why producers employ the least costly techniques of production. If the price of labor rises relative to the price of capital and other inputs, how would this affect a competitive seller's combination of resources employed in production?

4. Education in the United States is provided by both the private and public sectors. Why?

5. Describe what is meant by efficiency and equity in taxation.

■ CHAPTER ANSWERS

The Chapter in Brief

1. Capitalism 2. Price system 3. Profit 4. Economic rivalry 5. Barter 6. Double coincidence of wants 7. Is not 8. Circular flow diagram 9. Profitable 10. Least costly 11. Public goods 12. Negative 13. More 14. Positive 15. Little 16. Significant 17. Mixed economies 18. Federal government 19. Stabilization of the economy 20. National parks 21. Welfare benefits 22. Regressive 23. Progressive 24. Proportional 25. Marginal 26. Average 27. Excess burden

Key Terms Review

1. Public goods 2. Price system 3. Capitalism 4. Barter 5. Externalities 6. Mixed economy 7. Free market 8. Federal system of government 9. government transfers 10. Government failure 11. Taxes 12. Regressive tax 13. Progressive tax 14. Proportional tax 15. Average tax rate 16. Marginal tax rate 17. Excess burden

Concept Review

1. a. Private ownership
    b. Freedom of choice and enterprise
    c. Limited economic role for government
    d. Reliance on the price system to allocate resources
    e. Profit motive
    f. Economic rivalry

2. a. 2 b. 3 c. 4 d. 1 e. 5 f. 6

3. a. Subsidies
    b. Taxes
    c. Government services
    d. Purchases of goods and services
    e. Expenditures
    f. Resources
    g. Payments
    h. Income support
    i. Taxes
    j. Government services

4. a. Externalities
    b. Lack of competition in markets

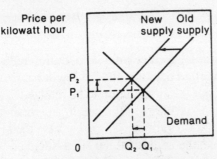

Quantity of kilowatt hours
supplied and demanded
(millions of hours per month)

109

c. Skewed distribution of income
d. Doesn't eliminate poverty or unemployment
5. a. Negative
   b. If power companies are required to bear the cost of cleaning their emissions, the market supply curve would shift leftward.

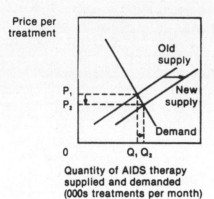

Price per treatment

Old supply

New supply

P_1

P_2

Demand

0   $Q_1 Q_2$

Quantity of AIDS therapy supplied and demanded (000s treatments per month)

c. Increases, decreases
6. a. Positive
   b. Few
   c. Government subsidies increase the net gain to those conducting AIDS research and developing therapies. In time there will be a rightward shift in the supply curve.
   d. Decreases, increases
   e. A market system relies on pricing to allocate resources. Market prices do not reflect the external benefits accruing to third parties. Markets will underproduce goods involving positive externalities. Governments can produce net gains for society by engaging in activities that reallocate more resources to the production of goods with positive externalities.

7. Ability-to-pay, benefits received

8. a. Progressive b. Regressive c. Regressive d. Proportional e. Regressive

9. a. The establishment of rights to use resources and the regulation of private actions
   b. Provision of goods and services
   c. Redistribution of income
   d. Stabilization of the economy

10. a. 1 b. 2 c. 1 d. 1 e. 2 f. 1 g. 1 h. 2 i. 2

11. a. Marginal benefits and costs become equal at three units of pollution reduction. This is the level of pollution that maximizes society's net gain. Sleaze E will have to treat 30,000 gallons of discharge for this level of pollution reduction to be realized.
    b. $10. A tax of $10 per unit of untreated discharge will result in a net gain to Sleaze E for each unit of treated discharge up to 30,000 gallons. This is because the marginal cost of treating a gallon of effluent is less than the additional benefit associated with not having to pay the pollution tax on that gallon. This holds true up to the level of 30,000 gallons at

which the marginal cost of treatment is $10. Treatment beyond this level would not take place because Sleaze E would be better off by paying the tax than treating the discharge.

12. Regarding economic stabilization policy, Robert Solow believes that government should be more involved in economic stabilization, although he also says that there is no consensus as to how much stabilization is appropriate. He notes that it is important for governments to coordinate their stabilization efforts, but that is difficult because "... national governments often have conflicting interests."

On balance, Solow thinks that there is still too much aggregate regulation. Some things are regulated excessively, whereas other areas such as the environment are regulated insufficiently. He favors market-based environmental regulation that relies upon economic incentives and the price system.

Mastery Test

1.c 2. d 3. b 4. c 5. d 6. b 7. c 8. d 9. c 10. b 11. d 12. b 13. d 14. c 15. b 16. d 17. c 18. b 19. e 20. c 21. b 22. b 23. a 24. c 25. b 26. c 27. b 28. d 29. c 30.d 31. d

Think It Through

1. Barter systems, whether or not they use computers, must develop "prices" or exchange ratios for the goods involved. This requires scarce resources. A double coincidence of wants is required, which reduces the efficiency of exchange. A middleman must be paid to provide a service that is naturally provided as part of the functioning of a market economy using money.

2. In a pure market system, there are no failures. There are no externalities, markets provide employment for everyone willing and able to work at prevailing wages, all markets involve economic rivalry, and incomes are based strictly on the resources that households supply to the market and the prices at which they sell. In short, the market operates efficiently without government interference. Government, nevertheless, performs a vital economic role by assigning property rights and enforcing those rights via a system of laws, courts, and police protection. Government also provides money and the basic infrastructure of roads, water supply, sewerage, etc., necessary for the efficient functioning of a market system.

3. Economic rivalry implies that sellers must operate at least cost. If they did not, in time they would incur insufficient profits to remain in business. Firms that stay in business in a pure market system are those that are able to use the least costly combination of inputs and technology in order to at least generate a minimally sufficient level of profit. If the price of labor rises relative to the cost of other inputs, a least cost producer will substitute the relatively less costly resources for labor. By making capital more productive relative to labor, technology reduces the cost of capital relative to labor in the production of output. This is what happened in American agriculture. Technology made farm labor more expensive relative to capital, inducing farmers to mechanize.

4. Education is a good involving positive externalities. A market system produces too little education from society's point of view. Government can increase the net gain to society by providing more education than that provided by a market system alone. But this does not necessarily mean the we have to have the current public-private system in order to achieve this outcome. Education could be entirely publicly provided or it could be provided entirely by a private sector encouraged to produce more with subsidies. Alternatively, students could be given education vouchers that supplement their own funds for education. These funds could be spent entirely in the private sector or even in the current public-private system.

111

5. Taxes can create an excess burden when there are tax-caused changes in individual and business behavior resulting from changes in net wages, net interest rates, and other prices or incomes. Efficiency can be improved if the tax is used to correct a negative externality. An efficient tax is one that raises tax revenue without causing an excess burden. The two basic concepts of equity in taxation are the ability-to-pay and benefits received concepts. The benefits received principle cannot be used where the benefits cannot be closely correlated with an individual's activity. The ability-to-pay criterion states that a fair tax is one for which an individual's tax liability is correlated with his or her ability to pay. Thus, higher income persons should pay more in taxes than those with lower incomes. This criterion does not indicate whether proportional, progressive, or regressive taxes are preferable, because ability-to-pay can be measured in absolute dollars or as a percentage of income.

PART III

INTRODUCTION TO MACROECONOMIC CONCEPTS

■ **PART EXERCISE**

Inside Information: *Where to Find Current Information and the Performance of the United States Economy*

In Part III, you will learn about the business cycle, unemployment, inflation, and measures of economic activity. Use the *Monthly Labor Review* and find the consumer price index for the past twelve months. Calculate the annual rate of inflation. Use *Employment and Earnings* and determine monthly earnings (current dollar or nominal earnings) for the past twelve months for an industry of your choice in your particular region. Calculate the annual rate of wage or earnings inflation.

Using your price index and earnings data, determine the change in monthly real earnings from the beginning to the end of the 12-month period. Also calculate the rate of change in real earnings over the period. If the above data reflected your earnings and the rate of inflation you face, are you better or worse off at the end of the 12-month period? Why?

6   GROSS DOMESTIC PRODUCT AND THE PERFORMANCE OF THE NATIONAL ECONOMY

■ CHAPTER CONCEPTS

After studying this chapter, attending class, and completing this chapter, you should be able to:

1. Explain what GDP is, how it can be viewed as the value added to intermediate products, and how real GDP differs from nominal GDP.

2. Understand why GDP must equal the sum of consumption, investment, government purchases, and net exports and how expenditure on the nation's output results in income to resource owners.

3. Explain how the concepts of gross domestic product, net national product, national income, personal income, and disposable income can be derived from GDP.

4. Understand how spending and income circulate among business firms, households, and governments and how international trade affects the economy.

5. Explain how national saving is computed and show the relationship to personal saving, business saving, and the government budget deficit and how foreign saving in the United States has helped finance domestic investment in recent years.

■ THE CHAPTER IN BRIEF

Fill in the blanks to summarize chapter content.

The National Income and Product Accounts are designed to measure economic activity—flows of income and expenditures over a period of time. The broadest measure of economic activity is (1)_____(gross domestic product, aggregate output). GDP is the market value of (2)_____(total, final) goods and services produced by workers and other resources located in a given country over a period of 1 year. It is designed to measure economic activity that gives rise to income, output, and employment. GDP includes income earned by foreigners from foreign-owned assets located in the United States, but excludes income earned by U.S. residents from U.S.-owned assets located abroad. Some transactions during the year do not affect production and employment and are thus excluded from GDP. These include changes in the value of existing assets, (3)_____ (nonfinancial, financial) transactions, sale of used goods, and most goods not sold in markets.

GDP can be thought of as the total value added in a nation over a given year. The market value of all products and services (4)_____(less, plus) the market value of all intermediate goods equals the value added in producing and making final goods and services available to the market. Value added (5)_____(is greater than, also equals) the payments to suppliers of labor, capital, and raw materials, including profit to entrepreneurs. Because GDP is defined in terms of its market value, inflation can cause the value of GDP to change. In order to remove this inflationary bias so as to uncover the movements in GDP that affect output and employment, it is necessary to deflate GDP—to remove the effect of inflation. This is accomplished by dividing a general price index into (6)_____ (nominal, real) GDP. Doing so yields (7)_____ (real, nominal)

GDP, a measure of the value of a nation's aggregate output of final products using market prices defined by the price index base year.

GDP should not be considered a perfect measure of a nation's well-being. It excludes nonmarket goods and services, such as the services of spouses in maintaining a home, that contribute to society's welfare. It also excludes the value of leisure, does not consider the impact of environmental damage caused by the production or consumption of output, (8)_____ (but does, and does not) reflect the market value of goods and services produced in the underground economy.

Gross domestic product can be measured by determining the total aggregate expenditures on final output during the year or by determining the income generated by the economy in producing that final output. GDP can be estimated by summing personal consumption expenditures of households, gross private domestic investment, government purchases of goods and services, and net (9)_____(exports, imports). Personal consumption expenditures are household expenditures on durable goods, nondurable goods, and services. Gross private domestic investment represents spending on producer durables, residential and nonresidential construction, and (10)_____ (the, changes in the) value of inventories. Government expenditures include the expenditures of all levels of government on goods and services (including labor services) less transfer payments. Net exports are total (11)_____ (exports, imports) less (12)_____(exports, imports).

Gross domestic product can also be determined by summing the incomes received by resource suppliers during the year. The four types of income are compensation of employees, profits, net interest, and rental income. Compensation of employees includes wages and salaries and employer-provided contributions to Social Security and pension plans. (13)_____ (Enterprise income, Proprietors' income) is the profit of unincorporated enterprises. Corporate profits are the incomes of corporations and equal the sum of dividends and retained earnings, and corporate profits taxes. Net interest includes the interest paid by business (14)_____ (and, but not) the interest paid by government. Rental income is received by those supplying land, mineral rights, and structures for the use of others. It (15)_____ (excludes, also includes) the imputed rent earned by homeowners. Adding these components of total income to indirect business taxes and depreciation (or consumption of fixed capital) gives GDP.

Other measures of income and expenditures are included in the National Income and Product Accounts. (16)_____ (Net national product, Gross national product) represents all output produced by a nation's residents regardless of the location of U.S.-owned assets. Income earned from the use of productive resources during the year is known as (17)_____ (personal income, national income). Income available after the payment of taxes is called (18) _____ (personal income, disposable income).

As can be shown in a circular flow diagram, total aggregate expenditures on final output generate the income necessary to sustain those expenditures. But if leakages from the circular flow exceed injections into the flow of spending, the level of economic activity will (19)_____(decline, increase). Leakages include net taxes, saving, and imports. These reduce the amount of funds available to purchase domestic output. Injections include gross private domestic investment, government spending on goods and services, and exports. These expenditures increase total spending on domestic output. If leakages are less than injections, economic activity will (20)_____(decline, increase). If leakages equal injections, the level of economic activity will just be maintained, neither increasing nor decreasing.

116

Saving is necessary for investment and economic growth. The total saving of households, business, and government is the national saving of the economy. National saving as a percent of GDP has (21)_____ (increased, decreased) in the 1980s from the levels that prevailed during the three previous decades. The national saving rate in the United States is markedly (22)_____ (higher, lower) than for other advanced nations. Investment spending in the 1980s as a percent of GDP exceeded the national saving rate. The difference was made up by a net inflow of foreign saving. Adding foreign saving to national saving gives total saving in the United States.

■ KEY TERMS REVIEW

Write the key term from the list below next to its definition.

Key Terms

Gross national product
Net exports
National Income and
   Product Accounts
Aggregates
Net taxes
Intermediate products
Aggregate expenditure
Total value added in
   a nation
Nominal GDP
Real GDP
Aggregate real income
Personal consumption
   expenditures
National saving
Total saving in the
   United States
Net national product

Gross private domestic
   investment
Depreciation
National income
Net private domestic
   investment
Government purchases of
   goods and services
Transfer payments
Leakages
Indirect business taxes
Corporate profits taxes
Disposable income
Injections
Personal saving
Value added
Final products
Gross domestic product
Personal income

Definitions

1. _____ : the market value of final goods and services produced by workers and other resources located within the border of a nation over a period of 1 year.

2. _____ : broad totals of economic variables such as production or unemployment.

3. _____ : the market value of a nation's final output based on current prices for the goods and services produced during the year.

4. _____ : the nominal (money) income of a nation, adjusted for inflation. Equivalent to real GDP.

5. _____ : investment purchases by business firms: expenditure on new machinery and equipment (producer durables), the value of new residential and nonresidential construction, and the change in business inventories during the year.

117

6. _____: expenditure on final products of business firms and all input costs, including labor costs, incurred by all levels of government in the United States.

7. _____: taxes levied on business firms that increase their costs and are therefore reflected in the market value of goods and services sold.

8. _____: the difference between taxes and transfer payments.

9. _____: a portion of income that is not used to purchase domestically produced goods during the year.

10. _____: the official system of accounting to measure the flows of income and expenditures in the United States.

11. _____: products produced by business firms for resale by other firms or for use as materials or services that will be included in the value of resold goods.

12. _____: a measure of the value of a nation's final products obtained by using market prices prevailing for products during a certain base or reference year.

13. _____: any excess of expenditure on exports over imports.

14. _____: an estimate of the value of capital goods that wear out or become obsolete over the year.

15. _____: payments for which no good or service is currently received in return and that therefore do not represent expenditures for the purchase of final products.

16. _____: those amounts corporations pay as taxes to governments out of their annual receipts from the sale of goods and services.

17. _____: the income individuals have to spend after payment of taxes.

18. _____: a purchase made by business firms, governments, or foreign buyers that increases the flow of income in a nation.

19. _____: the difference between the market value of *all* products of business firms and the market value of all intermediate products.

20. _____: the sum of consumption, investment expenditures, government purchases, and net exports during the year. Equivalent to real GDP.

21. _____: household and individual purchases of both durable and nondurable goods and services.

22. _____: gross private domestic investment less depreciation.

23. _____: the extra worth that a business firm adds to intermediate products: measured by the difference in the market value of a firm's sales and the market value of intermediate products purchased.

24. _____: goods and services sold to final users and not used as materials, parts, or services to be incorporated in the value of other items that are to be resold.

25. _____ : the sum of personal saving, business saving, and saving by the government sector.

26. _____ : the sum of national saving and the net foreign saving in the United States.

27. _____ : the market value of final output produced annually by all labor and property supplied by a nation's households no matter where those resources are employed. Measures the aggregate income of a nation's households.

28. _____ : GNP less capital consumption allowances.

29. _____ : the NIPA measure of annual household and business earnings from the use of productive resources.

30. _____ : the NIPA measure of annual income available to households.

31. _____ : the portion of household income that is not used to make purchases or pay taxes.

■ CONCEPT REVIEW

Concept 1: *GDP, value added, nominal GDP, and real GDP*

1. List four categories of items excluded from GDP.

   a. _____

   b. _____

   c. _____

   d. _____

2. The following table shows an economy producing one final product, gasoline. Complete the blanks.

Sales transactions	Intermediate purchases	Value added
$1 billion sale of oil by oil producers to refiners	None	(a) _____
$2 billion sale of gasoline by refiners to gas stations	$1 billion of oil	(b) _____
$2.5 billion sale of gasoline by gas stations to consumers	$2 billion of gasoline	(c) _____

Market value of all products	Market value of intermediate products	Total value added
(d) _____	(e) _____	(f) _____

   For this economy, GDP = _____ .

3. Consider the production and price data below for a nation producing only automobiles. (Assume that all automobiles are identical.)

119

Year	Price per Auto	Output (units)	Nominal GDP	Price Index	Real GDP
1	$10,000	1,000	_____	_____	_____
2	10,500	1,200	_____	_____	_____
3	11,000	1,400	_____	_____	_____
4	11,500	1,600	_____	_____	_____
5	12,000	1,800	_____	_____	_____

a. Complete the nominal GDP column.

b. Complete the price index column. Assume that year 3 is the base year. Price index = (current year price/base year price) x 100.

c. Prices have increased _____ % from year 3 to year 5.

d. Complete the real GDP column. (Hint: Divide the price index by 100 prior to dividing into nominal GDP.)

4. Indicate whether the following cause GDP to be understated or overstated as a measure of well-being.

a. _____GDP excludes most nonmarket goods.

b. _____GDP excludes the value of leisure.

c. _____The environmental damage that results from production is not accounted for in GDP.

d. _____GDP excludes the value of goods and services produced by the underground economy.

Concepts 2 and 3:   *GDP and the flow of expenditures and income*

5. a. List the components of personal consumption expenditures.

   (1) _____

   (2) _____

   (3) _____

b. List the components of gross private domestic investment.

   (1) _____

   (2) _____

   (3) _____

c. List the components of corporate profits.

   (1) _____

   (2) _____

   (3) _____

6. The following are national income and product accounts for a nation for a given year.

■ National Income and Product Accounts

Government purchases of goods and services	$ 580
Indirect business taxes	230
Personal consumption expenditures	1,530
Depreciation	310
Proprietors' income	175
Employer contributions to public and private pension plans	325
Net interest	98
Gross private domestic investment	410
Rental income	45
Exports	450
Imports	260
Corporate profits	225
Wages and salaries	1,302
Social security payroll taxes	235
Government transfer payments to individuals	300
Personal interest and dividends and business transfers to individuals	340
Personal taxes	325
Receipts of foreign income	75
Payments of income to foreigners	65

a. Using the expenditure side of GDP, determine GDP. _____

b. Using the income side of GDP, determine GDP. _____

c. Net private domestic investment = _____

d. Net exports = _____

e. National income = _____

f. Personal income = _____

g. Disposable income = _____

Concept 4: *Circular flow, leakages, and injections*

7. Regarding a circular flow diagram:

a. List the leakages from the flow of income.

(1) _____

(2) _____

(3) _____

b. List the injections to the flow of final expenditures on domestic output.

(1) _____

(2) _____

(3) _____

121

c. Economic activity _____ when leakages exceed injections. Economic activity _____ when leakages are less than injections. Economic activity _____ when leakages equal injections.

d. Total saving is composed of:

    (1) _____

    (2) _____

    (3) _____

    (4) _____

Concept 5: *National saving*

8. List the components of national saving.

    a. _____

    b. _____

    c. _____

Insights on Issues

9. a. Briefly summarize Professor Arrow's and Professor Litan's views regarding the belief by some that children today will in the future be worse off than their parents.

    b. According to Arrow and Litan, what could be done to increase future living standards?

Select the best answer.

1. Which of the following defines GDP?
    a. Total output produced by an economy
    b. Total final output produced by an economy
    c. The market value of the total final output produced by workers and other resources located in a given nation during a given year
    d. The market value of the total output produced by an economy during a given year

2. Which of the following are excluded from GDP?
    a. Changes in the value of existing assets
    b. Financial transactions
    c. Sale of used goods
    d. All of the above

3. The value added for a nation equals:
    a. all goods and services less the intermediate goods used in production.
    b. the market value of all products and services less the market value of all intermediate goods.
    c. input costs plus the value of intermediate goods.
    d. the market value of intermediate goods less the value of all goods and services.

4. The value added for a nation equals:
    a. GDP.
    b. the payments to suppliers of labor, capital, and raw materials, including profit to entrepreneurs.
    c. the market value of all products and services less the market value of all intermediate goods.
    d. All of the above.

5. Nominal GDP is:
    a. a preliminary estimate of GDP.
    b. GDP unadjusted for inflation.
    c. GDP adjusted for inflation.
    d. GDP less capital consumption allowances.

6. Real GDP is:
    a. the final estimate of GDP for a period.
    b. GDP unadjusted for inflation.
    c. GDP adjusted for inflation.
    d. total income minus indirect business taxes.

7. GDP overstates economic well-being if:
    a. nonmarket goods are included in GDP.
    b. leisure time is not included in GDP.
    c. production in the underground economy is included in GDP.
    d. the environmental damage caused by economic activity is not considered in GDP.

8. GDP can be estimated by summing :
   a. personal consumption expenditures, net private domestic investment, and federal government spending.
   b. personal consumption expenditures, gross private domestic investment, government spending on goods and services, and net exports.
   c. all services and goods purchased by households, businesses, and government.
   d. household spending, investment, financial transactions, and government transfers.

9. Gross private domestic investment equals the sum of:
   a. changes in the value of inventories, new residential and nonresidential construction, and producer durables.
   b. the value of inventories, residential construction, and machines.
   c. business structures and machines.
   d. plant and equipment.

10. Which of the following categories absorbs the largest percentage of household expenditures?
    a. Nondurable goods
    b. Services
    c. Durable goods
    d. Taxes

11. The most volatile components of GDP are:
    a. defense spending and net exports.
    b. personal consumption expenditures.
    c. services and government spending.
    d. investment and net exports.

12. Leakages from the flow of income include:
    a. saving.
    b. imports.
    c. taxes.
    d. All of the above.

13. Which of the following is not an injection to the flow of spending?
    a. Investment
    b. Government spending
    c. Imports
    d. Exports

14. If leakages exceed injections, economic activity will:
    a. expand.
    b. remain unchanged.
    c. decline.
    d. experience a slight decline, then a robust expansion.

15. If injections exceed leakages, economic activity will:
    a. expand.
    b. remain unchanged.
    c. decline.
    d. expand, then decline upon reaching the point of diminishing returns.

16. If injections equal leakages, economic activity will:
    a. expand.
    b. remain unchanged.
    c. decline.
    d. none of the above.

Answer questions 17 to 20 based upon the table of data below.

National Income and Product Accounts
(billions of dollars)

Government purchases	$1,160
Indirect business taxes	460
Personal consumption expenditures	3,060
Depreciation	620
Proprietor's income	350
Employer contributions to pension plans	650
Net interest	196
Gross private domestic investment	820
Rental income	90
Exports	900
Imports	520
Corporate profits	450
Wages and salaries	2,604
Social security payroll taxes	470
Government transfer payments	600
Personal interest and dividends and business transfers to individuals	680
Personal taxes	650
Receipts of foreign income	150
Payments of income to foreigners	130

17. Gross domestic product equals:
    a. $4,730
    b. $5,400
    c. $3,660
    d. $5,042

18. National income equals:
    a. $3,890
    b. $4,900
    c. $4,340
    d. $3,875

19. Personal income equals:
   a. $4,504
   b. $4,200
   c. $3,880
   d. $5,800
20. Disposable income equals:
   a. $3,550
   b. $3,230
   c. $2,710
   d. $3,854

■ THINK IT THROUGH

1. Discuss two methods of estimating gross domestic product.
2. If depreciation exceeds gross private domestic investment, what will happen to the nation's capital stock?
3. Discuss how the effect of inflation can be removed from GDP. Of what use is this?
4. Assume that the U.S. trade balance has improved. Exports are rising at a faster rate than imports. How is this likely to affect the U.S. economy?
5. Using the value added concept, explain why total expenditures on the nation's output of final goods and services are conceptually equal to the total income earned by suppliers of economic resources.

■ ANALYZING THE NEWS

Using the skills derived from studying this chapter, analyze the economic facts that make up the following article and answer the questions below.

1. What major bias is associated with the "fixed-weight" method of determining real GDP?
2. How can this bias be reduced?

126

National Economic Trends

Introducing Chain-Weight GDP Data in *National Economic Trends*

At the end of this year, the Department of Commerce will change the way it calculates real gross domestic product (GDP). For nearly 50 years, real GDP has been calculated using a fixed-weight index. This method of calculation will be replaced with a chain-weight index. Starting with this issue of *National Economic Trends*, we have added the chain-weight series to the charts on pages 4 and 5.

This change will more accurately measure the level of output and economic growth. To measure output in any year, the Department of Commerce first establishes a base year. In the base year, currently 1987, real GDP is set equal to nominal GDP. Under a fixed-weight index, the prices in the base year are used to determine real GDP in every year. Thus, real GDP of $5,344 billion in 1994 indicates how much the economy produced if goods and services cost the same as they did in 1987.

There are, however, problems with this method of calculation. As prices change, people and businesses alter their purchases, substituting away from goods whose prices are rising relative to others and toward goods whose relative prices are declining. Thus, output increases most for those goods whose relative prices are falling. Evaluating these goods at their previous higher prices overstates output growth. By contrast, growth may be understated in years before the base year. To lessen the bias in measuring current economic growth, the base year is regularly updated. Although such a revision presents a more accurate picture of the current economy, it further distorts the history of the series.

The chain-weight index will minimize the bias inherent in a fixed-weight index and eliminate the changes in historical growth rates that occur when a new base year is established. Under this method, real GDP is calculated using prices in years close to the year in question. For example, the calculation of 1991 real GDP uses the prices in 1990 and 1991 as weights. Real GDP for 1992 uses the prices in 1991 and 1992 as weights. Moving through time forms a chain of weights that gives the index its name.

The table below illustrates the difference in measured growth under the two indexes. In years close to the base year (1987), there is little substitution bias, so growth is the same using either index. As expected, however, the chain-weight index indicates higher growth in years prior to the base year and slower growth in years beyond the base year. Furthermore, as one moves further from the base, the substitution bias inherent in the fixed-weight index accumulates, resulting in an increasing divergence between the two indexes.

– Patricia S. Pollard

AVERAGE ANNUAL REAL GDP GROWTH			
Period	Chain-Weight	Fixed-Weight (1987 $)	Difference
1961-1975	3.75%	3.38%	0.37 % points
1975-1986	3.18	2.88	0.30
1986-1991	2.02	2.02	0
1991-1994	2.72	3.16	-0.44

Views expressed do not necessarily reflect official positions of the Federal Reserve System

Pollard, Patricia S. "Introducing Chain-Weight GDP Data in National Economic Trends," National Economic Trends. Federal Reserve Bank of St. Louis, October, 1995.

CHAPTER ANSWERS

Chapter in Brief

1. Gross domestic product 2. Final 3. Financial 4. Less 5. Also equals 6. Nominal 7. Real 8. And does not 9. Exports 10. Changes in the 11. Exports 12. Imports 13. Proprietors' income 14. But not 15. Also includes 16. Gross national product 17. National income 18. Disposable income 19. Decline 20. Increase 21. decreased 22. lower

Key Terms Review

1. Gross domestic product 2. Aggregates 3. Nominal GDP 4. Aggregate real income 5. Gross private domestic investment 6. Government purchases of goods and services 7. Indirect business taxes 8. Net taxes 9. Leakages 10. National income and product accounts 11. Intermediate products 12. Real GDP 13. Net exports 14. Depreciation 15. Transfer payments 16. Corporate profits taxes 17. Disposable income 18. Injections 19. Total value added in a nation 20. Aggregate expenditure 21. Personal consumption expenditures 22. Net private domestic investment 23. Value added 24. Final products 25. National saving 26. Total saving in the United States 27. Gross national product 28. Net national product 29. National income 30. Personal income 31. Personal saving

Concept Review

1. a. Changes in the value of existing assets
   b. Sale of used goods
   c. Financial transactions
   d. Most goods not sold in markets

2. a. $1 billion b. $1 billion c. $1/2 Billion d. $5 1/2 billion e. $3 billion f. 2 1/2 billion; 2 1/2 billion

3.

Nominal GDP	Price Index	Real GDP
$10,000,000	90.9	$11,001,100
12,600,000	95.5	13,193,717
15,400,000	100.0	15,400,000
18,400,000	104.5	17,607,656
21,600,000	109.1	19,798,350

   c. 9.1%

4. a. Understated
   b. Understated
   c. Overstated
   d. Understated

5. a. (1) Durable goods
      (2) Nondurable goods
      (3) Services
   b. (1) New residential and nonresidential construction
      (2) Producer durables
      (3) Changes in the value of inventories

c.   (1) Corporate profits taxes

      (2) Retained earnings

      (3) Dividends

6. a. $2,700

  b. $2,700

  c. $100

  d. $190

  d. $2,170

  f. $2,252

  g. $1,927

7. a.   (1) Saving

      (2) Net taxes

      (3) Imports

  b.   (1) Gross private domestic investment

      (2) Government purchases of goods and services

      (3) Exports

  c.   Declines, increases, remains unchanged

  d.   (1) Personal saving

      (2) Business saving

      (3) Foreign saving

      (4) Government saving

8. a.   Personal saving

  b.   Business saving

  c.   Government saving

9. a.   Professor Arrow notes that the growth of living standards have slowed over the last 15 years, but there is no reason to believe that standards of living will actually decline in the future. According to Professor Litan, that while living standards have grown less rapidly over the last 25 years, these trends are not unique to the United States, but have also occurred throughout the industrialized countries. Future conditions depend upon education and productivity.

  b.   Arrow suggests that to increase future living conditions, we must improve education, reverse the deterioration of the family unit, and increase national saving, in part, by reducing the federal budget deficit. Litan likewise advocates increasing saving, but in addition emphasizes increased investment in physical and human capital as well as in research and development.

Mastery Test

1. c 2. d 3. b 4. d 5. b 6. c 7. d 8. b 9. a 10. b 11. d 12. d 13. c 14. c 15. a 16. b 17. b
18. c 19. a 20. d

Think it Through

1. GDP can be estimated by summing the aggregate expenditures on the nation's final output or by summing the income generated by the economy in producing that output. The expenditure

approach requires the summation of personal consumption expenditures, government purchases of goods and services, gross private domestic investment, and net exports. The income approach involves the addition of the five types of income (proprietors' income, corporate profits, compensation of employees, rental income, and net interest) to indirect business taxes, consumption of fixed capital (or depreciation), and adjustments for net foreign income..

2. Although gross private domestic investment is positive, net private domestic investment is negative. Total investment is insufficient to replace the capital that has worn out during the year's production of GDP. The total capacity of the economy to produce output has declined. Future economic growth will likely be impaired.

3. Real GDP can be derived by dividing a general price index into nominal GDP. Changes in real GDP are the result of changes in output and not prices because real GDP is valued at a given set of prices as determined by the base year. Economists are interested in real GDP because changes in real GDP reflect real changes in economic activity that produce output and employment rather than the image of changes in economic activity caused merely by inflation.

4. If exports are rising faster than imports, net exports are rising. The total level of aggregate expenditures on domestic output is therefore also rising. In the context of the aggregate supply and demand model, aggregate demand is rising, causing an increase in real GDP and the price level.

5. Total expenditures on a nation's final output equal the market value of the final output produced. But the market value of all output less the market value of all intermediate products must equal the sum of the value added from each stage of production. This value added is made possible by the combined services of labor, raw materials, capital, and entrepreneurs. The value added just equals the payments to suppliers of labor, capital, and raw materials, including profits to owners. The sum of the value added at each stage of production equals GDP, but it also equals the total aggregate income generated in producing that value added. Thus total expenditures on a nation's final output are conceptually equal to the total income generated by the economy in producing that final output.

Analyzing the News

1. With a fixed-weight index, 1987 base-year prices are used to determine real GDP in every year. A fixed-weight index overstates the value of real output for years after the base year and understates it for prior years. Changing relative prices over time will cause a substitution away from relatively more expensive items to less expensive goods. Valuing the increased output of goods experiencing decreases in relative prices at the higher base-year prices will overstate the value of output.

2. One way to lessen this bias is to update the base year. But doing so frequently "distorts" the historical series. The Department of Commerce has decided to remedy the situation by using a "chain-weight" index that allows the use of more current prices (current and previous year prices). As shown on the table in the article, fixed-weight real GDP growth after the 1987 base-year is reduced using a chain-weight index.

7 BUSINESS CYCLES, UNEMPLOYMENT, AND ECONOMIC GROWTH

■ CHAPTER CONCEPTS

After studying this chapter, attending class, and completing this chapter, you should be able to:

1. Discuss the business cycle and give examples of recent periods of recession and expansion of the U.S. economy.
2. Explain how unemployment is measured and how the unemployment rate can be viewed as the sum of frictional, structural, and cyclical unemployment.
3. Define the concept of full employment and show how it is related to the natural rate of unemployment.
4. Explain potential real GDP and the difficulties involved in estimating it.
5. Discuss the social costs of unemployment and programs designed to cushion these costs.
6. Discuss the record and sources of economic growth in the United States.

■ THE CHAPTER IN BRIEF

Fill in the blanks to summarize chapter content.

The business cycle describes the ups and downs in real GDP over time. Although no two business cycles are identical, they all have four distinct phases: expansion, peak, contraction, and trough. An economy is in a recession or contraction when real GDP has declined for (1)_____(three, two) consecutive 3-month periods. Although real GDP fluctuates up and down, its long-run average annual growth trend is just over (2)_____(3%, 5%).

The unemployment rate is the percentage of the labor force that is unemployed. The labor force includes all persons over the age of 16 with jobs and those actively seeking employment. A person is considered unemployed if the person is over age 16 and is available for work (3)_____(but not, and) actively seeking employment. The unemployment rate may understate or overstate the true extent of unemployment. The unemployment rate (4)_____ (does not, does) include discouraged workers. Also, part-time employment is considered as full-time employment, not as partial employment or unemployment. People may respond to unemployment surveys that thcy are looking for work when in fact their expectations of a job will likely not materialize because those expectations are unrealistic.

The three types of unemployment are frictional unemployment, structural unemployment, and cyclical unemployment. (5)_____ (Structural, Frictional) unemployment is due to the length of time it takes to find employment upon entering the labor force or between jobs. (6)_____ (Structural, Frictional) unemployment results from changes in the composition of output produced by the economy or by technological changes that cause some industries to expand and others to decline. Cyclical unemployment is unemployment caused by economic decline or recession. Most cyclical unemployment is the result of layoffs. Full employment is defined as a level of economic activity where the actual unemployment rate (7)_____ (is less than, equals) the sum of structural and frictional unemployment and exists even when the economy is operating at the peak of the business cycle—at a high rate of capacity utilization. When the sum of

131

frictional and (8)_____ (structural, cyclical) unemployment is expressed as a percentage of the total labor force, the ratio is known as the natural rate of unemployment.

(9)_____(Actual, Potential) GDP is the level of output that results if the economy operates for an entire year at the natural rate of unemployment. Potential GDP (10)_____ (is, is not) the capacity level of output for an economy. An economy operating at capacity will, in time, produce conditions that will cause the economy to decline toward potential GDP. Potential GDP is (11)_____ (difficult, easy) to measure because it and an important variable upon which it depends, the natural rate of unemployment, are unobserved variables and have to be estimated. Potential GDP grows over time as a result of factors that contribute to economic growth such as improvements in technology and increases in the quantity and quality of resources.

When the economy is in a recession, such as the Great Depression of the 1930s or more recently the 1981-82 recession, unemployment (12)_____ (rises, falls). As the economy expands out of a trough, the unemployment rate (13)_____(rises, falls). If actual GDP falls short of potential GDP, the sacrificed output constitutes a major cost of cyclical unemployment. Other social costs of unemployment include the monetary and nonmonetary costs associated with suicide, crime, mental illness, physical illness, stress, and other problems attributed to unemployment.

Unemployment insurance was established in 1935 as part of the Social Security Act in order to soften the blow of unemployment. Generally, only those people who lose their jobs due to layoff, economic contraction, or (14)_____ (firings, plant closings) get unemployment benefits.

(15)_____ (Labor productivity, The quantity of labor supplied) is the key source of real GDP growth. It is influenced by the level of work experience, education, training, (16)_____ (the amount of profit, the amount of capital per worker), the age composition of the labor force, technological improvements, and improvements in managerial techniques. The growth of capital per worker is dependent on the rate of planned investment and the (17)_____ (stock market, rate of saving). According to the text, (18)_____ (two thirds, one half) of real GDP growth from 1929 to 1982 can be attributed to increases in labor productivity, with the remainder due to increases in the quantity of labor. Increases in (19)_____ (the quantity of labor supplied, labor productivity) are primarily due to improved technology and managerial techniques, increases in the quantity of capital, and improved education and training.

■ KEY TERMS REVIEW

Write the key term from the list below next to its definition.

Key Terms

Business cycle
Contraction
Recession
Layoff
Expansion
Productivity
Recovery
Discouraged worker
Labor force
Potential real GDP
Unemployment rate
Unemployed person

Overheated economy
Economic growth
Frictional
   unemployment
Structural
   unemployment
Cyclical
   unemployment
Natural rate of
   unemployment
Full employment

Definitions

1. _____: the term used to describe the fluctuations in aggregate production as measured by the ups and downs of real GDP.

2. _____: an upturn of economic activity between a trough and a peak during which real GDP increases.

3. _____: the sum of the number of persons over age 16 with jobs and workers who are actively seeking a job but currently do not have one.

4. _____: the temporary suspension of employment without pay for a period of 7 consecutive days or more.

5. _____: the amount of unemployment resulting from declines in real GDP during periods of contraction or recession or in any period when the economy fails to operate at its potential.

6. _____: the level that would prevail if the economy achieved the natural rate of unemployment over a period.

7. _____: a downturn from peak economic activity in the business cycle during which real GDP declines from its previous value.

8. _____: the term used to describe an expansion in economic activity after a trough if the expansion follows a period of contraction severe enough to be classified as a recession.

9. _____: measures the ratio of the number of people classified as unemployed to the total labor force.

10. _____: a worker who leaves the labor force (stops actively seeking work) after unsuccessfully searching for a job for a certain period.

133

11. _____ : the percentage of the labor force that can normally be expected to be unemployed for reasons other than cyclical fluctuations in real GDP.

12. _____ : exists when the decline in real GDP measured at an annual rate occurs for two consecutive 3-month reporting periods.

13. _____ : a person over age 16 who is available for work and has actively sought employment during the previous 4 weeks.

14. _____ : occurs when the actual rate of unemployment is no more the natural rate of unemployment.

15. _____ : represents the usual amount of unemployment resulting from people who have left jobs that did not work out and are searching for new employment, or people who are either entering or reentering the labor force to search for a job.

16. _____ : unemployment resulting from shifts in the pattern of demand for goods and services or changes in technology in the economy that affect the profitability of hiring workers in specific industries.

17. _____ : an economy in which the actual unemployment rate is less than the natural rate of unemployment.

18. _____ : expansion in production measured by the annual percentage increase in a nation's level of real GDP.

19. _____ : a measure of output per unit of input.

■ CONCEPT REVIEW

Concept 1: *Business cycle and record of recent fluctuations in the U.S. economy*

1. Identify the phases of the business cycle in the diagram below.

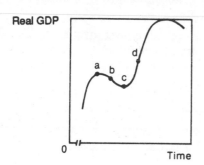

a. _____

b. _____

c. _____

d. _____

2. a. During the 1930s, the unemployment rate _____ to _____ and real GDP _____ by _____ of its 1929 value.

   b. As a result of World War II, the unemployment rate _____ and real GDP _____, but recessions did occur _____. The 1950s can be characterized as a period of _____, although _____ occurred in _____ and _____.

   c. The 1960s was a period of economic expansion lasting from _____ to _____, which was due in part to _____.

   d. The decade of the 1970s experienced periods of rising _____ and _____. The last half of the decade can be characterized as _____.

   e. There have been _____ recessions in the 1980s, with the most severe recession since the Great Depression occurring from _____ to _____. The remainder of the decade was characterized by _____ which began _____ and ended _____. The subsequent recession ended _____, but the ensuing expansion was _____.

Concept 2: *Unemployment rate*

3. Find the size of the labor force, the number of unemployed persons, and the unemployment rate from the data below.

1.	Total population	200 million
2.	Persons over age 16 working	95
3.	Institutional population (prisons, hospitals, etc.)	12
4.	Discouraged workers	2
5.	Persons over age 16 actively seeking work and available for employment	5

   a. Total labor force = _____

   b. Unemployed persons = _____

   c. Unemployment rate = _____

4. List three reasons why the unemployment rate may not reflect the true extent of unemployment.

   a. _____

   b. _____

   c. _____

5. Identify each of the following as either frictional, structural, or cyclical unemployment.

a. _____ You quit your job and spend time searching for new employment.

b. _____ You are temporarily unemployed due to layoff.

c. _____ Advances in office automation reduce the need for secretaries.

d. _____ Movie theaters reduce employment because more people are watching home videos.

e. _____ You graduate from high school and begin your search for a job.

f. _____ A decline in demand for the nation's output causes both GDP and employment to decline.

Concept 4: *Potential GDP*

6. Identify three basic facts regarding potential real GDP.

a. _____

b. _____

c. _____

Concept 5: *Social costs of unemployment*

7. In addition to losses in jobs, wages, profits, and tax revenue, other social costs of unemployment include the costs associated with:

a. _____

b. _____

c. _____

d. _____

Concept 6: *Economic Growth*

8. List four sources of economic growth.

a. _____

b. _____

c. _____

d. _____

Select the best answer.

1. Which of the following best defines the business cycle?
   a. Recessions and expansions
   b. Ups and downs in business activity
   c. Ups and downs in real GDP
   d. None of the above

2. The phase of a business cycle just following a trough is called a/an:
   a. recession.
   b. decline.
   c. expansion.
   d. peak.

3. The economy is defined as being in a recession if:
   a. economic activity declines.
   b. real GDP declines.
   c. real GDP declines for four consecutive 3-month periods.
   d. real GDP declines for two consecutive 3-month periods.

4. Since the turn of the century, real GDP has expanded at an average annual rate of:
   a. 2%.
   b. 3%.
   c. 4%.
   d. 5%.

5. Unemployment rises in _____ and declines in _____.
   a. expansions, recessions
   b. recessions, expansions
   c. expansions, expansions
   d. recessions, recessions

6. The total labor force consists of:
   a. all persons working plus those not working.
   b. all persons over age 16 working.
   c. discouraged workers, part-time and full-time workers, and the armed forces.
   d. all persons over age 16 either working or actively seeking work and available for employment.

7. The unemployment rate is defined as:
   a. the percentage of the population that is unemployed.
   b. the percentage of the labor force that is unemployed.
   c. all unemployed workers, including discouraged workers, divided by the total labor force.
   d. all unemployed workers, including discouraged workers, divided by the total population.

8. Which of the following is not a reason why the unemployment rate may not reflect the true extent of unemployment?
   a. Discouraged workers are excluded.
   b. Part-time work is considered as full-time work.
   c. People may respond to employment surveys that they are looking for work when in fact the likelihood of their finding employment that meets their expectations is remote.
   d. None of the above.

9. Unemployment due to the length of time it takes to find employment upon entering the labor force or voluntarily between jobs is called:
   a. cyclical unemployment.
   b. frictional unemployment.
   c. structural unemployment.
   d. natural unemployment.

10. Unemployment that results from changes in the composition of output produced by the economy or from technological changes is called:
   a. cyclical unemployment.
   b. frictional unemployment.
   c. structural unemployment.
   d. natural unemployment.

11. Unemployment caused by economic decline or recession is called:
   a. cyclical unemployment.
   b. frictional unemployment.
   c. structural unemployment.
   d. natural unemployment.

12. Most cyclical unemployment is the result of:
   a. layoffs.
   b. voluntary job separations.
   c. job findings.
   d. firings.

13. The unemployment rate that exists even when the economy is at the peak of a business cycle is:
   a. the sum of the frictional and structural unemployment rates.
   b. the actual unemployment rate.
   c. the cyclical unemployment rate.
   d. the natural rate of unemployment.
   e. a and d.

14. Today most economists consider the natural rate of unemployment to be:
   a. 4%.
   b. 8%.
   c. 6%.
   d. 2%.

15. _____ is the level of output that would result if the economy operated for an entire year at the natural rate of unemployment.
    a. Real GDP
    b. Natural rate of GDP
    c. Capacity GDP
    d. Potential real GDP

16. Costs associated with unemployment include:
    a. lost jobs, wages, profits, and tax revenue.
    b. costs associated with suicide and mental illness.
    c. costs associated with stress, physical illness, and crime.
    d. All of the above.

17. Unemployment insurance:
    a. covers all workers.
    b. is federally administered.
    c. primarily covers those workers who lose their jobs due to layoff, economic contraction, or plant closings.
    d. was established in 1970.

18. Which of the following is a key to the process of economic growth?
    a. Improvements in labor productivity
    b. Increases in the stock of resources
    c. Increases in the money supply
    d. Reducing the federal budget deficit

19. In order of importance, what factors are responsible for the growth in labor productivity in the United States from 1929 to 1982?
    a. Improvements in education, increases in the amount of capital per worker, increases in investment spending
    b. Increases in the capital stock, saving, cuts in income tax rates
    c. Improvements in technology and management, increases in the amount of capital per worker, improvements in education and training
    d. Saving and investment, technological improvements, increases in the quantity of labor and other resources

20. An increase in saving reduces _____ in the short run but if it is invested in physical and human capital over the long run, the level of potential real GDP will _____ .
    a. aggregate supply, decrease
    b. aggregate supply, increase
    c. aggregate demand, decrease
    d. consumption, increase

21. If an economy has a population of 250 million people, 115 million persons over age 16 working, an institutional population (prisons, hospitals, etc.) of 25 million, 4 million discouraged workers, and 10 million persons over age 16 actively seeking work and available for employment, what is the rate of unemployment?
    a. 4%
    b. 6%
    c. 8%
    d. 10%

22. Which of the following is true regarding frictional unemployment?
    a. Frictional unemployment results from changes in technology and taste and preferences that affect the composition of GDP.
    b. Frictional unemployment is most appropriately viewed as involuntary unemployment.
    c. Frictional unemployment falls in business cycle expansions and rises in contractions.
    d. Frictional unemployment rises in business cycle expansions and falls in contractions.

23. If actual real GDP exceeds potential real GDP:
    a. the natural rate of unemployment exceeds the actual rate.
    b. the natural rate of unemployment is less than the actual rate.
    c. cyclical unemployment exceeds the natural rate of unemployment.
    d. the sum of frictional and cyclical unemployment must exceed structural unemployment.

24. Which of the following is not a "basic" fact about potential real GDP?
    a. Potential real GDP is not the economy's "capacity" output.
    b. Potential real GDP is the economy's "capacity" output.
    c. It's not easy to measure potential real GDP.
    d. Potential real GDP grows over time.

25. If improvements in technology, education, training, and work experience increase labor productivity:
    a. actual real GDP will surpass potential real GDP.
    b. potential real GDP will rise.
    c. the natural rate of unemployment will rise.
    d. the natural rate of unemployment consistent with actual real GDP will fall.

■ THINK IT THROUGH

1. Define the unemployment rate and discuss why it may not accurately reflect the true extent of unemployment.
2. Discuss the factors that influence the unemployment rate.
3. Of what use is the concept of the natural rate of unemployment?
4. What are the social costs associated with unemployment?
5. Discuss one way in which society softens the blow of unemployment.

CHAPTER ANSWERS

The Chapter in Brief

1. Two 2. 3% 3. And 4. Does not 5. Frictional 6. Structural 7. Equals 8. Structural 9. Potential 10. Is not 11. Difficult 12. Rises 13. Falls 14. Plant closings 15. Labor productivity 16. The amount of capital per worker 17. Rate of saving 18. Two thirds 19. Labor productivity

Key Terms Review

1. Business cycle 2. Expansion 3. Labor force 4. Layoff 5. Cyclical unemployment 6. Potential real GDP 7. Contraction 8. Recovery 9. Unemployment rate 10. Discouraged worker 11. Natural rate of unemployment 12. Recession 13. Unemployed person 14. Full employment 15. Frictional unemployment 16. Structural unemployment 17. Overheated economy 18. Economic growth 19. Productivity

Concept Review

1. a. Peak b. Recession c. Trough d. Expansion

2. a. Increased, 25%, fell, one third
   b. Fell, increased, at the end of the war and in 1949; growth and stability, recessions, 1954, 1958
   c. 1961, 1970; military expansion and the Vietnam War
   d. Inflation, unemployment; growth and rampant inflation
   e. Two, 1981, 1982; expansion; November, 1982; July, 1990; March, 1991; less rapid than previous expansions

3. a. 100 million
   b. 5 million
   c. 5%

4. a. Discouraged workers are excluded.
   b. Part-time work is counted as full-time work.
   c. Survey responses may be misleading.

5. a. Frictional b. Cyclical c. Structural d. Structural e. Frictional f. Cyclical

6. a. Potential real GDP is not the economy's "capacity" output.
   b. It is difficult to measure potential real GDP.
   c. Potential real GDP grows over time.

7. a. Crime b. Suicide c. Mental illness d. Physical illness

8. a. Increases in the quantity of resources available to a nation
   b. Increases in resource productivity
   c. Improved technology and managerial techniques
   d. Improvements in the efficiency with which resources are used

Mastery Test

1. c 2. c 3. d 4. b 5. b 6. d 7. b 8. d 9. b 10. c 11. a 12. a 13. e 14. c 15. d 16. d 17. c 18. a 19. c 20. d 21. c 22. d 23. a 24. b 25. b

Think it Through

1. The unemployment rate is the percentage of the total labor force that is unemployed. The labor force consists of all persons over age 16 either working or actively seeking employment but not currently employed. Unemployed persons are those individuals over age 16 available for work and actively searching for employment. The unemployment rate may not reflect the true extent of unemployment because discouraged workers are unemployed but not counted as part of the labor force. Also, part-time work is counted as full-time employment. Further, employment surveys include responses from individuals that may be misleading.

2. The factors that influence the unemployment rate are the factors that influence frictional, structural, and cyclical unemployment. The rates of voluntary job separation and job finding affect frictional unemployment. The length of time that it takes to find a job varies with the business cycle. The decision to enter or reenter the labor force may also be associated with the level of economic prosperity. Technological progress often displaces certain workers who have skills specific to the obsolete technologies. Changes in society's preferences regarding the composition of GDP will cause some industries to expand and some to decline, even at a state of full employment in the economy as a whole. Broad forces causing economic contraction or expansion will decrease or increase the cyclical component of the unemployment rate.

3. The natural rate of unemployment is a useful benchmark for determining the potential output of the economy. Policies that are intended to spur economic activity and reduce unemployment must have a benchmark indicating possible courses of action in the short run.

4. The social costs of unemployment include the output that is forgone when an economy operates at a level of unemployment above the natural rate of unemployment. Other social costs include the costs associated with crime, suicide, mental and physical illness, and stress.

5. Unemployment insurance was established as part of the Social Security Act of 1935 in order to alleviate to some extent the problems associated with unemployment. Unemployment benefits replace some of the lost purchasing power resulting from unemployment, although there is not universal coverage of unemployed workers. Critics contend that the benefits are too high and available for too many weeks, thus reducing the urgency with which workers search for employment.

8   THE PRICE LEVEL AND INFLATION

■ CHAPTER CONCEPTS

After studying your text, attending class, and completing this chapter, you should be able to:

1. Understand how price indexes are used to measure the price level and inflation.
2. Deflate nominal income using a price index to derive real income and know the distinction between real and nominal wages.
3. Explain how inflation can affect workers, employers, creditors, and debtors.
4. Explain how inflation affects interest rates and know the distinction between real and nominal interest rates.
5. Explain how inflation can affect economic decisions and the functioning of the economy.

■ THE CHAPTER IN BRIEF

Fill in the blanks to summarize chapter content.

A price index is used to measure the price level. The (1)_____ [producer price index, consumer price index (CPI)] is used to measure the impact of changes in prices on households. It is determined by dividing the (2)_____ (current, base-year) value of a market basket of products and services by the value of the same market basket in the (3)_____ (current, base) year. The quotient is then multiplied by 100. In the (4)_____ (current, base) year, the price index is always 100. The CPI is actually a weighted average of a number of component price indexes. The weights are determined from household expenditure surveys conducted every (5)_____ (year, 10 years). A broader measure of inflation is the GDP deflator. The (6)_____ (producer price index, GDP deflator) is used in calculating real GDP.

Inflation is the percentage increase from period to period in a price index. If the price index is decreasing, the percentage change in the index is called (7)_____ (disinflation, deflation). From 1913 until 1950, the CPI exhibited periods of both inflation and deflation. (8)_____ (Deflation, Inflation) usually occurred immediately following wars and depressions. Since 1950, the CPI has shown a consistent (9)_____ (decrease, increase), although the rate of inflation has been variable. From 1960 to the 5-year period ending in 1979, the 5-year average rate of inflation increased from 1.26% to 8%. Between 1980 and 1984 inflation decreased to an average of 7.5%, and between 1985 and 1989 inflation decreased further to (10)_____ (3.6%, 5.5%). In the 1990s, inflation has averaged 3.5%

Price indexes can be used to remove the effect of inflation from nominal variables such as nominal income, nominal wages, and nominal GDP. Inflation (11)_____ (increases, erodes) the purchasing power of a dollar. Since nominal variables are defined in terms of current dollars, changes in the purchasing power of nominal variables (12)_____ (are necessarily, are not necessarily) fully reflected by dollar changes in the variable. For instance, if a household's nominal income doubled over a 10-year period but the level of prices confronting the household also doubled, the household's purchasing power would (13)_____ (remain unchanged, double).
Nominal values can be converted to real values by dividing the nominal variable by the relevant price index itself (14)_____ (multiplied, divided) by 100. By removing the effect of inflation, we can determine how much of an increase in a nominal variable is due to inflation and how

143

much is due to real increases in purchasing power. During periods of rapid inflation, nominal wage inflation (15)_____ (lags behind, exceeds) price inflation, causing real wages to (16)_____ (rise, fall). In effect, income is redistributed from workers to employers. Over the long run, however, wage inflation has exceeded price inflation, resulting in an/a (17)_____ (increase, decrease) in real wages.

In addition to reducing purchasing power, inflation can redistribute income and wealth. Borrowers (18)_____ (lose, benefit) during a period of inflation because the future dollars that they pay in principal and interest are worth (19)_____ (more, less) in purchasing power than the dollars at the time they were borrowed. The government borrows vast sums of money to finance its annual budget deficit. During periods of inflation, the purchasing power of the federal debt actually decreases. Over time, inflation may transfer purchasing power (20)_____ (to, away from) government (or taxpayers that are not creditors of government) and (21)_____ (to, away from) those holding government debt. Because households headed by young individuals and those with middle incomes tend to have large debt as a percentage of income relative to other age and income groups, inflation benefits young and middle-income households relative to other households. In general, if inflation is unanticipated, debtors benefit at the expense of creditors.

(22)_____ (Anticipated, Unanticipated) inflation affects present choices. If expectations of inflation are in error, choices are likely to result in a (23)_____ (more, less) efficient allocation of the economy's resources. If anticipated inflation is greater than the nominal interest rate, the real rate of interest is negative. If anticipated inflation increases more than the nominal rate of interest, the real rate of interest (24)_____ (falls, rises). Planned investment spending depends in part on the real rate of interest. Changes in anticipated inflation that cause changes in real rates of interest will affect planned investment. If those expectations are in error, businesses will likely over- or underinvest.

Similarly, expected inflation might cause households to consume (25)_____ (later rather than now at current prices, now rather than wait for prices to rise). Given a level of income, an increase in consumption of goods and services means that saving will decline. If anticipated inflation reduces saving, economic growth is (26)_____ (promoted, impaired). Also during periods of anticipated inflation, individuals tend to purchase goods that rise in value as fast as or faster than the general price level. If funds are being used to purchase real estate, gold, art, and other similar goods, those funds are not available as saving for use by businesses for capital investment. Inflation also redistributes wealth to households having these inflation-hedging assets away from those having assets that do not inflate in value as rapidly. Inflation can also increase the cost of capital, increase the real rate of interest, and excessive inflation can lead to a recession. By affecting important economic variables, inflation influences the decisions of business and government managers and policy makers.

KEY TERMS REVIEW

Write the key term from the list below next to its definition.

Key Terms

Price level

Price index

Inflation

Deflation

Consumer price
index (CPI)

Pure inflation

GDP deflator

Purchasing power of a dollar

Nominal income

Real income

Nominal wages

Real wages

Nominal interest rate

Real interest rate

Hyperinflation

Definitions

1. _____: an index for all final products, derived as the ratio of nominal GDP to real GDP (multiplied by 100); an index of the average of the prices used to deflate nominal GDP.

2. _____: inflation at very high rates of usually 200 percent or more prevailing for at least one year.

3. _____: a measure of how much a dollar can buy.

4. _____: occurs when the prices of all goods rise by the same percentage over the year.

5. _____: the actual number of dollars of income received over a year.

6. _____: the price index most commonly used to measure the impact of changes in prices on households. The index is based on a standard market basket of goods and services purchased by a typical urban family.

7. _____: hourly payments to workers in current dollars.

8. _____: the rate of downward movement in the price level for an aggregate of goods and services.

9. _____: nominal wages deflated to adjust for changes in the purchasing power of the dollar since a certain base year.

10. _____: the rate of upward movement in the price level for an aggregate of goods and services.

11. _____: the annual percentage amount of money that is earned on a sum loaned or deposited in a bank.

12. _____: a number used to measure the price level. The value of the index is set at 100 in the base period.

13. _____: the actual annual percentage change in the purchasing power of interest income earned on a sum of money that is loaned out.

14. _____: an indicator of how high or low prices are in a given year compared to prices in a certain base period.

15. _____: the purchasing power of nominal income.

■ CONCEPT REVIEW

Concept 1: *Price indexes and inflation*

1. a. Given the annual values of a given market basket of goods and services, compute the price index assuming the base year is year 3.

Year	Current Value of Market Basket	Price Index (base year = 3)
1	$18,000	_____
2	20,000	_____
3	24,000	_____
4	27,000	_____
5	29,500	_____
6	33,000	_____

   b. Determine the rate of inflation from the price index values above:

   (1) From year 3 to year 4 _____%

   (2) From year 4 to year 5 _____%

   (3) From year 5 to year 6 _____%

2. If housing has a weight of 42.6% in the CPI and housing prices increase 20% over the year, assuming all other prices rise at 5%, what is the rate of inflation for the year as measured by the rate of change in the CPI?_____%

Concept 2: *Nominal and real income*

3. a. Suppose you cleaned your closet and found income tax records for several consecutive years. Assuming your nominal income was shown in the table below and given the consumer price index, determine your real income for each year in the table.

Year	Nominal Income	CPI	Real Income (base year = year 1)
1	$29,000	100	$_____
2	31,000	110	_____
3	34,100	125	_____
4	35,000	131	_____
5	37,200	144	_____
6	39,500	160	_____

   b. Are you better off in year 6 as compared to year 1?

4. The data below consist of a household's nominal hourly wage and the CPI for given consecutive years.

Year	Nominal Hourly Wage	CPI	Real Hourly Wage
1	$ 6.25	110	_____
2	7.50	115	_____
3	8.50	125	_____
4	10.00	133	_____
5	12.00	145	_____

146

a. Complete the table.

b. Assume nominal wage growth is the result of two factors—inflation and increases in labor productivity. Determine what portion of the year-to-year change in the nominal hourly wage is due to inflation and what portion is due to increases in labor productivity.

Year 1 to 2: _____% due to inflation, _____% due to labor productivity.

Year 2 to 3: _____% due to inflation, _____% due to labor productivity.

Year 3 to 4: _____% due to inflation, _____% due to labor productivity.

Year 4 to 5: _____% due to inflation, _____% due to labor productivity.

Concepts 3, 4, and 5: *Consequences of inflation*

5. Identify how inflation affects purchasing power, the distribution of income and wealth, and economic choices.

a. Purchasing power:

b. Distribution of income and wealth:

c. Economic choices:

MASTERY TEST

Select the best answer.

1. Which of the following is an indicator of how high or low prices are in a given year compared to prices in a certain base year?
   a. Inflation
   b. Deflation
   c. Price level
   d. Price index

2. Which of the following is defined as a rate of downward movement in the price level for an aggregate of goods and services?
   a. Inflation
   b. Deflation
   c. Price level
   d. Price index

3. Which of the following price indexes measures the impact of changes in prices on households?
   a. Inflation index
   b. CPI
   c. Producer price index
   d. GDP deflator

4. A price index has a value of _____ in the base year.
   a. 100
   b. 10
   c. 50
   d. 1000
   e. 0

5. A price index for a market basket of goods can be found by:
   a. multiplying the value of the market basket by the rate of inflation.
   b. dividing the value of the market basket by the rate of inflation.
   c. dividing the current-year value of the market basket by the base-year value of the basket and multiplying the result by 100.
   d. dividing the base-year cost of the basket by the current-year cost of the basket.

6. If the CPI in year 1 equals 100 and the CPI in year 2 equals 113, it can be concluded that:
   a. year 2 is the base year.
   b. the rate of inflation from year 1 to year 2 is 113%.
   c. the rate of inflation from year 1 to year 2 is 13%.
   d. more information is needed to determine the rate of inflation.

7. Which of the following is not true regarding the consumer price index?
   a. The CPI is a weighted average.
   b. Most households actually experience rates of inflation somewhat different from that measured by percentage changes in the CPI.
   c. The CPI covers all goods consumed by households.
   d. Since 1950 the CPI has risen, although prior to that time there were times when consumer prices fell.

8. Beginning in 1960, the 5-year average rate of inflation in the United States:
   a. has continually increased.
   b. has continually decreased.
   c. increased until 1975-1979 and then decreased to the present.
   d. increased until 1980-1984 and then decreased to the present.

9. If the rate of inflation for a year is 10% but the rate of nominal income growth is 5%, real income:
   a. will rise.
   b. will fall.
   c. will remain the same.
   d. cannot be determined.

10. Over the long run _____ has exceeded _____, resulting in _____ real hourly wages in the United States.
    a. inflation, the rate of wage growth, rising
    b. the rate of wage growth, inflation, falling
    c. the rate of wage growth, inflation, rising
    d. inflation, the rate of wage growth, rising
    e. income, wages, falling

11. During periods of rapid inflation, _____ lags _____, causing real wages to _____.
    a. inflation, wage growth, rise
    b. wage growth, inflation, rise
    c. inflation, wage growth, fall
    d. wage growth, inflation, fall

12. Debtors benefit during periods of unanticipated inflation because:
    a. the money they pay lenders is worth more than the money originally borrowed.
    b. inflation outpaces wage growth.
    c. interest rates fall.
    d. the purchasing power of the dollars borrowed is greater than the purchasing power of the dollars repaid to lenders.

13. Which of the following groups lose as a result of unexpected inflation?
    a. Lenders
    b. Savers
    c. Taxpayers holding government debt
    d. Retirees on fixed pensions
    e. All of the above

149

14. Which of the following defines the anticipated real rate of interest?
    a. The nominal interest rate less the expected rate of inflation
    b. Inflation less the nominal rate of interest
    c. The nominal rate of interest plus the ex post rate of interest
    d. The real rate of interest adjusted for inflation

15. Anticipated inflation:
    a. affects the choices we make as individuals.
    b. constitutes a perfect forecast of actual inflation.
    c. may result in too much saving.
    d. may cause errors in consumption, but planned investment levels will always be correct because profit-maximizing producers use marginal analysis.
    e. None of the above.

16. Anticipated inflation:
    a. results in less funds available for productive investment.
    b. causes individuals to buy inflation "hedges" such as real estate, art and gold.
    c. may cause individuals to consume now rather than wait until prices rise.
    d. if erratic causes problems for planning and designing long-term contracts.
    e. All of the above.

17. Extremely high inflation such as that experienced by Germany in 1922 is called:
    a. deflation.
    b. inflation.
    c. stagflation.
    d. disinflation.
    e. hyperinflation.

18. Assume the rate of inflation as measured by the percentage change in the Consumer Price Index is 5%. If transportation and medical care have weights of 18.7% and 4.8%, respectively, and transportation prices rise by 10%, medical care prices rise by 20%, and all other prices rise by 5%, what will happen to the rate of inflation?
    a. The rate of inflation will rise to 7.5%.
    b. The rate of inflation will rise to 6.7%.
    c. The rate of inflation will rise to 8.0%.
    d. The rate of inflation will rise to 10.2%.

19. Over a 5-year period your salary has increased from $20,000 to $30,000 and the Consumer Price Index has fallen from 100 to 90. Determine the percentage change in your real income over the period.
    a. 50%
    b. 55%
    c. 46%
    d. 67%

20. Assume that the number of hours you work is positively related to the real wage. If your current nominal wage is $10.00 per hour and the Consumer Price Index is 125, but you expect wages to rise to $12.00 per hour and the price index to rise to 160, you will:
   a. work additional hours because the nominal wage has increased.
   b. work additional hours because the real wage has increased.
   c. work fewer hours because the nominal wage has increased.
   d. work fewer hours because the real wage has decreased.

21. If the level of real investment expenditures is inversely related to the real interest rate and the nominal rate of interest and rate of inflation rise from 8 to 10% and 6% to 8%, respectively, investment expenditures will:
   a. rise.
   b. fall.
   c. not change.
   d. be indeterminate.

22. Regarding the effects of inflation:
   a. inflation may increase the cost of capital.
   b. inflation may increase the real rate of interest.
   c. hyperinflation can lead to recession.
   d. All of the above
   e. None of the above

■ THINK IT THROUGH

1. It is likely that you experience a rate of inflation different from that derived from the rate of change in the consumer price index. Explain.

2. Explain the difference between nominal and real GDP. Can you think of any reasons why it is necessary to distinguish between nominal and real GDP? Discuss.

3. Explain what is meant by the following statement: " Inflation is a distorter of choices and a capricious redistributor of income."

■ ANALYZING THE NEWS

Using the skills derived from studying this chapter, analyze the economic facts that make up the following article and answer the questions below.

1. What is core inflation?

2. Is there a better way to measure core inflation?

National Economic Trends

A Better Measure of Core Inflation

Measures of core inflation are meant to capture the underlying inflation trend. The Bureau of Labor Statistics and the press routinely report the Consumer Price Index (CPI) excluding food and energy prices when they describe the underlying trend in the inflation rate. Historically, food and energy prices have been quite volatile, with large changes reflecting such factors as bad weather conditions or oil supply shocks (either positive or negative). Since the largest shocks have typically occurred in the food and energy sectors, excluding these components often gives a better picture of the underlying inflation trend.

Much of the month-to-month variation in the CPI is associated with shocks to individual markets in the economy. Although the net effect of such shocks should be zero over time, at monthly intervals the effect on reported inflation can be large. Since most of the month-to-month variation in the CPI is not due to monetary policy and likely to be self-correcting, it is important that policymakers not overreact to it. Thus, it is important to find ways to measure the underlying trend.

Researchers Stephen Cecchetti and Michael Bryan have constructed a measure called the median CPI, which they suggest does a better job of measuring core inflation than does the CPI excluding food and energy prices.[1] In principle, the median eliminates all goods and services except the item for which the price change is in the middle; that is, half the price changes are higher and the other half are lower. Thus, the median excludes all the items that have extreme price changes,

both positive and negative. For practical reasons, Bryan and Cecchetti start by grouping the price changes into 36 categories. To account for the fact that there are vast differences in the number of commodities in the different components, each component is weighted by its relative expenditure share in 1985.

The median price change, along with the CPI, is displayed in the chart below. The median CPI corrects for extreme movements in energy prices, which occurred in 1986 and 1990, as well as for shocks to other sectors. For practical purposes, the CPI excluding food and energy prices is quite similar to the median. However, in forecasting experiments, Bryan and Cecchetti found that the median CPI was a better predictor of future inflation – that is, a better measure of the inflation trend – than either the CPI itself or the CPI excluding food and energy.

—William T. Gavin

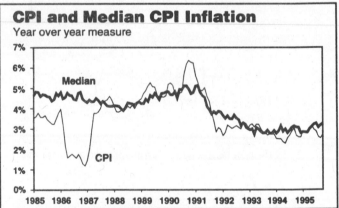

CPI and Median CPI Inflation
Year over year measure

[1]See "Measuring Core Inflation" by Michael F. Bryan and Stephen G. Cecchetti in *Monetary Policy* edited by N. Gregory Mankiw, Chicago: The University of Chicago Press, 1994, pp. 195-215.

Views expressed do not necessarily reflect official positions of the Federal Reserve System

Gavin, William T. "A Better Measure of Core Inflation," National Economic Trends. Federal Reserve Bank of St. Louis, December, 1995.

■ CHAPTER ANSWERS

The Chapter in Brief

1. Consumer price index (CPI) 2. Current 3. Base 4. Base 5. GDP deflator 7. Deflation 8. Deflation 9. Increase 10. 3.6% 11. Erodes 12. Are not necessarily 13. Remain unchanged
14. Divided 15. Lags behind 16. Fall 17. Increase 18. Benefit 19. Less 20. To 21. Away from
22. Anticipated 23. Less 24. Falls 25. Now rather than wait for prices to rise 26. Impaired

Key Terms Review

1. GDP deflator 2. Hyperinflation 3. Purchasing power of the dollar 4. Pure inflation 5. Nominal income 6. Consumer price index (CPI) 7. Nominal wages 8. Deflation 9. Real wages 10. Inflation
11. Nominal interest rate 12. Price index 13. Real interest rate 14. Price level 15. Real income

Concept Review

1. a.   Price Index (base year = year 3)
    75.0
    83.3
    100.0
    112.5
    122.9
    137.5
  b.   (1) 12.5% (2) 9.2% (3) 11.9%

2. Compute a weighted-average inflation rate as follows:
$$.426(20\%) + .574(5\%) = 11.39\%$$

3. a.   Real Income
    $29,000.00
    28,181.82
    27,280.00
    26,717.56
    25,833.33
    24,687.50
  b.   You are worse off in year 6 as compared to year 1 because your real income has declined.

4. a.   Real Hourly Wage
    $5.68
    6.52
    6.80
    7.52
    8.28

b. In order to determine the year-to-year percentage change in nominal hourly wages due to increases in labor productivity, find the year-to-year change in real hourly wages and divide this by the year-to-year change in nominal hourly wages. Subtract the result from 1 to determine the year-to-year percentage change in nominal hourly wages due to inflation.

	Due to Inflation	*Due to Increases in Productivity*
Year 1 to 2	32.8%	67.2%
2 to 3	72.0	28.0
3 to 4	52.0	48.0
4 to 5	62.0	38.0

5. a. Inflation reduces the purchasing power of a dollar and reduces the purchasing power of all nominal variables, such as nominal wages, nominal income, and nominal GDP.

  b. Unexpected inflation harms creditors such as financial institutions, savers, and holders of government debt, but benefits borrowers, including the federal government. It also benefits those households with a high debt burden such as middle-income households and households headed by young individuals. Inflation redistributes wealth from households having assets that do not increase in value as rapidly as the price level to households having assets that rise in value at a rate faster than the general price level.

  c. Anticipated inflation affects economic choices in the present. Expectations of inflation may cause an increase in consumption in an effort to beat the expected price increase. Or it may induce people to purchase inflation-hedging assets. Both forms of spending reduce current saving, impairing future economic growth. Errors are likely to be made in decision making because long-term plans and contracts will be based in part on an expected rate of inflation that may or may not materialize. Because of the uncertainty regarding future price levels, planned investment may be lower.

Mastery Test

1. c 2. b 3. b 4. a 5. c 6. c 7. c 8. c 9. b 10. c 11. d 12. d 13. e 14. a 15. a 16. e 17. e 18. b 19. d 20. d 21. c 22. d

Think it Through

1. The consumer price index is a weighted average of several price indexes for certain classes of goods or services such as housing or food and beverages. The weight for each class of goods represents the percentage of a typical urban family's budget that is spent on that class of goods. For instance, the weight for housing is .426, meaning that the typical urban family spends 42.6% of its budget on housing. These weights are based upon a 1982 to 1984 survey. These surveys are updated once a decade.

    If you differ in any way in your spending as compared to the "typical" urban family, you will face a different rate of inflation than that given by percentage changes in the CPI. The further in time we are away from the date of the survey, the less accurate are the weights. New products such as VCRs and personal computers and the changing spending patterns in response to these new goods would not be reflected in the weights of the CPI until the next survey.

2. Nominal GDP is the current-dollar value of GDP. Increases in prices or output will cause GDP to rise. While economists and others are certainly interested in inflation, it is of value to know how much real output the economy produces from year to year. It is increases in real output not inflation that ultimately result in increased employment and living standards. To remove the

effect of rising prices from nominal GDP in order to reveal the changes in real output, nominal GDP can be divided by a price index (the GDP deflator) itself divided by 100. The result is real GDP, which is a much better indicator of economic growth over time than is nominal GDP.

3. See question 5 in the Concept Review section for the answer. Inflation is "capricious" in its redistribution of income in that there are gainers and losers and it is difficult to assess the net outcome. Further, these changes in income distribution result not from public policy, but from unanticipated changes in price levels.

Analyzing the News

1. Core inflation represents the underlying trend in inflation. Because food and energy prices have often been volatile, they are removed from the CPI to give a measure of core inflation.

2. The median CPI is a better measure of core inflation than the CPI less food and energy. The median CPI omits all goods that experience wide price swings, not just food and energy. As shown in the figure, the trend in the median CPI is smoother than movements in the CPI.

PART IV

AGGREGATE DEMAND/ AGGREGATE SUPPLY

■ PART EXERCISE

Inside Information: *The State of the "Stats": How Accurate are Government Economic Statistics?*

In this section of the text, you will learn about macroeconomic models and their use in assessing economic impacts of changes in autonomous economic variables. These models are also used for government and business planning. Many of the variables used in macroeconomic models come from the National Income and Product Accounts and from other sources. For planning, it is important to obtain the latest data. But the most recently released data for some economic variables may be "preliminary" or "flash" estimates, which are subsequently revised at a future date. What are some implications for management and government planning when macroeconomic forecasts are based on preliminary data?

9 AGGREGATE DEMAND AND AGGREGATE SUPPLY

■ CHAPTER CONCEPTS

After studying your text, attending class, and completing this chapter, you should be able to:

1. Distinguish an aggregate demand curve from a market demand curve and discuss changes in aggregate demand.

2. Distinguish an aggregate supply curve from a market supply curve and discuss changes in aggregate supply.

3. Use aggregate supply and demand analysis to show how we determine the equilibrium level of real GDP and the price level over a given year.

4. Use aggregate supply and demand analysis to show how changes in aggregate demand and aggregate supply affect the equilibrium levels of real GDP and the price level for a given year and to explain the possible causes of recessions, excessive unemployment, and inflation.

■ THE CHAPTER IN BRIEF

Fill in the blanks to summarize chapter content.

Macroeconomics is concerned with explaining the forces affecting aggregate production and the general level of prices rather than with specific market quantities and prices. Aggregate supply and demand analysis is used to explain the factors that cause aggregate production and the price level to change. The aggregate demand curve shows the relationship between (1)_____ (the general price level, aggregate income) and the aggregate domestic production demanded. The aggregate quantity demanded is (2)_____ (positively, inversely) related to the general price level—the aggregate demand curve is (3)_____ (downward sloping, upward sloping). A change in the price level will change the aggregate quantity demanded, but influences other than the change in the price level that affect aggregate quantity demanded will (4)_____ (result in a movement along an aggregate demand curve, shift the aggregate demand curve).

The aggregate demand curve shows an inverse relationship between the price level and aggregate quantity demanded. As the price level rises, real wealth falls, causing saving to (5)_____ (increase, decrease) and consumption to (6)_____ (increase, decrease). Higher prices increase the demand for credit, thus increasing real interest rates which (7)_____ (increases, reduces) planned investment. Finally, a higher price level reduces exports and increases imports. Thus a higher price level (8)_____ (increases, reduces) aggregate purchases.

Factors that shift the aggregate demand curve include: (a) real interest rates, (b) the quantity of money in circulation, (c) changes in the international value of the dollar, (d) wealth, (e) government purchases, taxes and transfers, (f) expectations about the future, and (g) income and other factors affecting demand in foreign countries. If changes in these factors reduce aggregate demand, the aggregate demand curve shifts to the (9)_____ (right, left). If changes in these factors cause aggregate demand to increase, the aggregate demand curve shifts (10)_____ (rightward, leftward).

The aggregate supply curve shows an/a (11)_____(inverse, positive) relationship between aggregate output produced (real GDP) and the price level as potential real GDP is approached. As the price level rises, individual producers experience rising prices for the products that they produce. If input prices are not rising, opportunities for additional profits arise, causing some producers to increase production. Because producers confront (12)_____ (falling, rising) marginal costs with increases in output, they must have higher product prices to cover the (13)_____ (falling, rising) marginal and unit costs of production. At output levels associated with considerable cyclical unemployment, increases in production do not increase unit production costs. As potential real GDP is approached, unit production costs begin to (14)_____ (rise, fall). If output expands beyond potential real GDP, unit production costs rise even faster for given increases in output.

Changes in input prices and the quantity or productivity of inputs shift the aggregate supply curve. Higher input prices shift the aggregate supply curve vertically (15)_____ (downward, upward) and vice versa. Rightward shifts in the aggregate supply curve result from (16)_____ (more, fewer) inputs or (17)_____ (less, more) productive inputs. A decrease in the quantity or productivity of inputs will shift the aggregate supply curve leftward.

Macroeconomic equilibrium occurs when the quantity of real GDP demanded equals the quantity of real GDP supplied—where the aggregate demand and supply curves intersect. In equilibrium, there are no tendencies for the price level or aggregate output level to change (18)_____ (and there will be no, even though there may be) shortages or surpluses in individual product or resource markets. If aggregate demand rises relative to aggregate supply, unintended inventories fall, inducing firms to eventually (19)_____ (increase, decrease) production. If aggregate demand falls relative to aggregate supply, unintended inventories (20)_____ (rise, fall) causing firms to eventually (21)_____ (increase, cut) production and employment.

If aggregate demand decreases, real GDP falls relative to potential real GDP. An/a (22)_____ (inflationary, recessionary) gap arises equal to the difference between the potential and actual levels of real GDP. If aggregate demand increases, the aggregate demand curve shifts rightward and both real output and the price level will increase. Continual increases in aggregate demand cause (23)_____ (demand-pull, cost-push) inflation. The increase in the price level and the level of real GDP depend on the point on the aggregate supply curve at which the economy is operating. If actual real GDP exceeds potential real GDP, an/a (24)_____ (inflationary, recessionary) gap exists by the amount of the difference between the potential and actual levels of real GDP.

Changes in aggregate supply will alter the equilibrium level of real GDP and the price level. If aggregate supply decreases relative to aggregate demand, the price level will (25)_____ (fall, rise) while the level of employment and output will fall. If aggregate supply increases relative to aggregate demand, output (26)_____ (decreases, increases) and the price level falls. Rising input prices shift the aggregate supply curve (27)_____ (leftward, rightward), causing the price level to increase and employment and real GDP to (28)_____ (rise, fall). Continual decreases in aggregate supply cause (29)_____ (demand-pull, cost-push) inflation.

■ KEY TERMS REVIEW

Write the key term from the list below next to its definition.

Key Terms

Aggregate demand curve
Aggregate quantity demanded
Aggregate supply curve
Aggregate quantity supplied
Aggregate supply
Aggregate demand
Macroeconomic equilibrium

Inflationary GDP gap
Change in aggregate supply
Recessionary GDP gap
Cost-push inflation
Change in aggregate demand
Demand-pull inflation

Definitions

1. _____: inflation caused by increases in aggregate demand.

2. _____: a change in the amount of a nation's final product that will be purchased caused by something other than a change in the price level.

3. _____: the difference between equilibrium real GDP and potential real GDP when the economy is overheated.

4. _____: the difference between the equilibrium level of real GDP and potential real GDP when the economy is operating at less than full employment.

5. _____: a change in the amount of national production resulting from something other than a change in the price level.

6. _____: occurs when aggregate quantity demanded equals the quantity supplied.

7. _____: inflation caused by continual decreases in aggregate supply.

8. _____: the quantity of final products that will be supplied by producers at a given price level.

9. _____: shows the aggregate output of final products, as measured by real GDP, that will be produced at each possible price over a given period.

10. _____: the amount of final products that buyers are willing and able to purchase at each possible price level.

11. _____: shows how the amount of aggregate domestic production demanded, measured by real GDP, will vary with the price level.

12. _____: a relationship between aggregate quantity demanded and the economy's price level.

13. _____: a relationship between the price level and aggregate quantity supplied.

■ CONCEPT REVIEW

Concept 1: *Slope of the aggregate demand curve; shifts in the aggregate demand curve*

1. Assume that the economy is currently operating at a level of real GDP of $2200 billion with a price level equal to 120. Plot this coordinate on the figure below.

a. An increase in the price level to 180 will cause real wealth to _____, causing saving to _____ and consumption to _____ by $200 billion.

b. This price level increase will also cause real interest rates to _____, resulting in a/an _____ in planned investment of $100 billion.

c. The increase in the price level _____ imports by $80 billion and _____ exports by $20 billion, causing net exports (exports minus imports) to _____ by $100 billion.

d. The total change in aggregate quantity demanded due to the increase in the price level to 180 is $_____. Plot this new price level-aggregate quantity demanded coordinate on the figure above. The aggregate demand curve has a/an _____ slope.

2. List eight factors that shift the aggregate demand curve and indicate whether an increase in the factor shifts the aggregate demand to the right or left.

a. _____

b. _____

c. _____

d. _____

e. _____

f. _____

g. _____

h. _____

Concept 2: *Aggregate supply*

3. Match the statement with the proper segment of the aggregate supply curve shown in the figure below.

a. _____: Output can increase without much upward pressure on unit costs of production.

b. _____: Unit production costs rise very rapidly.

c. _____: Higher prices are required by producers to cover the rising unit costs of production as potential real GDP is approached.

d. _____: There is idle capacity and much cyclical unemployment.

e. _____: The economy is overheated.

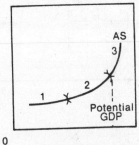

Concepts 3 and 4: Changes in aggregate demand and supply; macroeconomic equilibrium

4. The economy shown in the figure below is currently operating at its potential level of real GDP.

a. Show on the figure below the effect of an increase in aggregate demand and label the new AD curve AD1. Identify on the figure the change in real GDP and the price level. Real GDP _____ potential real GDP, resulting in a/an _____ gap.

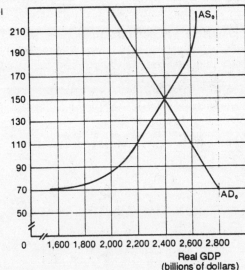

163

b. Given ADo as the initial aggregate demand curve, show on the figure above the effect of a decrease in aggregate demand and label the new AD curve AD2. Identify the changes in real GDP and the price level. Real GDP _____ potential GDP, resulting in a/an _____ gap.

5. The economy shown in the figure below is currently operating at its potential level of real GDP.

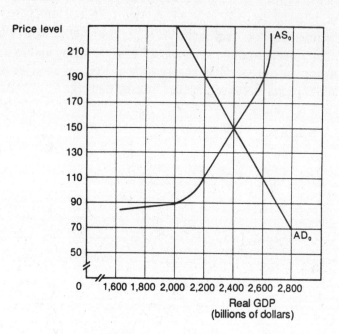

a. If the nation experiences a significant increase in oil prices, the aggregate supply curve will shift _____ by $200 billion dollars at every price level. Show this in the figure above and label the new aggregate supply curve AS1.

b. Real GDP _____ potential GDP by $_____, causing a/an _____ gap. The price level _____ to _____.

c. Assume that the economy is currently at potential real GDP. Show the effect of a decline in input prices and label the new aggregate supply curve AS2. Real GDP _____, and the price level _____.

■ MASTERY TEST

Select the best answer.

1. The aggregate demand curve shows a(n):
   a. positive relationship between prices and quantities.
   b. inverse relationship between the price level and the aggregate quantity demanded.
   c. independent relationship between the price level and the aggregate quantity demanded.
   d. inverse relationship between the product price and the quantity of a good demanded.

2. Which of the following will not shift the aggregate demand curve?
   a. Changes in exports
   b. Changes in planned investment by businesses
   c. The price level
   d. Changes in government spending

3. A higher price level:
   a. reduces real wealth and the level of consumption.
   b. increases real interest rates and decreases planned investment.
   c. increases imports and reduces exports.
   d. All of the above.
   e. a and b.

4. The aggregate _____ curve shows a relationship between real GDP produced and the price level. As potential real GDP is approached this curve _____.
   a. demand, is downward sloping
   b. supply, becomes steeper
   c. supply, becomes flatter
   d. demand, becomes steeper

5. The price level rises more rapidly as potential real GDP is approached along an aggregate supply curve because:
   a. profit-taking firms are exploiting their market size and power.
   b. of the profit incentive.
   c. the costs of additional units of aggregate output begin to rise more rapidly, causing firms to seek higher prices to cover these rising costs.
   d. None of the above.

6. Macroeconomic equilibrium occurs when:
   a. aggregate demand equals price.
   b. price equals the value of the marginal product.
   c. market demand equals market supply.
   d. aggregate quantity demanded equals aggregate quantity supplied.

7. Starting initially at potential real GDP, an increase in aggregate demand shifts the aggregate demand curve _____, causing real GDP to _____ and the price level to _____.
   a. rightward, rise, rise
   b. rightward, rise, fall
   c. leftward, fall, fall
   d. rightward, fall, fall
   e. leftward, fall, rise

8. If actual real GDP exceeds potential real GDP:
   a. the economy is overheated.
   b. prices rise more rapidly.
   c. an inflationary gap exists.
   d. real GDP increases less for given increases in aggregate demand.
   e. All of the above.

9. Starting initially at potential real GDP, a decrease in aggregate demand shifts the aggregate demand curve _____, causing real GDP to _____ and the price level to _____.
   a. rightward, rise, rise
   b. rightward, rise, fall
   c. leftward, fall, fall
   d. rightward, fall, fall
   e. leftward, fall, rise

10. If actual real GDP is below potential real GDP:
   a. the economy is overheated.
   b. prices rise more rapidly.
   c. an inflationary gap exists.
   d. a recessionary gap exists.

11. If domestic consumers reduce their demand for imports, aggregate demand will _____, causing real GDP to _____.
   a. fall, rise
   b. fall, fall
   c. rise, fall
   d. rise, rise

12. Demand-pull inflation:
   a. is caused by rising prices.
   b. is caused by rising input prices.
   c. is due to the decline over time in aggregate demand.
   d. is caused by continual increases in aggregate demand beyond the potential real GDP level.

13. An increase in input prices shifts the aggregate _____ curve _____, causing real GDP to _____ and the price level to _____.
    a. demand, upward, fall, rise
    b. demand, leftward, rise, rise
    c. demand, rightward, rise, fall
    d. supply, leftward, fall, rise
    e. supply, rightward, rise, fall

14. Which of the following causes cost-push inflation?
    a. A one-time increase in aggregate demand
    b. Continual increases in aggregate demand
    c. A one-time decrease in aggregate supply
    d. Continual decreases in aggregate supply

15. Which of the following will not shift the aggregate demand curve?
    a. A change in the price level
    b. An increase in the money supply
    c. A decrease in the international value of the dollar
    d. An increase in taxes
    e. Changes in household expectations

16. What will happen to the equilibrium price level and real GDP if the international value of the dollar increases and at the same time a major union wage settlement increases the average wage level?
    a. Real GDP rises, but the price level falls.
    b. real GDP and the price level increase.
    c. Real GDP falls, but the change in the price level is indeterminate.
    d. The price level rises, but the change in real GDP is indeterminate.

17. If the stock market crashes, reducing real wealth, at the same time that energy prices are falling, what will likely happen to real GDP and the price level?
    a. Real GDP rises, but the price level falls.
    b. Real GDP and the price level fall.
    c. Real GDP falls, but the change in the price level is indeterminate.
    d. The price level falls, but the change in real GDP is indeterminate.

18. Which of the following scenarios can cause demand-pull inflation?
    a. Favorable expectations regarding future employment and income
    b. An oil price shock
    c. An increase in the international value of the dollar
    d. An increase in the labor force

19. Which of the following scenarios can cause cost-push inflation?
    a. An increase in net taxes
    b. A major union wage settlement that increases average wage levels
    c. A decrease in real interest rates
    d. An increase in government purchases
    e. An oil price shock that reduces oil prices

167

THINK IT THROUGH

1. Distinguish between demand-pull and cost-push inflation.
2. Discuss the macroeconomic effects of a significant increase in the price of oil.

■ CHAPTER ANSWERS

The Chapter in Brief

1. The general price level 2. Inversely 3. Downward sloping 4. Shift the aggregate demand curve
5. Increase 6. Decrease 7. Reduces 8. Reduces 9. Left 10. Rightward 11. Positive 12. Rising
13. Rising 14. Rise 15. Upward 16. More 17. More 18. Even though there may be 19. Increase
20. Rise 21. Cut 22. Recessionary 23. Demand-pull 24. Inflationary 25. Rise 26. Increases
27. Leftward 28. Fall 29. Cost-push

Key Terms Review

1. Demand-pull inflation 2. Change in aggregate demand 3. Inflationary GDP gap 4. Recessionary
GDP gap 5. Change in aggregate supply 6. Macroeconomic equilibrium 7. Cost-push inflation
8. Aggregate quantity supplied 9. Aggregate supply curve 10. Aggregate demand 11. Aggregate
quantity demanded 12. Aggregate demand 13. Aggregate supply

Concept Review

1.

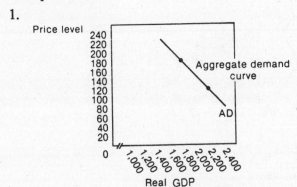

    a. Decrease, increase, decrease
    b. Rise, decrease
    c. Increases, decreases, decrease
    d. $400 billion; negative

2. a. Increase in real interest rates, left
    b. Increase in the quantity of money in circulation, right
    c. Increase in the international value of the dollar, left
    d. Increase in wealth, right
    e. Increase in tax rates, left
    f. Increase in government purchases or transfers, right
    g. Improved expectations of the future, right
    h. Increase in income in foreign countries, right

3. a. 1 b. 3 c. 2 d. 1 e. 3

4. a. Exceeds, inflationary

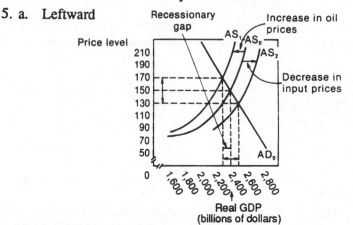

b. Falls below, recessionary

5. a. Leftward

b. Falls below, $100 billion, recessionary; rises, 170
c. Increases, decreases

Mastery Test

1. b 2. c 3. d 4. b 5. c 6. d 7. a 8. e 9. c 10. d 11. d 12. d 13. d 14. d 15. a 16. c 17. d 18. a 19. b

Think it Through

1. Demand-pull inflation results from continual increases in aggregate demand when the economy is close to or beyond potential GDP. The price level rises more rapidly when the economy is overheated along the very steep portion of the aggregate supply curve beyond potential real GDP. In contrast to demand-pull inflation where high inflation is associated with low unemployment, cost-push inflation results in the simultaneous occurrence of inflation and rates of unemployment above the natural rate of unemployment. Cost-push inflation results from continual decreases in aggregate supply caused by increases in input prices.

2. An increase in oil prices shifts the aggregate supply curve leftward. The aggregate supply curve shifts leftward (or upward) because businesses require higher prices to cover rising oil prices in order to be induced to continue producing at their current levels of output. If prices do not rise sufficiently to fully cover the increase in oil prices, firms will cut back production. As the aggregate supply curve shifts leftward, real GDP falls, unemployment rises, and the price level increases.

10 AGGREGATE DEMAND—AGGREGATE SUPPLY ANALYSIS OF ECONOMIC FLUCTUATIONS AND GROWTH

■ CHAPTER CONCEPTS

After studying your text, attending class, and completing this chapter, you should be able to:

1. Understand the classical model of macroeconomic equilibrium and explain why the self-correction mechanism implied by the model does not always work quickly and reliably.

2. Discuss the Keynesian model of macroeconomic equilibrium and explain why Keynes thought that the economy could stagnate in equilibrium at a level of real GDP well below potential real GDP.

3. Discuss the process of self-correction in an overheated economy and explain how such a process results in a wage-price spiral and a period of stagflation.

4. Explain how supply-side shocks affect the economy and understand the consequences of a supply-side induced recession.

5. Use aggregate demand-aggregate supply analysis to explain how changes in the international value of the dollar affect macroeconomic equilibrium.

6. Discuss the process of economic growth using aggregate demand-aggregate supply analysis.

■ THE CHAPTER IN BRIEF

Fill in the blanks to summarize chapter content.

The (1)_____ (Keynesian, classical) model of macroeconomic equilibrium assumes that any departure of real GDP from its full-employment level will cause wages and prices to adjust in such a way as to quickly restore full employment. If the economy is initially at potential real GDP and aggregate demand increases, the price level will rise, inducing firms to increase production. But in time, input prices (2)_____ (fall, rise), shifting the aggregate supply curve leftward, and real output falls back to its potential level. In the long run, real GDP is fixed at (3)_____ (an inflationary level, its potential level) regardless of the price level. The classical long-run aggregate supply curve is therefore (4)_____ (vertical, upward sloping) at the potential level of real GDP.

(5)_____ (Keynesian, Classical) macroeconomic analysis criticizes the (6)_____ (Keynesian, classical) model's assumption of flexible wages and prices. If wages and prices are rigid in the downward direction, a decline in aggregate demand will not result in sufficient wage and price level changes to restore full employment. As a result, Keynes argued that (7)_____ (government policies, the economy's self-adjustment mechanism) could be used to increase aggregate demand to move the economy toward its potential level of real GDP.

If a nation's aggregate supply curve is upward sloping, increases in aggregate demand increase both real GDP and the price level. The rate of increase in the price level is likely to (8)_____ (increase, remain the same) as the economy approaches potential real GDP. If increases in aggregate demand cause an inflationary GDP gap, rising prices eventually will induce labor and other input suppliers to demand higher wages and resource prices to compensate for the loss in

171

purchasing power due to the price level increase. This shifts the aggregate supply curve (9)_____ (rightward, leftward), thus returning the economy to (10)_____ (its potential, a recessionary) level of real GDP. But this results in still higher prices. A wage-price spiral will occur if further increases in aggregate demand take place.

(11)_____ (Expansion, Stagflation) results when the aggregate supply curve shifts to the left. Unemployment is rising while the price level is rising. If workers begin to anticipate continued increases in inflation, they ask for even higher wages, shifting the aggregate supply curve (12)_____ (rightward, leftward) by an even larger amount. Prices can be rising even when unemployment falls below the natural rate of unemployment. Stagflation can also result from (13)_____ (adverse, favorable) supply-side shocks such as sharp increases in the cost of resources that shift the aggregate supply curve leftward.

Increases in the international value of the dollar causes U.S. exports to (14)_____ (rise, fall) and U.S. imports from to rise. U.S. net exports (15)_____ (fall, rise), causing the aggregate demand curve to shift (16)_____ (rightward, leftward). But an appreciation of the dollar also reduces the dollar prices of imported raw materials and other inputs, which shifts the aggregate supply curve (17)_____ (rightward, leftward). It is expected that the change in aggregate demand is larger than the change in aggregate supply, causing equilibrium real GDP and the price level to (18)_____ (rise, fall).

Conversely, a decrease in the international value of the dollar makes U.S. goods (19)_____ (more, less) price competitive abroad while increasing the relative prices of imports to the United States. U.S. exports (20)_____ (fall, rise) and imports (21)_____ (fall, rise), causing net exports to rise. An increase in net exports shifts the aggregate demand curve (22)_____ (rightward, leftward). The aggregate supply curve shifts leftward because the prices of imported inputs (23)_____ (decrease, increase). On net, the increase in aggregate demand will outweigh the decrease in aggregate supply, causing equilibrium real GDP and the price level to (24)_____ (fall, rise).

In the long run, as wages and other input prices adjust to the prevailing rate of inflation and assuming that there are no other forces influencing the level of real GDP, the economy will eventually return to its potential level of real GDP at the natural rate of unemployment. The (25)_____ (long-run aggregate supply, short-run aggregate demand) curve is vertical at the potential level of real GDP. In the long run, this curve will shift to the right due to (26)_____ (decreases, increases) in the quantity of resources available for use by the economy, (27)_____ (decreases, increases) in resource productivity, improvements in technology, and improvements in the efficiency with which inputs are used.

Over time, even though aggregate demand is subject to cyclical variation, it exhibits a long-term upward trend. But in the long run, aggregate supply increases as well. The increase in a nation's aggregate supply satisfies its rising aggregate demand, but also (28)_____ (increases, moderates) the rate at which prices rise.

172

■ KEY TERMS REVIEW

Write the key term from the list below next to its definition.

Key Terms

Wage-price spiral
Stagflation
Supply-side shock
Keynesian model of
  macroeconomic equilibrium

Long-run aggregate supply curve (LRAS)
Classical model of macroeconomic
  equilibrium

Definitions

1. _____: a theory implying that excessive unemployment and unused productive capacity would set up forces that would eventually result in increases in real GDP and eliminate the unemployment of workers.

2. _____: a sudden and unexpected shift of the aggregate supply curve.

3. _____: a situation that exists when higher product prices result in higher wages, which in turn increase prices still further through a decrease in aggregate supply.

4. _____: term coined to describe an economy in which real GDP stagnates at a given level or actually declines from one period to the next while inflation ensues at relatively high rates.

5. _____: a curve showing the relationship between the aggregate quantity supplied and the price level that would be observed if nominal wages and other money prices were flexible enough to allow the classical self-correction mechanism to work.

6. _____: a model assuming that because of rigid nominal wages the economy can be in equilibrium at less that full employment.

Concepts 1 and 2:   **Classical and Keynesian models and macroeconomic equilibrium**

1. The economy shown in the figure below is currently operating at its potential level of real GDP.

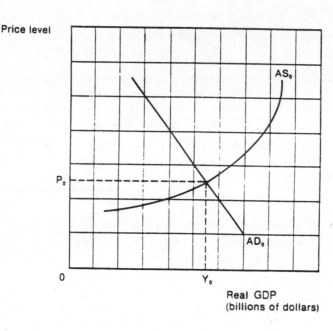

a. Show the effect of an increase in aggregate demand. Label the new aggregate demand curve AD1.

b. According to classical macroeconomics, in the short run real GDP will_____ and the price level will _____. In the long run wages and prices will _____, ensuring that real GDP _____ potential real GDP. Graphically, in the long run the short-run aggregate supply curve will shift _____.

c. Show on the figure above the classical long-run aggregate supply curve and label it LRAS.

d. Keynes argued that in a recessionary GDP gap, wages and prices _____ and automatic forces in the economy _____ (will, will not) quickly restore full employment. Keynes argued that full employment could be restored by _____ aggregate demand with _____ in government spending.

Concept 3: *Wage-price spiral and the long-run aggregate supply curve*

2. Suppose the economy shown in the figure below is currently in equilibrium at its potential
level of real GDP.

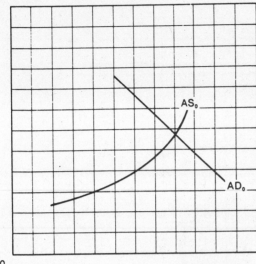

Price level

Real GDP
(billions of dollars)

a. On the figure above, show a new aggregate demand curve reflecting an increase in demand
and label it AD1. The price level _____ while real GDP _____. Identify the
new price level and level of real GDP on the figure above.

b. Eventually, workers and other input suppliers will react to the loss of purchasing power
resulting from the increase in the price level by _____. Show the impact
on the aggregate supply curve assuming that input suppliers have completely adjusted to
the new price level and label the curve AS1. The price level _____ while the level
of real GDP _____. Identify graphically the new equilibrium price and real GDP
levels.

c. Suppose that aggregate demand increases again, shifting the AD curve from AD1 to AD2.
Show graphically and identify the new price level and level of real GDP. Workers will
again eventually respond by _____, which causes the AS curve to shift
_____. Show the new AS curve and label it AS2.

d. The process described above produces a _____-_____ spiral.

e. In the long run, when input suppliers have completely adjusted to the price level, the equilibrium level of real GDP equals _____. Find the long-run aggregate supply
curve in the figure above and label it AS3. The long-run aggregate supply curve is (upward sloping, vertical).

Concepts 3 and 4:   *Stagflation, price expectations, and supply-side shocks*

3. The figure below shows an economy at its potential level of real GDP. Assume that this economy has been experiencing a wage-price spiral such that input suppliers begin to anticipate a higher price level.

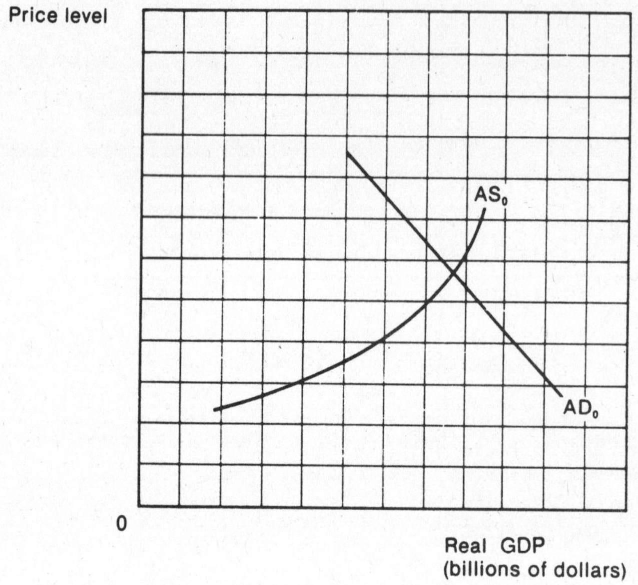

Price level

AS_0

AD_0

0

Real GDP
(billions of dollars)

a.   Show on the figure above, what happens to the aggregate supply curve when workers begin to anticipate higher prices. Label the new AS curve AS1. Real GDP _____, and the price level _____.

b.   Given the aggregate demand curve and the new AS curve, AS1, assume that an oil price shock occurs. Show the effect on the AS curve. Label the new AS curve AS2. The oil price shock is known as a _____. Equilibrium real GDP _____ while the price level _____.

c.   Rising price-level expectations and adverse supply-side shocks produce the dual incidence of _____ and _____, which is otherwise known as _____.

Concept 5: *International value of the dollar and macroeconomic equilibrium*

4. The figure below represents an economy.

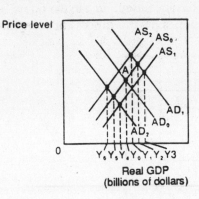

a. A depreciation of the U.S. dollar relative to the Canadian dollar makes U.S. goods _____ price competitive in Canada and Canadian goods _____ price competitive in the United States. U.S. exports _____, imports _____, and net exports _____.

b. Given the initial aggregate demand and supply curves, ADo and ASo, the change in net exports indicated above shifts the AD curve to _____ (AD1, AD2).

c. The price of imported inputs in U.S. dollars _____, causing the AS curve to shift to _____ (AS1, AS2).

d. Equilibrium real GDP _____ from Yo to _____.

5. Refer to the figure above in answering this question.

a. An appreciation of the U.S. dollar relative to the Canadian dollar makes U.S. goods _____ price competitive in Canada and Canadian goods _____ price competitive in the United States. U.S. exports _____, imports _____, and net exports _____.

b. Given the initial aggregate demand and supply curves, ADo and ASo, the change in net exports indicated in part a above shifts the AD curve to _____ (AD1, AD2).

c. The prices of imported inputs in U.S. dollars _____, causing the AS curve to shift to _____ (AS1, AS2).

d. Equilibrium real GDP _____ from Yo to _____.

Concept 6: *Aggregate supply and demand analysis and the process of economic growth*

6. In the United States, aggregate demand and aggregate supply have both exhibited a long-term increase. Because of downward wage-price rigidity or the sluggishness with which prices and wages fall, the price level over the long run has increased. In a in the figure below, show this process of economic growth. In b in the figure, show this process of economic growth.

a. Price level

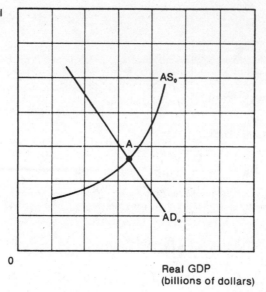

Real GDP
(billions of dollars)

b. Government goods per year

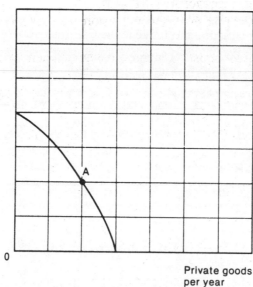

Private goods
per year

178

■ MASTERY TEST

Select the best answer.

1. Which of the following assumptions is crucial to the classical macroeconomic model's assertion that the economy has built-in forces that automatically eliminate unemployment and quickly move the economy to its potential level of real GDP?
   a. Profit motive
   b. Rigid wages and prices
   c. Flexible wages and prices
   d. Natural rate of unemployment

2. The classicists argued that an increase in aggregate demand would _____ in the short run, but in the long run real GDP would _____.
   a. decrease real GDP, increase
   b. increase real GDP, return to its potential level
   c. increase real GDP, rise further, causing inflation
   d. decrease aggregate supply, rise

3. The classical long-run aggregate supply curve is:
   a. vertical at a level of output below potential real GDP.
   b. upward sloping.
   c. upward sloping at the level of potential real GDP.
   d. vertical at the level of potential real GDP.

4. John Maynard Keynes argued that:
   a. downward nominal-wage rigidity prevented the classical self-correction mechanism from working to eliminate recessionary GDP gaps.
   b. the automatic forces of the market would restore the economy to full employment very quickly.
   c. the classical macroeconomists' argument that government spending should be used in recessions would not eliminate a recessionary GDP gap.
   d. fluctuations in aggregate demand were the primary cause of recessions.
   e. a and d.

5. For an economy operating on the upward sloping portion of the aggregate supply curve, an increase in aggregate demand will _____ the price level and _____ real GDP.
   a. increase, decrease
   b. increase, increase
   c. decrease, increase
   d. decrease, decrease

6. If an economy is currently operating at its potential level of real GDP, an increase in aggregate demand will:
   a. increase the price level and produce an inflationary gap.
   b. decrease the price level and produce a recessionary gap.
   c. cause stagflation.
   d. produce long-run economic growth.

179

7. When an economy is currently at its potential level of real GDP and experiences an increase in aggregate demand, input suppliers will eventually _____, causing the aggregate supply curve to shift _____.
   a. withdraw from resource markets, leftward
   b. press for higher input prices, rightward
   c. press for higher input prices, leftward
   d. increase the productivity of their resources, rightward

8. The process of increases in aggregate demand followed by input price pressures followed by increases in aggregate demand is called:
   a. a recession.
   b. stagflation.
   c. the business cycle.
   d. the real output cycle.
   e. a wage-price spiral.

9. Stagflation results from which of the following?
   a. Increases in aggregate demand
   b. Increases in aggregate supply
   c. Increases in input price expectations
   d. Adverse supply-side shocks
   e. c and d

10. An oil price shock that reduces oil prices shifts the _____ curve rightward, causing real GDP to _____ and the price level to_____.
    a. aggregate demand, fall, rise
    b. aggregate supply, fall, rise
    c. aggregate supply, rise, rise
    d. aggregate supply, rise, fall
    e. aggregate demand, rise, fall

11. An adverse supply-side shock shifts the aggregate supply curve _____ causing real GDP to _____ and the price level to _____.
    a. leftward, fall, rise
    b. rightward, fall, rise
    c. leftward, rise, fall
    d. rightward, rise, fall
    e. leftward, fall, fall

12. Which of the following increases potential real GDP over the long run?
    a. An increase in demand
    b. Inflation
    c. Government spending
    d. Consumption
    e. None of the above

13. Which of the following shift the long-run aggregate supply curve rightward?
    a. Increases in the quantity of resources available to a nation
    b. Increases in the productivity of productive resources
    c. Improvements in technology
    d. Improvements in the efficiency with which resources are used
    e. All of the above

14. The long-run aggregate supply curve is:
    a. upward sloping.
    b. horizontal.
    c. downward sloping.
    d. vertical.

15. An increase in the international value of the dollar causes aggregate demand to _____ and aggregate supply to _____, resulting in a/an _____ in real GDP.
    a. decrease, decrease, decrease
    b. increase, increase, increase
    c. increase, decrease, decrease
    d. increase, increase, decrease
    e. decrease, increase, decrease

16. A decrease in the international value of the dollar causes aggregate demand to _____ and aggregate supply to _____, resulting in a/an _____ in real GDP.
    a. decrease, decrease, decrease
    b. increase, increase, increase
    c. increase, decrease, increase
    d. increase, increase, decrease
    e. decrease, increase, decrease

17. In a growing economy, both _____ and _____ increase, but because prices do not fall as quickly or easily as they rise, the general price level over the long run _____.
    a. aggregate demand, aggregate supply, falls
    b. aggregate supply, unemployment, falls
    c. inflation, unemployment, rises
    d. aggregate demand, aggregate supply, rises

18. Supply-side shifts in the aggregate supply curve resulting from economic growth serve to:
    a. increase inflation.
    b. reduce the price level over time.
    c. moderate inflation resulting from shifts in the aggregate demand curve.
    d. increase real GDP beyond the level possible by shifts in the aggregate demand curve alone.
    e. c and d.

19. Which of the following best describes the classical long-run adjustment process? (Assume that the economy is initially at its potential level of real GDP)

   a. An increase in aggregate demand causes the price level to rise and level of unemployment to rise above the natural rate of unemployment. In time, the aggregate supply curve will shift downward as input suppliers press for higher input prices. Eventually, the price level will return to its initial level.

   b. An increase in aggregate demand will cause both the price level and real GDP to rise. In time, the aggregate supply curve will shift upward as input suppliers press for higher input prices. Eventually, real GDP will return to its potential level.

   c. A change in aggregate demand will always cause an opposite change in aggregate supply, ensuring that in the short run and long run, real GDP remains unchanged at its potential level of real GDP.

   d. As prices rise, workers win wage concessions from employers, causing the aggregate demand and aggregate supply curves to shift upward. In the long run, real GDP will be at a level consistent with the natural rate of unemployment.

20. Assume that the economy is at its potential level of real GDP. An increase in aggregate demand followed by the classical adjustment process and then again by another increase in aggregate demand causes:

   a. stagflation.
   b. deflation.
   c. a wage-price spiral.
   d. unemployment.

21. Assume that the economy is at its potential level of real GDP. Which one of the following will likely occur if a major oil find reduces the world price of oil by 50%?

   a. Stagflation
   b. Deflation
   c. A wage-price spiral
   d. Unemployment

22. An increase in the international value of the dollar:

   a. shifts the aggregate demand curve leftward and the aggregate supply curve downward, causing real GDP and the price level to fall.

   b. shifts the aggregate supply and demand curves leftward, causing real GDP to fall.

   c. shifts the aggregate demand curve rightward and the aggregate supply curve upward, causing real GDP and the price level to rise.

   d. shifts the aggregate demand curve rightward and the aggregate supply curve upward, causing the price level to rise, but reducing real GDP.

23. A decrease in the international value of the dollar:

   a. shifts the aggregate demand curve leftward and the aggregate supply curve downward, causing real GDP and the price level to fall.

   b. shifts the aggregate supply and demand curves leftward, causing real GDP to fall.

   c. shifts the aggregate demand curve rightward and the aggregate supply curve upward, causing real GDP and the price level to rise.

   d. shifts the aggregate demand curve rightward and the aggregate supply curve upward, causing the price level to rise, but reducing real GDP.

■ THINK IT THROUGH

1. Why did Keynes believe that government policies designed to change aggregate demand should be used in recessions?

2. Assume that an adverse-side supply shock occurs. Discuss the effects of the supply-side shock. Suppose that workers increase their expectations of inflation at the same time that the supply-side shock is occurring. Discuss the likely effects.

3. Why is the long-run aggregate supply curve independent of shifts in the aggregate demand curve?

4. Assume that the United States imports copper, which is used widely in business and industry. Discuss the effects on the U.S. economy of a major reduction in the world price of copper.

5. If the international value of the dollar decreases, what are the likely economic consequences?

■ ANALYZING THE NEWS

Using the skills derived from studying this chapter, analyze the economic facts that make up the following article and answer the question below.

Are wages flexible or "sticky"?

Wage Flexibility

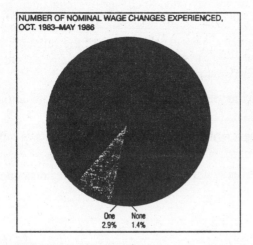

NUMBER OF NOMINAL WAGE CHANGES EXPERIENCED, OCT. 1983–MAY 1986

One 2.9%   None 1.4%

Upward and Downward Nominal Wage Changes, Oct. 1983–May 1986

Number of negative changes	Percent of workers experiencing negative change[a]	Number of positive changes	Percent of workers experiencing positive change[a]
0	22.0	0	2.1
1	27.9	1	5.9
2	26.2	2	19.9
3	17.4	3	30.4
4	5.6	4	27.5
5	0.8	5	11.6
6	0.0	6	2.4

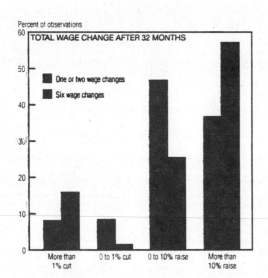

Percent of observations

TOTAL WAGE CHANGE AFTER 32 MONTHS

- One or two wage changes
- Six wage changes

More than 1% cut   0 to 1% cut   0 to 10% raise   More than 10% raise

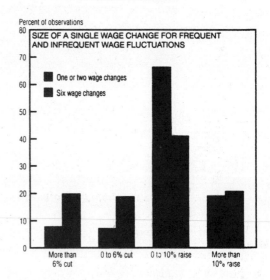

Percent of observations

SIZE OF A SINGLE WAGE CHANGE FOR FREQUENT AND INFREQUENT WAGE FLUCTUATIONS

- One or two wage changes
- Six wage changes

More than 6% cut   0 to 6% cut   0 to 10% raise   More than 10% raise

a. Numbers may not sum to 100 due to rounding.
SOURCE: Federal Reserve Bank of Cleveland calculations based on data from the Census Bureau's Survey of Income and Program Participation.

Economists are interested in whether wages are flexible or "sticky," because this question is central to the study of both business cycles and wage differences across regions. To shed light on this issue, the Census Bureau's Survey of Program Participation sampled 2,700 continuously employed hourly workers at four-month intervals between October 1983 and May 1986. Each person could have had as many as seven wage changes from the preceding interview.

The results showed that more than half of the sample experienced five or more changes during this two-and-a-half-year period. While most were positive nominal changes (which is consistent with the strong U.S. economic expansion during this time), more than three-quarters of the sample had at least one negative wage change as well. This seems to contradict concern about sticky downward wages.

Perhaps surprisingly, people whose wages changed less frequently were more likely to have smaller wage changes than those whose wages changed often. This was true not only for a single wage change, but also for the sum of all wage changes over the entire sample period. If a worker experienced a total of six wage changes, he was more than twice as likely to have a total wage increase exceeding 10% — about the average increase during the period—than to have a smaller pay hike. Likewise, a disproportionate share of workers who experienced fewer than three wage changes had increases below 10%.

Research Department of the Federal Reserve Bank of Cleveland. Economic Trends, Federal Reserve Bank of Cleveland, August, 1995, p.13.

CHAPTER ANSWERS

The Chapter in Brief

1. Classical 2. Rise 3. Its potential level 4. Vertical 5. . Classical 7. Government policies 8. Increase
9. Leftward 10. Its potential 11. Stagflation 12. Leftward 13. Adverse 14. Fall
15. Fall 16. Leftward 17. Rightward 18. Fall 19. More 20. Rise 21. Fall 22. Rightward 23. Increase
24. Rise 25. Long-run aggregate supply 26. Increases 27. Increases 28. Moderates

Key Terms Review

1. Classical model of macroeconomic equilibrium 2. Supply-side shock 3. Wage-price spiral
4. Stagflation 5. Long-run aggregate supply curve 6. Keynesian model of macroeconomic equilibrium

Concept Review

1. a.

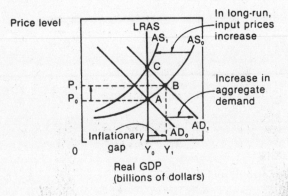

   b. Increase, rise; rise, equals; leftward
   c. On figure above
   d. Are rigid downward, will not; increasing, increases

2. a.

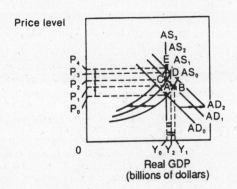

185

Increases, increases

b. Pressing for higher wages and other input prices; increases, falls back to its potential level of real GDP

c. Pressing for higher wages; leftward

d. Wage, price

e. The potential level of real GDP; vertical

3. a.

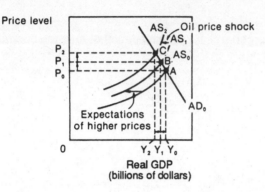

Decreases, increases

b. Supply-side shock; falls, increases

c. Rising unemployment and rising inflation; stagflation

4. a. More, less; rise, fall, increase

b. AD1

c. Rises, AS2

d. Increases, Y1

5. a. Less, more; fall, rise, decrease

b. AD2

c. Falls, AS1

d. Decreases, Y4

6.

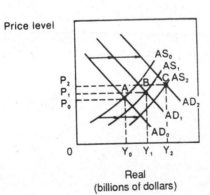

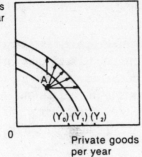

Government goods per year

A

(Y_0) (Y_1) (Y_2)

0

Private goods per year

Mastery Test

1. c 2. b 3. d 4. e 5. b 6. a 7. c 8. e 9. e 10. d 11. a 12. e 13. e 14. d 15. e 16. c 17. d 18. e 19. b 20. c 21. b 22. a 23. c

Think it Through

1. Keynes believed that in recessions wages and prices would not fall quickly enough to restore real GDP to its potential level without significant social costs of prolonged unemployment. Wages and prices are rigid in the downward direction in part because of institutional factors such as multi-year labor contracts. Keynes believed that recessions were due to inadequate levels of aggregate demand. Because the economy's self-adjustment mechanism would not eliminate a recessionary GDP gap in the short run, Keynes argued that government policies could be used to increase aggregate demand to a level that would restore higher levels of employment.

2. An adverse supply-side shock shifts the aggregate supply curve to the left. As aggregate supply falls relative to aggregate demand, real GDP falls and the price level rises. The dual incidence of rising inflation and rising unemployment is called stagflation. If at the same time workers have expectations of higher future price levels, the aggregate supply curve will shift even further leftward as workers press for higher wages to offset the expected higher prices. The equilibrium price level will increase even more, and the extent of unemployment will be greater. Therefore adverse supply-side shocks combined with rising price level expectations may produce a serious stagflation.

3. Shifts in aggregate demand cause short-run changes in real GDP, but if given enough time for product and resource prices to adjust completely, the economy will return to its potential level of real GDP. For instance, if an increase in aggregate demand causes inflation, workers and other resource suppliers will in time push for higher wages and resource prices. Businesses either will require higher product prices to cover the increases in resource prices or they will reduce output at given prices. Either way, the aggregate supply curve shifts leftward and real GDP returns to its potential level in the long run. The long-run aggregate supply curve is vertical at the potential level of real GDP. Only supply-side influences such as the quantity and productivity of resources can shift the long-run aggregate supply curve rightward.

4. A major reduction in the world price of copper is an example of a favorable supply-side shock. Businesses increase output because the profitability of producing goods has increased at given price levels. The aggregate supply curve shifts rightward, putting downward pressure on the

187

price level and increasing real GDP. In this case, a falling price level and unemployment rate occur simultaneously.

5. If the international value of the dollar decreases, U.S. goods become less costly in foreign currencies, increasing their price competitiveness in foreign markets. Likewise, foreign goods become more costly in dollars, decreasing their price competitiveness in the United States. U.S. imports of foreign goods decrease, and U.S. exports to foreign nations increase. The increase in net exports causes the aggregate demand curve to shift rightward. But foreign inputs now cost more in dollars. As production costs rise, the aggregate supply curve shifts leftward. On net, however, real GDP increases.

Analyzing the News

The Census Bureau's Survey of Program Participation, covering 2,700 workers over a period from October 1983 to May 1986, revealed that wages are quite flexible. More than half of the workers experienced more than five wage changes, both positive and negative changes. Three quarters of the surveyed workers experienced at least one negative wage change. Wages do not seem to be "sticky" downward.

11 KEYNESIAN ANALYSIS OF AGGREGATE PURCHASES

■ CHAPTER CONCEPTS

After studying your text, attending class, and completing this chapter, you should be able to:

1. Discuss the Keynesian consumption function and the distinction between induced consumption and autonomous consumption.

2. Know how to measure the marginal propensity to consume and the marginal propensity to save.

3. Explain why investment purchases are extremely unstable from year to year.

4. Understand why government purchases in a given year are independent of disposable income, discuss how imports are likely to vary with disposable income, and draw a nation's net export function graph.

5. Draw an aggregate purchases line and explain how it shows the way purchases of final products that comprise GDP will vary with disposable income in a given year.

■ THE CHAPTER IN BRIEF

Fill in the blanks to summarize chapter content.

Personal consumption purchases are the major component of aggregate demand, accounting for (1)_____ (one half, two thirds) of GDP. Consumption is primarily determined by the (2)_____ (level of disposable income, real interest rate). Households on average use about 95% of their disposable income for consumption purchases. Disposable income that is not consumed is saved. That percentage of consumption due to disposable income is referred to as (3)_____ (induced, autonomous) consumption. The percentage of consumption due to influences on other than disposable income is referred to as (4)_____ (induced, autonomous) consumption. Changes in autonomous consumption result from changes in aggregate household wealth, aggregate household debt, and household expectations about future income and wealth.

The consumption function is a line or curve showing an/a (5)_____ (independent, positive) relationship between consumption and disposable income. The saving function is also a line or curve showing an/a (6)_____ (independent, positive) relationship between disposable income and saving. Given that disposable income must be either consumed or saved, saving can be derived by subtracting consumption from disposable income and the saving function can be derived by subtracting the consumption function from the 45-degree line. The slope of the consumption function is called the (7)_____ (marginal propensity to consume, rate of change in consumption). For a linear curve (straight line), it is found by a change in consumption (8)_____ (divided, multiplied) by a change in disposable income. The marginal propensity to save is the slope of the saving function and is defined as a change in (9)_____ (disposable income, saving) divided by a change in (10)_____ (disposable income, saving). Because disposable income must be consumed or saved, the marginal propensities to consume and save must sum to (11)_____ (zero, one).

Autonomous changes in consumption shift the consumption function, but they also shift the saving function because the saving line is derived from the consumption line. An increase in wealth (12)_____ (increases, decreases) consumption and (13)_____ (increases, decreases) saving at a given level of disposable income. The consumption function shifts (14)_____ (downward, upward) by the same amount that the saving function shifts (15)_____ (downward, upward). An increase in household debt reduces consumption (increases saving) at a given level of disposable income and vice versa. Expectations can also shift the saving and consumption functions. Expectations of a decline in future income will likely cause some households to save more and consume less out of their current income.

Investment spending is a (16)_____ (volatile, stable) component of GDP. It includes expenditures on machines, structures, equipment, and inventories. (17)_____ (Unplanned, Planned) investment purchases are those investment purchases that businesses make on the basis of profit expectations. If businesses overproduce output relative to sales, the unsold output is added to inventories. This is an increase in inventory investment even though it is unplanned. Planned investment demand is determined by the real interest rate, the real marginal return to investment, and other factors that shift the investment demand curve. A profit-maximizing business will invest up to the point at which the expected return for each additional dollar invested (the real marginal return to investment) is (18)_____ (just equal to, greater than) the opportunity cost of using a dollar to make the investment (or the real interest rate). The (19)_____ (aggregate purchases, investment demand) curve shows an inverse relationship between the real interest rate and the level of investment. A decline in the real interest rate relative to the real marginal return to investment will cause businesses to (20)_____ (decrease, increase) investment purchases.

Several factors can change the level of investment at a given real interest rate. These include: (a) expectations about aggregate demand, (b) expectations about the profitability of investments, (c) (21)_____ (disposable income, capacity utilization), (d) technological change, and (e) the tax treatment of investment and income. When plotted against disposable income, the investment function is a horizontal line at the annual level of investment. Any of the influences listed above, including the real interest rate, will shift the investment function either up or down. For example, an increase in the real rate of interest will (22)_____ (reduce, increase) investment purchases at a given level of disposable income and will shift the investment function (23)_____ (upward by the increase, downward by the reduction) in investment spending.

Government spending, like investment, is assumed to be (24)_____ (independent of, dependent on) the current year's level of disposable income. Government purchases of goods and input services constitute (25)_____ (40%, 17.5%) of real GDP. The government purchases function is horizontal and shifts either up or down depending upon the change in government spending. An increase in government spending shifts the curve upward and vice versa. Government can also influence aggregate demand by changing taxes and transfer payments. An increase in taxes or a reduction in transfers (26)_____(increases, reduces) disposable income and consumption and vice versa.

The last component of aggregate demand is net exports. Net exports are defined as the difference between exports and imports. If the difference is positive, international trade results in an/a (27)_____ (increase, decrease) in domestic aggregate demand. If the difference is negative, trade (28)_____ (reduces, increases) aggregate demand. Net exports are determined by the level of disposable income and the prices of imported goods relative to domestic prices. A/An (29)_____ (decrease, increase) in disposable income increases imports and reduces net ex-

190

ports. If the international value of the dollar (30)_____ (increases, decreases) relative to foreign currencies, U.S. exports become less price competitive in foreign markets, reducing net exports. The net export function shows a/an (31)_____ (positive, inverse) relationship between net exports and disposable income.

■ KEY TERMS REVIEW

Write the key term from the list below next to its definition.

Key Terms

Wealth
Aggregate household wealth
Aggregate household debt
Consumption function
Autonomous consumption
Induced consumption
Real marginal return to
   investment

Marginal propensity to
   consume
Marginal propensity to
   save
Planned investment
   purchases
Aggregate purchases

Definitions

1. _____: purchases of new or replacement residential and nonresidential structures, producer durable equipment, and additions to inventories that business firms intentionally make during the year.

2. _____: an estimate of the percentage of each dollar invested that will be returned to a firm as additional revenue per year (adjusted for the effects of changes in the price level).

3. _____: the fraction of each additional dollar of annual disposable income that is saved.

4. _____: the market value of final goods and services that will be purchased at any given level of income.

5. _____: the fraction of each additional dollar of annual disposable income that is allocated to consumer purchases.

6. _____: the portion of annual consumer purchases in a given year that responds to changes in current disposable income.

7. _____: the purchasing power of the sums of money outstanding that households have borrowed and are currently obligated to repay.

8. _____: the portion of annual consumer purchases that is independent of current disposable income.

9. _____: the purchasing power of all assets owned by households.

10. _____: a relationship between aggregate consumer purchases and disposable income in a certain year given all other determinants of consumption.

11. _____: the sum of the current values of all assets a person owns.

■ CONCEPT REVIEW

Concepts 1 and 2:   *Consumption, saving, and the consumption and saving functions*

1. Below are annual data for an economy.

Disposable Income ($ billions)	Consumption ($ billions)	Saving ($ billions)
$ 0	$ 200	$_____
250	350	_____
500	500	_____
750	650	_____
1,000	800	_____
1,250	950	_____
1,500	1,100	_____

   a. Complete the table.

   b. There exists a/an _____ relationship between disposable income and consumption and a/an _____ relationship between disposable income and saving.

   c. Marginal propensity to consume equals _____; marginal propensity to save equals _____. The sum of the marginal propensities to consume and save equal _____.

   d. Plot the consumption line in a in the figure below and plot the saving line in b. At what level of disposable income is saving zero? $_____

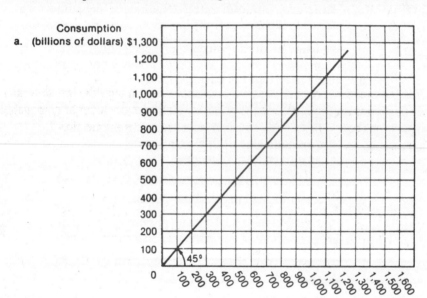

a. Consumption (billions of dollars)

192

b. Saving (billions of dollars)

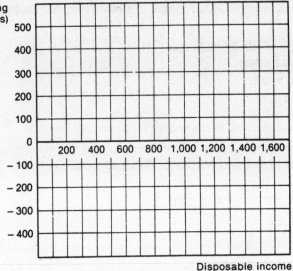

Disposable income
(billions of dollars)

2. List three factors that will shift the consumption and saving lines.

a. _____

b. _____

c. _____

3. The stock market has produced impressive gains in household wealth over the last several months. Because of this, consumption increased by $200 billion at every level of disposable income. Answer the questions below based upon the data reproduced from question 1.

Disposable Income	Consumption		Saving	
	Old	New (1)	Old (2)	New (3)
$ 0	$ 200	$_____	$_____	$_____
250	350	_____	_____	_____
500	500	_____	_____	_____
750	650	_____	_____	_____
1,000	800	_____	_____	_____
1,250	950	_____	_____	_____
1,500	1,100	_____	_____	_____

a. Reproduce the saving data that you derived for question 1 in column 2 above.
b. Complete the new consumption and saving schedule assuming a $200 billion increase in consumption at every level of disposable income.
c. Plot the new consumption and saving lines in the figure above.
d. The consumption line has shifted _____ by $_____, and the saving line has shifted _____ by $_____.
e. The level of disposable income at which saving is zero is $_____ assuming the new level of consumption.

193

4. Indicate for each of the following whether the consumption line and saving line will shift and in which direction.
   a. Expectations of higher future income
   b. Increase in disposable income
   c. Decline in household wealth
   d. Increase in household debt

Concept 3: *Investment demand and the investment purchases line*

5. The figure below represents the relationship between the real marginal return on investment and the aggregate level of investment purchases for an economy.

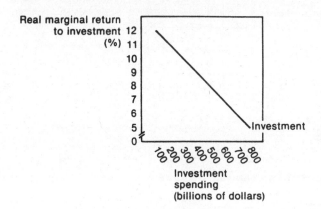

   a. Profit-maximizing firms will engage in investment spending up to the point at which the _____ is just equal to the _____.
   b. At a real interest rate of 10%, the level of investment purchases equals $_____. If the rate of interest falls to 8%, the level of investment _____ to $_____.

c. On the figure below, plot the economy's investment purchases line for a 10% real rate of interest.

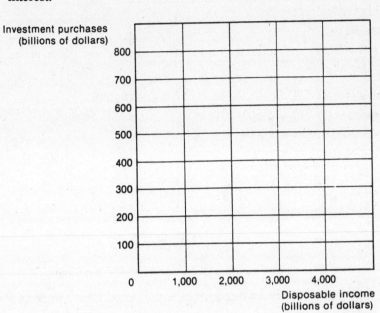

Investment purchases
(billions of dollars)

Disposable income
(billions of dollars)

d. On the figure above, plot the investment purchases line for an 8% rate of interest.
e. An increase in the real interest rate will shift the investment line _____, and a decrease in the real interest rate will shift the investment line _____.

6. List five factors other than the real interest rate that will shift the investment purchases line and discuss for two of the five factors how the investment purchases line is affected.

a. _____
b. _____
c. _____
d. _____
e. _____

Concept 4: *Government purchases and net exports*

7. The level of government spending is assumed to be independent of the level of disposable income. Plot the government purchases line in the figure below assuming annual government purchases equal $150 billion. An increase in government purchases will shift the government purchases line _____ and vice versa. Also show in the figure the effect of a $50 billion increase in government purchases.

195

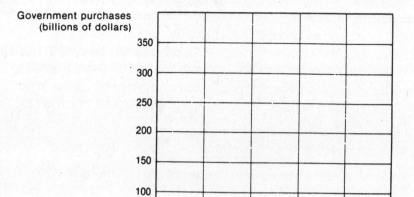

Government purchases
(billions of dollars)

Disposable income
(billions of dollars)

8. The data below show the relationship among disposable income, exports, and imports for an economy.

Disposable Inc. ($ billions)	Imports	Exports ($ billions)	Net Exports
$ 0	$ 0	$ 150	$_____
400	50	150	_____
800	100	150	_____
1,200	150	150	_____
1,600	200	150	_____
2,000	250	150	_____
2,400	300	150	_____

a. Complete the table.

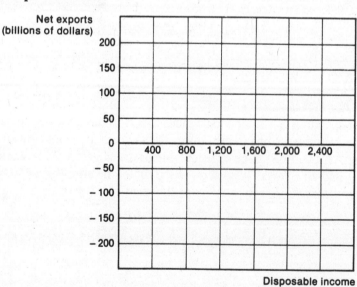

Net exports
(billions of dollars)

Disposable income
(billions of dollars)

b. Plot the net exports line in the figure above.
c. Net exports are _____ related to disposable income.
d. If the international value of the dollar falls relative to the foreign currencies of U.S. trading partners, assume that U.S. export goods become more price competitive abroad, resulting in an increase in exports of $50 billion at every level of disposable income. Show in the figure the effect on the net exports line. The level of disposable income at which net exports equal zero _____ to $_____.

Concept 5: *Aggregate purchases line*

9. Derive the aggregate purchases schedule and aggregate purchases line from the table below. (All data are in billions of dollars.)

Disposable Income	C	Ip	G	NE	Aggregate Purchases
$ 0	$200	$100	$150	$100	$_____
400	500	100	150	75	_____
800	800	100	150	50	_____
1,200	1,100	100	150	25	_____
1,600	1,400	100	150	0	_____
2,000	1,700	100	150	-25	_____
2,400	2,000	100	150	-50	_____

a. Complete the table.
b. Plot the aggregate purchases line in the figure below.

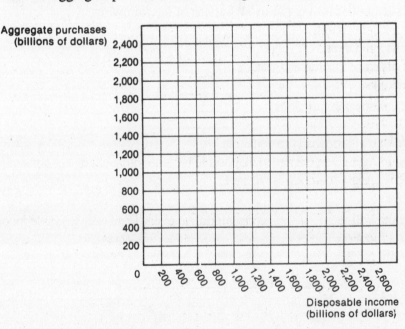

197

■ MASTERY TEST

Select the best answer.

1. Consumption represents what proportion of gross national product?
   a. One fourth
   b. One half
   c. Two fifths
   d. Two thirds
   e. Three fourths

2. From 1960 to 1995, Americans have used what percentage on average of their disposable income for household consumption?
   a. 60%
   b. 70%
   c. 80%
   d. 95%

3. Induced consumption is caused by which of the following?
   a. Aggregate household wealth
   b. Aggregate household debt
   c. Expectations of future income and wealth
   d. Disposable income
   e. Interest rate

4. Autonomous consumption is influenced by all but one of the following.
   a. Aggregate household wealth
   b. Aggregate household debt
   c. Expectations of future income and wealth
   d. Disposable income

5. The slope of the consumption function:
   a. is positive.
   b. is called the marginal propensity to consume.
   c. is found by dividing a given change in disposable income into a change in consumption.
   d. is one minus the marginal propensity to save.
   e. All of the above.

6. An increase in wealth will _____ consumption at every level of disposable income and will shift the saving function _____.
   a. decrease, upward
   b. decrease, downward
   c. increase, upward
   d. increase, downward

7. The level of disposable income where the consumption function intersects the 45-degree line:
   a. is the point of maximum returns to investment.
   b. is the point of maximum saving.
   c. is the point at which saving is zero.
   d. None of the above.

8. Expectations of future higher income and wealth will cause the consumption function to shift _____ and the saving function to shift _____.
   a. upward, upward
   b. downward, downward
   c. upward, downward
   d. downward, upward

9. Which of the following components of aggregate demand is the most unstable?
   a. Consumption
   b. Investment
   c. Government purchases
   d. Net exports

10. Which of the following is true of planned investment expenditures?
   a. Planned investment is inversely related to the real interest rate.
   b. Planned investment is positively related to the real interest rate.
   c. Planned investment includes inventory investment resulting from unexpectedly low sales.
   d. Profit-maximizing firms plan to invest on the basis of a comparison between the nominal rate of interest and the absolute cost of the investment project.
   e. None of the above.

11. If the real rate of interest increases relative to the real marginal return to investment:
   a. planned investment will decrease.
   b. there is an upward movement along a fixed investment demand curve.
   c. the investment line or function relating investment purchases to disposable income will shift downward.
   d. All of the above.

12. If the rate of capacity utilization falls markedly, investment spending will _____ and the investment purchases function will shift _____.
   a. decrease, downward
   b. increase, upward
   c. decrease, upward
   d. increase, downward

13. Which of the following will not shift the investment demand curve?
   a. Expectations about aggregate demand
   b. Changes in capacity utilization
   c. Changes in the real interest rate
   d. Technological change
   e. Changes in the tax treatment of investment purchases

14. In 1995, government purchases accounted for what percentage of GDP?
   a. 10%
   b. 20%
   c. 30%
   d. 40%
   e. 26%

15. The government purchases function is :
    a. horizontal.
    b. upward sloping.
    c. downward sloping.
    d. vertical.

16. Given the level of exports, as disposable income rises, imports _____ and net exports
    _____.
    a. rise, rise
    b. fall, rise
    c. fall, fall
    d. rise, fall

17. If the international value of the dollar increases relative to foreign currencies, U.S. exports will
    _____, causing both net exports and aggregate purchases to _____.
    a. rise, rise
    b. fall, rise
    c. fall, fall
    d. rise, fall

18. An increase in exports will shift the net exports curve _____ and shift the aggregate pur-
    chases line _____.
    a. upward, downward
    b. downward, upward
    c. upward, upward
    d. downward, downward

19. Which of the following defines aggregate purchases?
    a. GDP + C - S + NE
    b. C + G - NE - S + Ip
    c. C + G + Ip - S
    d. C + NE + G + Ip

20. The market value of final goods and services that will be purchased at any given level of in-
    come is known as:
    a. aggregate purchases.
    b. aggregate household wealth.
    c. aggregate household debt.
    d. aggregate household disposable income.

Answer the following two questions based upon the data below.

Disposable income ($billions)	Consumption ($billions)
$ 500	$ 700
1,000	1,000
1,500	1,300
2,000	1,600
2,500	1,900

21. The marginal propensity to save is:
    a. .10
    b. .25
    c. .40
    d. .35

22. If consumption increases by $200 billion at every level of disposable income, saving equals zero at what level of disposable income?
    a. $ 500
    b. $1,000
    c. $1,500
    d. $2,000
    e. $2,500

23. The real rate of interest currently equals the real marginal return to investment. If the current level of capacity utilization is low and businesses have expectations of rising sales, what will likely happen to the level of investment?
    a. Investment will increase.
    b. Investment will decrease.
    c. Investment will not change.
    d. The change in investment is indeterminate.

24. If depreciation rules change, increasing the after-tax return to investment, and at the same time the international value of the dollar decreases, what will happen to the level of aggregate purchases?
    a. Increase
    b. Decrease
    c. Will not change
    d. Indeterminate

25. Assume that disposable income in the United States is increasing faster than disposable income in Canada. Canada is a major trading partner of the United States. Other influences held constant, what is the impact of these income changes on United States net exports and the level of aggregate purchases?
    a. Imports will rise and exports will fall, causing net exports and aggregate purchases to rise.
    b. Imports will increase more than exports, causing net exports and aggregate demand to rise.
    c. Imports will increase more than exports, causing net exports and aggregate purchases to fall.
    d. Imports will increase less than exports, causing net exports and aggregate purchases to fall.

■ THINK IT THROUGH

1. Discuss the likely consequences of a crash in the stock market that results in large losses in the value of household real wealth.
2. Can you think of any reasons why it is not uncommon for businesses to invest *more* as interest rates rise?
3. How can government influence the level of aggregate purchases other than by changing the level of government spending on goods and input services?

4. Explain how the nation's aggregate purchases function is affected when the international value of the dollar falls relative to the value of foreign currencies.

■ ANALYZING THE NEWS

Using the skills derived from studying this chapter, analyze the economic facts that make up the following article and answer the question below.

What caused the slowdown in consumption spending during March and April 1995?

National Economic Trends

Did Big Tax Payments and Late Tax Refunds Decrease Consumption?

Nominal personal consumption expenditures grew 0.1 percent between March and April after growing 0.7 percent between February and March. Many analysts attributed this slowdown in consumption to a large increase in personal income tax payments and slower-than-usual tax refunds. Early this year, the IRS was slow in issuing some refund checks, partly because of a new program implemented to reduce fraudulent claims for tax refunds. According to one estimate, the dollar value of the delay reached $6 billion. At the same time, personal tax payments in April were nearly 10 percent higher than the payments made in April of last year because of lower deductions for mortgage interest paid and payments for back taxes arising from the Omnibus Reconciliation Act of 1993.

Households, faced with large tax payments and slow refunds, saw their disposable personal income fall. (Disposable personal income is personal income minus tax and non-tax payments.) Any increase in tax payments or delay in tax refunds decreases disposable personal income, but does not affect personal income. So, if households consumed less to offset their tax payments or slow refunds, the ratio of consumption to personal income would have fallen because consumption would have declined while personal income would have remained constant. In contrast, the ratio of consumption to disposable income would have remained nearly unchanged because both quantities would have fallen.

Households could have left their consumption unchanged and absorbed the higher net tax payments by reducing their savings. The ratio of consumption to personal income would then have remained constant, but the ratio of consumption to disposable personal income would have risen because the tax payments and slow refunds would have reduced their disposable personal income.

As the graph below shows, between March and April of this year (the last data plotted), consumption remained unchanged relative to personal income but rose relative to disposable personal income. This contradicts the story that higher taxes and slow tax refunds lowered consumption. It does support the hypothesis that households absorbed the tax payments and slow refunds by saving less. In fact, personal saving fell $50 billion between March and April, remarkably close to the $54 billion increase in net tax payments between the same two months.

— Peter Yoo

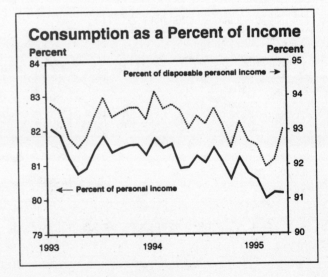

Consumption as a Percent of Income

Yoo, Peter. "Did Big Tax Payments and Late Tax Refunds Decrease Consumption? National Economic Trends. Federal Reserve Bank of St. Louis, July, 1995.

■ CHAPTER ANSWERS

The Chapter in Brief

1. Two thirds 2. Level of disposable income 3. Induced 4. Autonomous 5. Positive 6. Positive
7. Marginal propensity to consume 8. Divided 9. Saving 10. Disposable income 11. One
12. Increases 13. Decreases 14. Upward 15. Downward 16. Volatile 17. Planned 18. Just equal to
19. Investment demand 20. Increase 21. Capacity utilization 22. Reduce 23. Downward by the
reduction 24. Independent of 25. 17.5% 26. Reduces 27. Increase 28. Reduces 29. Increase
30. Increases 31. Inverse

Key Terms Review

1. Planned investment purchases 2. Real marginal return to investment 3. Marginal propensity to
save 4. Aggregate purchases 5. Marginal propensity to consume 6. Induced consumption 7. Aggregate household debt 8. Autonomous consumption 9. Aggregate household wealth 10. Consumption function 11. Wealth

Concept Review

1. a.   Saving
      $-200
       -100
         0
       100
       200
       300
       400

  b.   Positive, positive c. .6, .4; 1 d. $500 billion

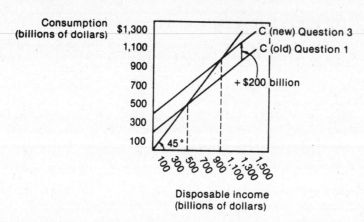

2. a.   Changes in aggregate household wealth

b. Changes in aggregate household debt

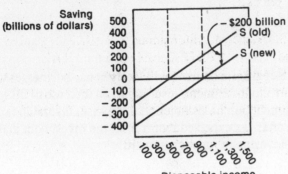

Saving
(billions of dollars)

c. Expectations of future income and wealth

3. a. Shown above in answer 1. a
   b.

New Conumption	New Saving
$ 400	$ -400
550	-300
700	-200
850	-100
1,000	0
1,150	100
1,300	200

   c. Shown in figure above
   d. Upward, $200 billion, downward, $200 billion
   e. $1,000 billion

4. a. The consumption function will shift upward and the saving function downward.
   b. Neither the consumption nor saving functions will shift.
   c. The consumption function will shift downward and the saving function will shift upward.
   d. The consumption function will shift downward and the saving function will shift upward.

5. a. Real rate of interest, real marginal return to investment
   b. $300 billion, rises, $500 billion
   c. Shown on figure below
   d. Shown on figure below
   e. Downward, upward

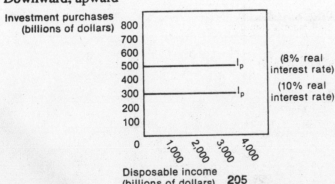

Investment purchases
(billions of dollars)

Disposable income
(billions of dollars)   205

6. a. Expectations about changes in aggregate demand
   b. Expectations about input and product prices
   c. Capacity utilization
   d. Technological change
   e. Tax treatment of investment purchases
      Expectations of higher levels of future aggregate demand will likely cause businesses to revise upward their real marginal returns to investment, resulting in an increase in investment and an upward shift in the investment purchases function. Likewise, favorable tax treatment of investment increases the after-tax expected return from the investment making it more attractive. This also shifts the investment function upward.

7. Upward

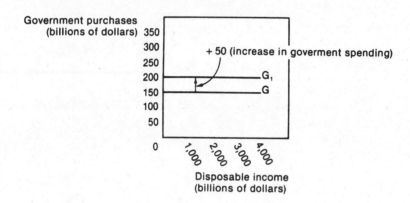

8. a. Net Exports
      $150
       100
        50
         0
       -50
      -100
      -150

   b.

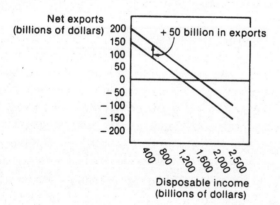

206

c. Inversely

d. Shown in figure above, increase, $1,600 billion

9. a. Aggregate Purchases

$ 550

825

1,100

1,375

1,650

1,925

2,200

b.

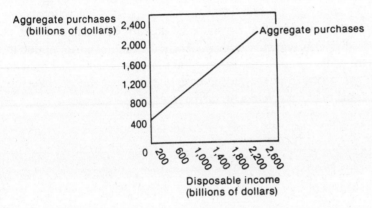

Mastery Test

1. d 2. d 3. d 4. d 5. e 6. d 7. c 8. c 9. b 10. a 11. d 12. a 13. c 14. b 15. a 16. d 17. c 18. c 19. d 20. a 21. c 22. c 23. d 24. a 25. c

Think It Through

1. If households experience large losses in household wealth, they will reduce consumption expenditures and increase saving. The consumption function will shift downward, and the saving function will shift upward. The October 1987 crash reduced real consumer spending for a short period, but other forces that cause consumption to increase eventually offset the impact of the decline in wealth.

2. The real rate of interest is just one of several influences affecting investment. In an expansion, interest rates at some point usually rise, but other factors affecting investment in the opposite direction are also changing. In an expansion, capacity utilization is rising and expectations of future growth in aggregate demand may be optimistic. Further, there may be expectations of rising product prices and profitability of expanded capacity. In other words, the real marginal return to investment is being revised upward faster than the increase in real interest rates.

3. In addition to changing the level of government purchases, the government can influence the level of aggregate demand by influencing the level of disposable income and therefore consumption. An increase in income taxes reduces disposable income and causes a reduction in household consumption and aggregate purchases and vice versa. An increase in transfer pay-

ments to households supplements household disposable income, resulting in an increase in consumption and aggregate purchases. A decrease in transfers reduces aggregate purchases.

4. When the international value of the dollar falls relative to the value of foreign currencies, the prices of U.S. exports become relatively lower to foreigners as compared to their foreign-produced output. Foreigners purchase more U.S. goods and less of their own output. As U.S. exports rise, net exports and aggregate purchases increase. The net export function shifts upward and, since the net export function is a component of the aggregate purchases function, the aggregate purchases function likewise shifts upward.

Analyzing the News

Some analysts have argued that slow tax refunds and larger personal tax payments early in 1995 caused the slow growth in consumption during March and April. Smaller refunds and higher tax payments reduce disposable income and consumption. If this is what happened, the ratio of consumption to disposable income should have remained constant and the ratio of consumption to personal income should have decreased. But between March and April, the ratio of consumption to personal income remained constant while the ratio of consumption to disposable income increased. This is possible if households reduce saving to offset the decrease in disposable income. Personal saving fell by an amount almost equal to the net change in tax payments, $54 billion.

12   KEYNESIAN ANALYSIS OF MACROECONOMIC EQUILIBRIUM

■ CHAPTER CONCEPTS

After studying your text, attending class, and completing this chapter, you should be able to:

1. Show how macroeconomic equilibrium is influenced by the level of aggregate purchases of domestic products by consumers, investors, governments, and foreigners.

2. Show how decrease in aggregate purchases associated with any given level of real income can cause equilibrium real GDP to decline.

3. Understand the concept of the multiplier and how it is related to the rate at which income is respent on the final products of domestic sellers.

4. Show how an increase in the price level can affect aggregate purchases and discuss Keynes' analysis of the causes of inflation.

■ THE CHAPTER IN BRIEF

Fill in the blanks to summarize chapter content.

In Keynesian analysis of the macroeconomy, (1)_____ (aggregate demand, inflation) is the key cause of fluctuations in real GDP. Macroeconomic equilibrium occurs when aggregate production (2)_____ (exceeds, equals) aggregate purchases. For an economy without government purchases, taxes or net exports, another condition for equilibrium is that planned investment equal (3)_____ (consumption, saving) and unintended inventory investment (4)_____ (exceed, equal) zero. If aggregate purchases exceed aggregate production, planned investment will exceed saving and unintended inventory investment will be (5)_____ (positive, negative). This puts (6)_____ (upward, downward) pressure on real GDP. Just the opposite is true of levels of income where aggregate purchases are less than aggregate production. In equilibrium, there is no tendency for real GDP to rise or fall.

Graphically, macroeconomic equilibrium occurs where the aggregate purchases line intersects the (7)_____ (45-degree, consumption) line and where the saving function intersects the planned investment line.

In Keynesian analysis, shifts in the aggregate purchases line cause expansions and recessions. For example, a/an (8)_____ (decline, increase) in planned investment will reduce aggregate purchases relative to aggregate production, resulting in an unintended (9)_____ (decline, increase) in inventory investment. Businesses will (10)_____(increase, cut) production due to the increase in unsold output. As production and income fall, real GDP, saving, and unintended inventory investment will fall. When saving falls to equal the new and lower level of planned investment, unintended inventory investment is zero and aggregate purchases are once again equal to aggregate production but at a lower level of real GDP—a recessionary level. As real GDP falls, employment also falls. Anything that causes a downward shift in the aggregate purchases line will cause equilibrium real GDP to (11)_____ (rise, fall). Conversely, anything that causes the aggregate purchases function to shift upward will cause equilibrium real GDP to (12)_____ (increase, decrease). In the short run, the economy can attain a recessionary level of equilibrium real

GDP and employment. Keynes believed that recessionary levels of employment would persist for long periods unless government intervened by stimulating aggregate demand.

A change in (13)_____ (induced, autonomous) purchases (a shift in the aggregate purchases curve) produce larger changes in equilibrium real GDP. This is known as the multiplier effect. The (14)_____ (marginal propensity to consume, multiplier) is a number that when multiplied by either a positive or negative change in autonomous purchases gives the resulting change in equilibrium real GDP. The multiplier process occurs because income spent becomes the income of input suppliers to the industries in which the income was originally spent. Input suppliers in turn spend a portion of the new income and save a portion. When they spend, input suppliers elsewhere in the economy receive income, a portion of which they eventually spend. For the case of an economy without government or foreign sectors, this process of spending and respending continues until the change in saving (15)_____ (just equals, is greater than) the initial change in planned investment. The multiplier can be found by taking the reciprocal of (16)_____ [(1 - MPC), (1 - MPS)] or the reciprocal of the (17)_____ (MPS, MPC).

Adding the government and international sectors to the Keynesian model requires reflecting all four components of aggregate purchases in the aggregate purchases curve: C, Ip, G, and NE. The conditions for macroeconomic equilibrium also change. Aggregate production must still equal aggregate purchases, now defined as including G and NE, (18)_____ (and S = Ip continues to be, but S = Ip is no longer) valid as a condition for equilibrium. The sum of the uses of income for purposes other than purchasing domestic output (saving, taxes less transfers, and imports) must just be offset by the sum of planned investment, government purchases, and exports. That is, Ip + G + E = S + T + M or, alternatively, Ip + G + NE = S + T. The multiplier must also be modified because like saving, imports and taxes are positive functions of real income. The new multiplier can be defined as (19)_____ [the reciprocal of (1 - MRR), MRR times MPC] where the marginal respending rate (MRR) is influenced by the marginal propensity to consume (MPC), the marginal propensity to import (MPI), and the tax rate. Fluctuations in real GDP can be caused by autonomous changes in any of the components of aggregate purchases, including G and NE.

Thus far, Keynesian analysis has assumed that the price level is constant. In order to understand the inflationary implications of fluctuations in autonomous purchases, it is necessary to introduce a price variable to the Keynesian model. As an initial step, the aggregate demand curve must be derived. The aggregate demand curve shows a relationship between the (20)_____ (real disposable income, price level) and aggregate purchases. An increase in the price level will (21)_____ (increase, reduce) aggregate purchases because real wealth decreases, causing consumption to (22)_____ (rise, fall); real interest rates, rise causing planned investment to (23)_____ (rise, fall); and the prices of U.S. goods relative to foreign goods rise, causing exports to (24)_____ (rise, fall) and imports to (25)_____ (rise, fall). The aggregate demand curve is downward sloping. When the aggregate purchases curve shifts upward, causing an inflationary gap where real GDP exceeds potential GDP, the price level rises. This will eventually cause the aggregate purchases line to shift (26)_____ (to a level higher than; back down to) its original position where real GDP equals potential GDP. Thus the price variable acts as a long-run corrective mechanism, eventually returning real GDP to its potential level.

KEY TERMS REVIEW

Write the key term from the list below next to its definition.

Key Terms

Multiplier   Marginal respending rate (MRR)
Autonomous purchases   Marginal propensity to
 import (MPI)

Definitions

1. _____: the fraction of each extra dollar of income used to purchase imported products.

2. _____: the extra purchases that result from each extra dollar of income.

3. _____: a number that indicates how many dollars of increase in real GDP results from each dollar of new autonomous purchases.

4. _____: purchases such as investment or autonomous consumption that cause the economy's aggregate purchases line to shift.

CONCEPT REVIEW

Concept 1: *Macroeconomic equilibrium*

1. Assume that an economy does not engage in international trade and there are no taxes, transfers, or government purchases. Answer the following questions based upon the data in the table below. (All data are in billions of dollars.)

Aggregate Production	Planned Investment	Consumption	Aggregate Purchases Investment	Unintended Inventory
$ 500	$300	$ 600	$_____	$_____
1,000	300	1,000	_____	_____
1,500	300	1,400	_____	_____
2,000	300	1,800	_____	_____
2,500	300	2,200	_____	_____
3,000	300	2,600	_____	_____
3,500	300	3,000	_____	_____

 a. Complete the table.

 b. The conditions for macroeconomic equilibrium are that _____ equal _____ and _____ equal zero. In equilibrium, planned investment must equal _____.

 c. Equilibrium GDP = $_____. In equilibrium, aggregate purchases = $_____, aggregate production = $_____, unintended inventory investment = $_____, saving = $_____, and planned investment = $_____.

211

d. Plot the aggregate purchases curve in the figure below and identify the equilibrium level of real GDP.

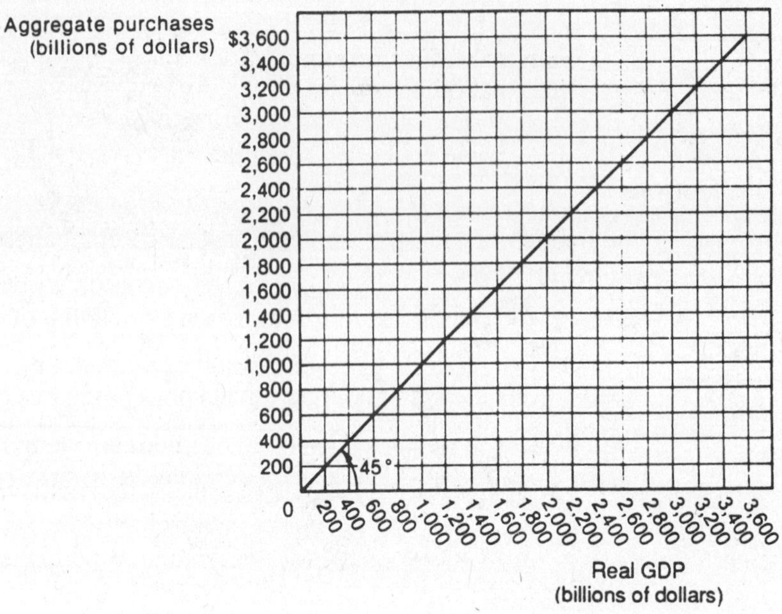

e. At a level of aggregate production of $1,500 billion, aggregate purchases _____ aggregate production by $_____, resulting in an unintended inventory investment of $_____. This causes the level of real GDP to _____.

f. At a level of aggregate production of $3,500 billion, aggregate purchases _____ aggregate production by $_____, resulting in an unintended inventory investment of $_____. This causes real GDP to _____.

Concepts 2 and 3:   **Changes in autonomous purchases, macroeconomic equilibrium, and the multiplier**

2. For the economy shown in the table above in question 1, analyze the effect of an increase in planned investment of $100 billion. (All data are in billions of dollars.)

Aggregate Production	Planned Investment		Consumption	Aggregate Purchases		Unintended Inventory Investment	
	Old	New		Old	New	Old	New
$ 500	$300	$400	$ 600	$___	$___	$___	$___
1,000	300	400	1,000	___	___	___	___
1,500	300	400	1,400	___	___	___	___
2,000	300	400	1,800	___	___	___	___
2,500	300	400	2,200	___	___	___	___
3,000	300	400	2,600	___	___	___	___
3,500	300	400	3,000	___	___	___	___

212

a. Complete the table.
b. For the new level of planned investment, equilibrium real GDP = $_____.
c. On the figure above, draw the new aggregate purchases curve and identify the new equilibrium real GDP.
d. Equilibrium real GDP has _____ from $_____ to $_____. Equilibrium autonomous purchases have _____ from $_____ to $_____. The multiplier = _____.
e. MPC = _____, MPS = _____. What is the reciprocal of the MPS or (1 - MPC)?

3. Complete the table.

Change in Autonomous Purchases	MPC	MPS	Multiplier	Change in Equilibrium Real GDP
$50 billion	.8	____	_____	$_____
-30 billion	.75	____	_____	_____
700 billion	____	.4	_____	_____
-80 billion	____	____	2	_____

4. In the figure below is an aggregate supply and aggregate demand model. Assuming the MPS is .25, show what will happen to the aggregate demand curve and the equilibrium level of real GDP given a decline in household wealth that reduces autonomous purchases by $75 billion.

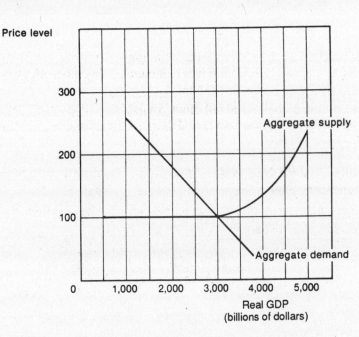

5. Show on the figure below the effect of an increase in government purchases of $100 billion. Identify the new equilibrium real GDP. The multiplier = _____. If after the increase in government spending the level of equilibrium real GDP is short of potential GDP by $200 billion and government desires to increase its spending to move the economy to its potential level, how much more of an increase in government purchases is required? $_____

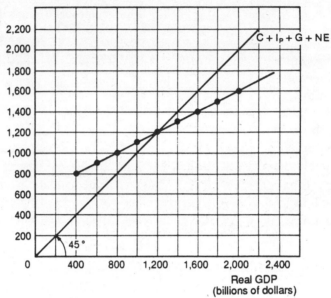

6. Given the initial level of aggregate purchases in the figure above, show on the figure the effect of a decline in exports of $50 billion. Equilibrium real GDP _____ from $_____ to $_____.

Concept 4:   *Aggregate demand and the price level*

7. List three reasons why an increase in the price level will reduce aggregate purchases.

   a. _____

   b. _____

   c. _____

8. In the figure below, a represents three aggregate purchases curves, each associated with a different price level. Curve 1 is associated with price level P1, curve 2 with P2, and curve 3 with P3. In b, find the price level-real GDP coordinates consistent with macroeconomic equilibrium. (Plot the aggregate demand curve.)

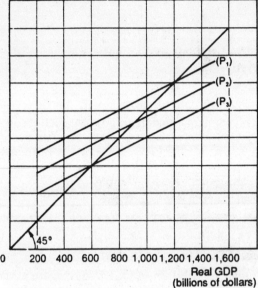

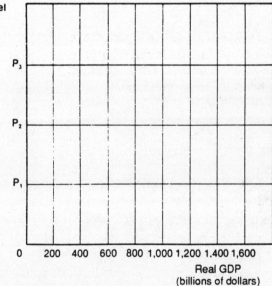

■ MASTERY TEST

Select the best answer.

1. In Keynesian analysis, the key determinant of real GDP is:
   a. profits.
   b. investment.
   c. inflation.
   d. aggregate demand.

2. For an economy without international trade, taxes, transfers and government spending, equilibrium real GDP is achieved when:
   a. planned investment equals saving.
   b. aggregate production equals aggregate purchases.
   c. consumption and planned investment equal aggregate production.
   d. All of the above.
   e. None of the above.

3. Graphically, macroeconomic equilibrium occurs where:
   a. the consumption function and saving line intersect.
   b. the planned investment line and the government spending line intersect.
   c. spending equals saving.
   d. the aggregate purchases curve intersects the 45-degree line.

4. At a level of real GDP greater than equilibrium real GDP, aggregate production _____ aggregate purchases and unintended inventory investment _____.
   a. equals, equals zero
   b. exceeds, is positive
   c. is less than, is negative
   d. equals, is negative
   e. exceeds, equals zero

5. At a level of real GDP less than equilibrium real GDP, aggregate production _____ aggregate purchases and unintended inventory investment _____.
   a. equals, equals zero
   b. exceeds, is positive
   c. is less than, is negative
   d. equals, is negative
   e. exceeds, equals zero

6. A decline in planned investment:
   a. causes aggregate purchases to increase and aggregate production to decrease.
   b. reduces aggregate purchases relative to aggregate production causing unintended inventories to rise and putting pressure on real GDP to rise.
   c. increases aggregate purchases relative to aggregate production causing unintended inventories to rise and putting pressure on real GDP to fall.
   d. reduces aggregate purchases relative to aggregate production causing unintended inventories to rise and putting pressure on real GDP to fall.

7. If households experience a substantial increase in aggregate household wealth:
   a. unintended inventory investment falls initially, but eventually equilibrium real GDP will rise.
   b. unintended inventory investment rises initially, but eventually equilibrium real GDP will fall.
   c. unintended inventory investment falls initially, but eventually equilibrium real GDP will fall.
   d. initially equilibrium real GDP will rise, but eventually unintended inventory investment will fall.

8. If the economy is operating at a level of equilibrium real GDP below its potential real GDP:
   a. the economy is experiencing inflation.
   b. government can move the economy toward its potential level by reducing government purchases.
   c. the economy is at full employment, but is at least not experiencing inflation.
   d. government can move the economy toward its potential level by increasing government purchases.

9. A change in autonomous purchases produces a larger change in real GDP. This concept is represented by the:
   a. MPC.
   b. MRR.
   c. multiplier.
   d. 1/MPI.
   e. c and d.

10. Which of the following expressions represents the multiplier?
    a. 1/MPI
    b. 1/MPC
    c. 1/MPS
    d. 1/(1 - MPC)
    e. C and d

11. If the current level of equilibrium real GDP is $2,000 billion and the MPS equals .25, an increase in planned investment of $50 billion will change real equilibrium GDP to:
    a. $1,800 billion.
    b. $2,300 billion.
    c. $3,200 billion.
    d. $2,200 billion.
    e. $2,100 billion.

12. If the MPC is .8 and a decline in consumer wealth reduces aggregate purchases by $100 billion, equilibrium real GDP will change by:
    a. -$200 billion.
    b. $200 billion.
    c. $400 billion.
    d. -$500 billion.

13. Which of the following equilibrium conditions applies to an economy with foreign trade, government spending, taxes, and transfers?
    a. Aggregate production = aggregate purchases
    b. C + Ip + G + NE = real GDP
    c. Ip + G + E = S + T + M
    d. All of the above
    e. B and c

14. The multiplier for an economy with taxes and imports as a function of income:
    a. is larger than the multiplier for an economy without foreign trade, taxes, transfers, and government spending.
    b. is expressed as the reciprocal of the MRR.
    c. is expressed as the reciprocal of (1 - MRR).
    d. is smaller than the multiplier for an economy without foreign trade, taxes, transfers, and government purchases.
    e. c and d

15. A/An _____ in exports can cause a/an _____ gap.
    a. decrease, recessionary
    b. decrease, inflationary
    c. increase, recessionary
    d. increase, will leave real GDP unchanged

16. Which of the following is not a reason why aggregate purchases and the price level are inversely related?
    a. Higher prices cause higher wages, inducing firms to cut employment and production.
    b. Higher prices reduce real wealth, decreasing consumption and aggregate purchases.
    c. Higher prices increase real interest rates, reducing planned investment and aggregate purchases.
    d. Higher prices reduces exports and increase imports, reducing aggregate purchases.

17. A point on the aggregate demand curve represents a price level- real GDP coordinate at which:
    a. aggregate purchases equal aggregate government spending.
    b. aggregate demand equals aggregate purchases.
    c. aggregate purchases equal aggregate production.
    d. S + C = Ip + real GDP.

18. An inflationary gap exists where equilibrium real GDP _____ potential or full-employment GDP. In the long run, an inflationary gap will cause the aggregate purchases curve to shift _____.
    a. equals, upward
    b. equals, downward
    c. is less than, downward
    d. is greater than, downward
    e. is greater than, upward

Answer the following questions based upon the data below. All data are in billions of dollars.

Aggregate Production	Investment	Consumption	Government	Net Exports
$1,000	$300	$1,000	$200	$250
2,000	300	1,800	200	200
3,000	300	2,600	200	150
4,000	300	3,400	200	100
5,000	300	4,200	200	50
6,000	300	5,000	200	0

19. For the economy described above, equilibrium real GDP equals:
   a. $2,000
   b, $3,000
   c. $4,000
   d. $5,000
   e. $6,000

20. For the economy described above, the marginal respending rate is:
   a. .40
   b. .75
   c. .90
   d. .80

21. For the economy described above, the multiplier is:
   a. 2
   b. 1.5
   c. 4
   d. 5

22. What will happen to equilibrium real GDP for the economy described above if autonomous consumption increases by $250 billion at each level of aggregate production?
   a. Real GDP will increase to $5,000 billion.
   b. Real GDP will increase to $4,000 billion.
   c. Real GDP will not change because the consumption curve does not shift.
   d. Real GDP will increase to $3,000 billion.

23. What will happen to equilibrium real GDP for the economy described above if a decrease in the international value of the dollar increases net exports by $30 billion?
   a. Real GDP will decrease to $5,000.
   b. Real GDP will increase to $5,000.
   c. Real GDP will increase to $4,120.
   d. Real GDP will decrease to $4,880.
   e. Real GDP will increase to $3,660.

THINK IT THROUGH

1. Suppose that the international value of the dollar on foreign exchange markets increases, causing the prices of U.S. goods abroad to become less competitive. If exports fall, what is the likely impact on the economy?

2. If business becomes more optimistic regarding future sales such that the expected marginal rate of return to investment rises relative to the real interest rate, discuss the likely macroeconomic effects.

3. Explain intuitively the multiplier process.

ANALYZING THE NEWS

Using the skills derived from studying this chapter, analyze the economic facts that make up the following article and answer the questions below.

1. Distinguish between planned and unplanned inventories.

2. "Most post-war recessions have been preceded by a rise in inventory levels. Does the 1994 buildup of inventory portend another downturn?"

National Economic Trends

Inventory Changes and the Business Cycle

The robust growth of Gross Domestic Product (GDP) in 1994 was due in large part to a buildup of business inventory. The 1994 increase in business inventory was $47.8 billion in 1987 dollars, contributing 1 percentage point of the 4.1 percent increase in GDP, and following a $15.3 billion increase in 1993. Most post-war recessions have been preceded by a rise in inventory levels. Does the 1994 buildup of inventory portend another downturn? Not necessarily.

The impact of inventory increases on the business cycle depends on whether they are planned or unplanned. *Unplanned* increases in inventory are undesirable and are usually followed by scaled-back production or purchases until inventory levels return to normal. Such decreases in production can trigger layoffs and sluggish demand throughout the economy. *Planned* increases in inventory, on the other hand, contribute positively to economic expansions and do not lead to corrections.

Inventory increases before recessions usually coincide with *increases* in the business inventory-to-sales ratio, but the ratio is at its lowest level in 20 years. Low inventory-to-sales ratios in 1994 suggest that firms have been economizing by maintaining a minimum level of inventory. Last year's unexpectedly large increase in consumer spending caught some firms under-stocked. For example, automakers like Ford and GM experienced shortages of popular models. Such stock-outs would result in a *planned* attempt to raise inventory levels. The retail sector, however, may have experienced some unplanned increases in inventory due to lower than anticipated holiday sales. We would then expect some inventory decumulation in the retail sector during the first quarter of 1995.

Fundamental changes in inventory management methods may also have permanently changed the relationship between inventory and recessions. The accompanying chart shows the inventory-to-sales ratio (number of months' sales in stock) of the manufacturing, wholesale and retail trade sectors for the last 20 years, with recessions shaded. The manufacturing sector has adopted more efficient inventory management techniques and contributed heavily to the decline in the aggregate inventory-to-sales ratio. Innovations like just-in-time delivery allow production to respond faster to changes in demand, minimizing unplanned inventory accumulation. Some analysts believe this will reduce the severity of business cycles over the long run.

— Donald S. Allen

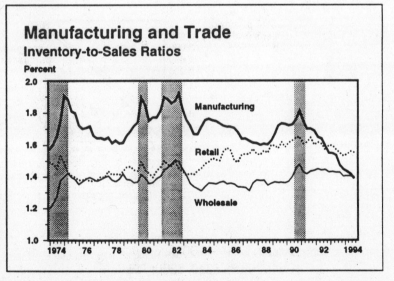

Manufacturing and Trade
Inventory-to-Sales Ratios

Views expressed do not necessarily reflect official positions of the Federal Reserve System.

Allen, Donald S. "Inventory Changes and the Business Cycle." National Economic Trends. Federal Reserve Bank of St. Louis, April, 1995.

CHAPTER ANSWERS

The Chapter in Brief

1. Aggregate demand 2. Equals 3. Saving 4. Equal 5. Negative 6. Upward 7. 45-degree 8. Decline 9. Increase 10. Cut 11. Fall 12. Increase
13. Autonomous 14. Multiplier 15. Just equals 16. (1 - MPC) 17. MPS 18. But S = Ip is no longer 19. The reciprocal of (1 - MRR) 20. Price level 21. Reduce 22. Fall 23. Fall 24. Fall 25. Rise 26. Back down to

Key Terms Review

1.Marginal propensity to import 2. Marginal respending rate (MRR) 3. Multiplier 4. Autonomous purchases

Concept Review

1. a.

Aggregate Purchases	Unintended Inventory Investment
$ 900	$-400
300	-300
1,700	-200
2,100	-100
2,500	0
2,900	100
3,300	200

   b. Aggregate purchases, aggregate production, unintended inventory investment; saving
   c. $2,500; $2,500, $2,500, $0, $300, $300
   d.

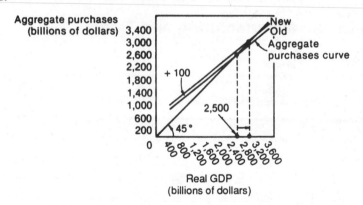

   e. Exceed, $200, -$200; rise
   f. Are less than, $200, $200; fall

2. a.

Aggregate Purchases		Unintended Inventory Investment	
Old	New	Old	New
$ 900	$1,000	$-400	$-500
1,300	1,400	-300	-400
1,700	1,800	-200	-300
2,100	2,200	-100	-200
2,500	2,600	0	-100
2,900	3,000	100	0
3,300	3,400	200	100

b. $3000

c.   On figure above

d.   Increased, $2,500, $3,000; increased, $2,500, $3,000; 5

e.   .8, .2; the multiplier

3.

Change in Autonomous Purchases	MPC	MPS	Multiplier	Change in Equilibrium Real GDP
$50 billion	.80	.20	5.0	$250 billion
-30 billion	.75	.25	4.0	-120 billion
700 billion	.60	.40	2.5	1,750 billion
-80	.50	.50	2.0	-160 billion

4.

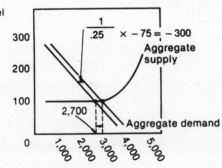

5.

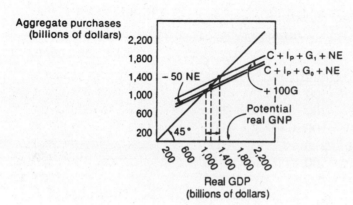

2, $100 billion

6. Shown on figure above; decreases, $1,200, $1,100

7. a. An increase in the price level will reduce real wealth, reducing consumption and aggregate purchases.

   b. An increase in the price level will increase real interest rates, reducing planned investment and causing aggregate purchases to fall.

   c. An increase in the prices of U.S. goods relative to foreign goods increases imports and decreases exports, causing aggregate purchases to decline.

8.

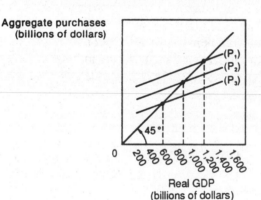

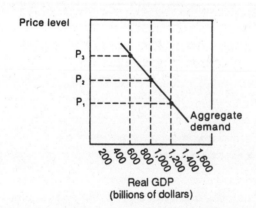

224

Mastery Test

1. d 2. d 3. d 4. b 5. c 6. d 7. a 8. d 9. c 10. e 11. d 12. d 13. d 14. e 15. a 16. a 17. c 18. d 19.c
20. b 21. c 22. a 23. c

Think it Through

1. If exports fall, net exports and aggregate purchases will decline. As aggregate spending declines relative to the current level of real GDP, unintended inventory investment increases. Businesses will eventually reduce the rate of production, causing real GDP to fall. As long as real GDP exceeds aggregate purchases, unintended inventory investment will be positive putting downward pressure on real GDP. Real GDP will fall to a lower equilibrium level where aggregate production and aggregate purchases are equal and unintended inventory investment is zero.

2. If because of an optimistic outlook regarding future sales businesses revise upward their expected marginal real returns to investments, the expected marginal returns will exceed the prevailing real interest rate, causing profit-maximizing firms to increase planned investment. This will cause an autonomous increase in aggregate purchases, which in turn will produce a multiple increase in real GDP assuming that the economy initially was in equilibrium at less than full employment. If the economy was initially at full employment, the increase in planned investment will cause an inflationary gap.

3. An increase in autonomous expenditures causes an equal increase in output and income. Businesses produce output to meet increases in spending, and households receive income for supplying inputs to the industry experiencing the autonomous spending. Input suppliers save a portion of the new disposable income and spend a portion. But when they spend, they create a demand for goods and services, which causes producers of those items to increase production. In order to increase production, firms must hire additional inputs, providing another round of income increases to input suppliers. The multiplier process results from the spending and respending of income. At each round, output produced by the economy increases. This process continues until the initial increase in autonomous spending just equals the growth of saving. At this point, there is no additional income created and consequently no growth in spending or production.

Analyzing the News

1. Planned changes in inventories result from expectations of future sales and other profit considerations whereas unplanned inventory changes occur when production (based on expected sales) does not match actual sales.

2. Inventory buildups have preceded most post-war recessions. These inventory increases were unplanned and resulted in subsequent decreases in production, causing declines in real GDP. There is reason to believe, however, that the 1994 inventory buildup was planned. The 1994 inventory-to-sales ratio was at a 20 year low. Larger than expected levels of consumption caused unplanned inventory decreases from already low levels, inducing some firms to increase planned inventory levels. This suggests that the 1994 inventory increase does not signal another recession.

225

APPENDIX TO CHAPTER 12
A COMPLETE KEYNESIAN MODEL

■ THE APPENDIX IN BRIEF

Fill in the blanks to summarize appendix content.

The complete Keynesian model considers aggregate purchases to be the sum of C + Ip + G + NE. Consumption, C, is a function of disposable income. In determining disposable income, DI, a net tax function is employed where net taxes collected equal the marginal tax rate times the level of (1)_____ (consumption, income). The (2)_____ (average, marginal) tax rate is the fraction of each extra dollar of income earned in a nation that is collected as taxes. Planned investment, Ip, and government purchases, G, are treated as autonomous variables. The net exports function, NE, is an/a (3)_____ (inverse, positive) function of income. Specifically, NE = exports - imports where imports are a (4)_____ (negative, positive) function of income. Thus as national income rises, imports rise relative to exports, causing net exports to (5)_____ (rise, fall).

A condition for economic equilibrium is that aggregate purchases equal aggregate production.

Aggregate purchases = C + Ip + G + (E - M)

Aggregate production = Y = C + S + T

Setting aggregate production equal to aggregate purchases and simplifying yields:

(E - M) + (G - T) = S - Ip

The sum of the foreign trade balance and the government budget balance must equal the difference between saving and planned investment. This can be alternatively stated as:

Balance of trade deficit = S - (Ip + budget deficit)

If a nation has a balance of trade deficit, domestic saving (6)_____ (falls short of, exceeds) the sum of planned investment purchases and the budget deficit.

In order to algebraically solve for the equilibrium level of real GDP and the multiplier, the individual functions for the components of aggregate purchases must be summed to obtain the aggregate purchases function. This is then set equal to the level of aggregate production, Y, and solved for Y—the equilibrium level of real GDP. The collection of coefficients preceding autonomous C, Ip, G, and E are the multipliers pertaining to each component.

$$Y = C + Ip + G + NE$$
$$Y = A + MPC[(1 - t)]Y + Ip + G + [E - MPI(Y)]$$
$$Y = [1/(1 - MRR)]A + [1/(1 - MRR)]Ip + [1/(1 - MRR)]G + [1/(1 - MRR)]E$$
$$\text{where MRR} = [MPC(1 - t) - MPI]$$

A change in planned investment, for instance, would change real GDP by

$[1/(1 - MRR)]$ times the change in (7)_____ (planned investment, real GDP).

■ CONCEPT REVIEW

Answer questions 1, 2, and 3 given the values below.

A = $300 billion, Ip = $400 billion, G = $500,
E = $200, MPC = .9, t = .3, MPI = .15

1. MRR = _____

   Multiplier = _____

   Equilibrium real GDP = $_____

2. If the marginal tax rate, t, is reduced to .2, what is the impact on real GDP? Real GDP
   _____ from $_____ to $_____.

3. If the international value of the dollar falls relative to the values of foreign currencies, exports
   rise. If exports rise by $50 billion, by how much will equilibrium income change?
   (Assume t = .2.) $_____

■ MASTERY TEST

Select the best answer.

1. The fraction of each extra dollar of income earned in a nation that is collected as taxes is called:
   a. net taxes.
   b. average tax rate.
   c. marginal tax rate.
   d. marginal income.

2. In the complete Keynesian model, which of the following represents the consumption function?
   a. $C = A - (MPC)Y$
   b. $C = A + (MPC - t)Y$
   c. $C = MPC - A(1 - t)Y$
   d. $C = A - MPC[(1 - t)]Y$

3. In the complete Keynesian model, the multiplier is expressed as:
   a. $1/MPC$.
   b. $1/(1 - MPS)$.
   c. $1/(MRR - 1)$.
   d. $1/(1 + MRR)$.
   e. $1/\{1 - [MPC(1 - t) - MPI]\}$.

4. The equilibrium condition can be expressed to yield an implication regarding a nation running
   a balance of trade deficit. Which of the following is a statement of that implication?
   a. Real GDP is always larger given balance of trade deficits.
   b. A balance of trade deficit implies that planned investment and the budget deficit exceed
      saving.
   c. A balance of trade deficit implies that domestic saving falls short of the sum of planned in-
      vestment purchases and the budget deficit.
   d. None of the above.

CHAPTER APPENDIX ANSWERS

The Appendix in Brief

1. Income 2. Marginal 3. Inverse 4. Positive 5. Fall 6. Falls short of 7. Planned investment

Concept Review

1. .48, 1.923, $2,692.3 billion
2. Increases, $2,692.3 billion, $3,255.8 billion
3. +$116.28 billion

Mastery Test

1. c 2. d 3. e 4. c

PART V

MONEY, FINANCIAL MARKETS, AND MACROECONOMIC EQUILIBRIUM

■ **PART EXERCISE**

Inside Information: *Federal Reserve Bulletin*

In Part V, you will learn about the money supply and the role of the banking system in the process of money growth. Use the most recent issue of the *Federal Reserve Bulletin* and find M1. Also, find a consolidated balance sheet for all commercial banks and list each asset as a percentage of all assets and each liability and capital account as a percentage of all liabilities and capital. Do the same thing using the same monthly issue of the *Federal Reserve Bulletin*, but for a year earlier. During the previous twelve months, what has happened to M1? What is the annual rate of growth of M1? Has the composition of commercial bank assets, liabilities, and capital changed? Please detail any changes. Are these changes consistent with the changes in M1? Explain.

13   THE FUNCTIONS OF MONEY

■ CHAPTER CONCEPTS

After studying your text, attending class, and completing this chapter, you should be able to:

1. List the four major functions of money in the economy.

2. Discuss the major components of the money stock in an economy, the concept of near money, and the official measures of the U.S. money stock.

3. Discuss the determinants of the demand for money.

4. Explain how, given the demand for money, changes in the available money stock can affect credit and interest rates and influence spending decisions and how, given the stock of money, changes in the demand for money can affect interest rates.

■ THE CHAPTER IN BRIEF

Fill in the blanks to summarize chapter content.

In order to understand the operation of the macroeconomy, it is necessary to understand the role of money. But first it is necessary to define money, identify its functions, consider operational measures of money, and explain how changes in the demand for and supply of money affect interest rates and spending in the economy.

Money is defined according to its functions. Money serves as a medium of (1) _exchange_ (exchange, value), a standard of value, a standard of deferred payment, and a store of (2) _value_ (exchange, value). Anything performing these functions is money. Money does not have to have intrinsic value such as (3) _commodity_ (fiat, commodity) money in order to perform these functions. Fiat money and checkable deposits are considered money not because they have intrinsic value, but because they are accepted as a medium of exchange and fulfill the other functions of money. Bonds and credit cards are (4) _not_ (not, also) money. Money is an asset—a store of value. Even though credit cards can be used as a medium to facilitate exchange, a liability or debt is incurred when credit cards are used.

Three of the official definitions of money are M1, M2, and M3. M1 is the sum of (5) _checkable_ (checkable, savings) deposits, currency, and traveler's checks held by the public on a given day. M2 is the sum of M1 and near monies. Near monies are assets that can easily be converted to money because they can be liquidated easily, quickly, and at little cost. M3 is the sum of M2 and (6) _large_ (small-, large-) denomination certificates of deposit.

Individuals and businesses hold money for two reasons: to carry out transactions in the economy and because money is an asset. Modern economies require a medium of exchange to facilitate transactions. As an economy experiences growth in nominal GDP, the number and volume of transactions increase, causing the transaction demand for money to (7) _increase_ (increase, decrease). The degree to which receipts and payments are synchronized also affects the need for transaction money balances. In addition, expectations of future interest rates will affect the desire to hold transaction money balances because interest rates influence the (8) _opportunity cost_ (liquidity, opportunity cost) of holding money.

Money, like other assets, has certain characteristics that make it more or less attractive to hold relative to other financial assets. Money is held as an asset not because of its income, return, or yield, but because it is (9) _liquid_ (totally riskless, liquid). Because individuals and businesses have a (10) _precautionary_ (hedging, precautionary) and speculative motive for holding money, liquidity is required to satisfy these motives. Expectations of future interest rates and bond prices affect the desire to hold money relative to other assets. Even expectations of future rates of inflation affect the desirability of holding money as an asset.

The total demand for money is the sum of the transaction and asset demands for money. The quantity of money demanded varies (11) _inversely_ (inversely, directly) with the interest rate. Higher interest rates (12) _decrease_ (decrease, increase) the opportunity cost of holding money and therefore reduce the quantity of money demanded and vice versa. The factors mentioned above that influence either the transaction or asset demand for money will affect the total demand for money. The money demand curve is (13) _downward sloping_ (upward sloping, downward sloping), but will shift to the right or left depending upon changes in the noninterest rate determinants of money demand, which include (a) the degree to which receipts and payments are synchronized, (b) expectations of future interest rates, stock and bond prices, and rates of inflation, and (c) the level of nominal GDP.

The interest rate is determined by the supply of and demand for loanable funds. A change in the stock of money or demand for money influences the market rate of interest. A change in the interest rate in turn influences the level of spending in the economy and GDP. For instance, given the demand for money, an increase in the supply of money will create a (14) _surplus_ (surplus, shortage) of money at the current rate of interest. Since (15) _more_ (more, less) money is on hand than is desired for transactions or as assets, saving and the buying of bonds are likely to (16) _increase_ (decrease, increase). This (17) _increases_ (decreases, increases) the supply of loanable funds resulting in an/a (18) _increase_ (increase, decrease) in the interest rate. Interest rates must (19) _fall_ (fall, rise) in order to increase the quantity of money demanded to equal the higher level of the money stock. Likewise, a decline in the money stock (20) _decreases_ (increases, decreases) the interest rate.

Given the stock of money, a change in the demand for money will create either a shortage or a surplus of money at the current market rate of interest, causing the loanable funds market to be influenced such that interest rates change in the direction necessary to once again equate the supply of and demand for money. Changes in the interest rate affect interest-sensitive expenditures and thus the level of aggregate demand and GDP.

■ KEY TERMS REVIEW

Write the key term from the list below next to its definition.

Key Terms

Money
Commodity money
Fiat money
Checkable deposits
Commercial banks
Saving and loan associations
Mutual savings banks
Credit unions
Bonds

M1
Near monies
M2
Time deposits
M3
Transaction demand for money
Demand for money
Money demand curve
Change in money demanded

Definitions

1. __Fiat money__ : money that is accepted as a medium of exchange because of government decree rather than because of its intrinsic value as a commodity.

2. __Credit Unions__ : depository institutions whose depositors belong to a particular organization; they make loans only to their members.

3. __Near monies__ : assets that are easily converted to money because they can be liquidated at low cost and little risk of loss.

4. __M3__ : the sum of M2 and large-denomination ($100,000 and more) certificates of deposit.

5. __Demand for money__ *Trans.* : the sum of money people wish to hold per day as a convenience in paying their bills.

6. __Money demand curve__ : shows a relationship between the level of interest rates in the economy and the stock of money demanded at a given point in time.

7. __Change in money demanded__ : a change in the relationship between the level of interest rates and the stock of money demanded in the economy caused by a change in economic conditions.

8. __Commodity money__ : an item that serves the functions of money but also has value in uses other than as the medium of exchange.

9. __Mutual savings bank__ : depository institutions operating in some states that are similar to savings and loan associations in that they primarily attract savings deposits and in the past have specialized in making mortgage loans.

10. __M1__ : the stock of money measured by the sum of currency, traveler's checks, and checkable deposits held by the public on a particular day of the year in the United States.

11. __Time deposits__ : interest-bearing accounts at commercial banks and thrift institutions for which the bank can legally request a 30-day notice before paying out the funds.

12. _Demand for Money_: the relationship between the sums of money people willingly hold and the level of interest rates in the economy given all other influences on the desirability of holding money instead of other assets.

13. _Money_ : anything that is generally accepted as payment for goods or services; also serves as a standard of value, a standard of deferred payment, and a store of value.

14. _Savings + Loans_ : depository institutions that acquire funds chiefly through attracting savings deposits and have in the past specialized in making mortgage loans.

15. _Bonds_ : securities issued by corporations and governments representing the promise to make periodic payments of interest and repay a debt of borrowed funds at a certain time.

16. _M2_ : the sum of M1 and certain near monies; a measure of liquid assets held by the public.

17. _Commercial banks_: firms that acquire funds by accepting checkable deposits and savings deposits of households and business firms and use these funds to make loans to businesses and individuals.

18. _Checkable deposits_ represents money deposited in bank accounts that can be used to write checks that are accepted to pay debts, or that can easily be converted to currency.

■ **CONCEPT REVIEW**

Concept 1: *Functions of money*
1. List four functions of money.
   a. _Store of value_
   b. _medium of exchange_
   c. _standard of value_
   d. _standard of deferred payment_

Concept 2: *Definitions of money; measures of money*
2. Using the items given below, define M1, M2, and M3.
   - Currency held by the public
   - Money market mutual funds
   - Money market deposit accounts
   - Traveler's checks held by the public
   - Checkable deposits held by the public
   - Large-denomination certificates of deposit
   - Savings accounts, small-denomination certificates of deposit, and certain other near monies
   a. M1 = _Currency, TC, Checkable deposits_

   b. M2 = _Saving accounts + M1 + mutual funds + deposit accounts_

236

c.   M3 = _large-denomination + M2_____

d.   Near monies = _Mutual funds + savings accounts_

_____

e.   Silver dollars are examples of _commodity_ money.
f.   Federal Reserve Notes are examples of _fiat_ money.
g.   Why are credit cards not considered money? _They incur debt_

Concept 3:   *Determinants of the demand for money; money demand curve*

3. a.   List and discuss three factors that influence the transaction demand for money.
    (1) _price level_
    (2) _interest rate_
    (3) _____

    b.   List and discuss three factors that influence the asset demand for money.
    (1) _____
    (2) _____
    (3) _____

4. The data below show the relationship between the quantity of money demanded and the nominal interest rate holding all other influences unchanged.

	Quantity of Money Demanded per Day ($ billions)		Interest Rate (%)
(a)	*(b)*	*(c)*	*(d)*
$740	740	680	12%
760	800	700	11
780	820	720	10
800	840	740	9
820	860	760	8
840	880	780	7

a. Plot the money demand curve on the diagram below.

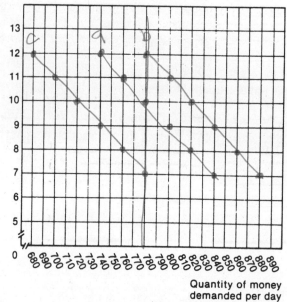

Nominal interest rate (%)

Quantity of money demanded per day (billions of dollars)

b. Why is the money demand curve downward sloping?

c. List the factors that shift the money demand curve.

(1) _interest rate_____

(2) _____

(3) _____

(4) _____

d. Assume that the data above are for a level of nominal GDP of $4 trillion. Assume nominal GDP increases, causing the demand for money to increase by $40 billion at each interest rate.
(1) Complete column b in the table above.

(2) Plot the new money demand curve on the figure above. The money demand curve has shifted _outward___.

e. Assume again that the current money demand data are reflected in column a. Assume that expectations of higher future inflation reduce the desirability of holding money as an asset, causing the demand for money to decrease by $60 billion at each interest rate.
(1) Complete column c in the table above.

(2) Plot the new money demand curve on the figure above. The money demand curve has shifted _inward___.

5. For each of the following, indicate whether the money demand curve will shift to the right or left.
   a. Technology and new banking regulations allow employers to electronically deposit paychecks in employees' checkable deposit accounts, and the accounts are automatically drafted to pay the employees' fixed monthly payments such as mortgage pay-ments. _left_
   b. Merchants allow customers to use "debit" cards whereby the merchant can electronically transfer funds for a purchase from the customer's checkable deposit account to the merchant's account. _left_
   c. Credit cards are used more frequently. _left_
   d. Employers and consumers coordinate their payments and receipts such that paychecks are received and payments are due the first of each month. _right_ _left_
   e. Nominal GDP increases. _right_
   f. The price level increases. _right_
   g. New highly liquid and safe financial assets become available earning a rate of interest in excess of that earned by checkable deposits. _left_

Concept 4: *Changes in the supply of and demand for money*

6. The data from question 4 above are reproduced below.

Quantity of Money Demanded ($ billions)			Interest Rate (%)
(a)	*(b)*	*(c)*	
$740			12%
760			11
780			10
800			9
820			8
840			7

   a. Assume that the stock of money is $780 billion. Draw the money stock curve on the diagram above. The equilibrium rate of interest is __10__ %.
   b. If the demand for money changes from that shown in column a to that in column b, interest rates will _increase_ to __12__ %.
   c. If the demand for money changes from that shown in column a to that in column c, interest rates will _decrease_ to __7__ %.

d. On the diagrams below:
   (1) Show the effect of an increase in the stock of money. Interest rates _decrease_.
   (2) Show the effect of a decrease in the stock of money. Interest rates _increase_.
   (3) Show the effect of an increase in both the demand for and supply of money by the same amount. Interest rates _increase_. unchanged

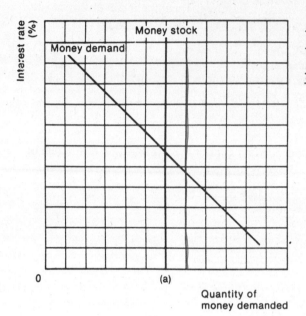

(a)

Quantity of money demanded

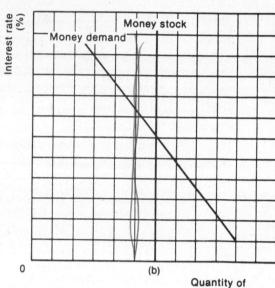

(b)

Quantity of money demanded

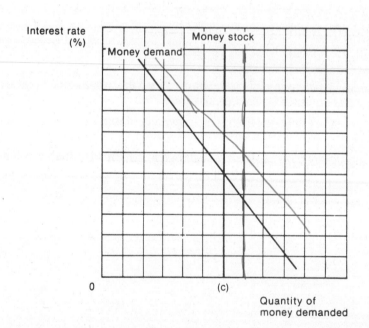

(c)

Quantity of money demanded

240

Advanced Application: The Supply of and Demand for Money

7. Let the supply of and demand for money be given by the equations below.

   MT = a - bR   where MT   = transaction demand
   MA = c - dR   MA   = asset demand
   MS = M1   MS   = money stock
                  M1   = currency, checkable deposits, and
                                traveler's checks held by the public
                  R   = interest rate

   Constants a and c reflect the impact of noninterest rate determinants on the transaction and asset money demands, respectively. Constants b and d are the slope terms indicating the magnitude of the effect that a change in R has on MT and MA, respectively.

   a. Find an equation for the total demand for money, MD.
   b. Find an equation for the equilibrium interest rate. (Hint: The condition for equilibrium is that MD = MS.)
   c. Using your equation for R, discuss the factors that cause R to rise or fall.
   d. Given the values below, plot MA, MT, and MD on the figure below. Draw in the money stock curve. Identify on the diagram the equilibrium rate of interest.

   a = $800 billion b = $10 billion c = $400 billion
   d = $40 billion M1 = $850 billion

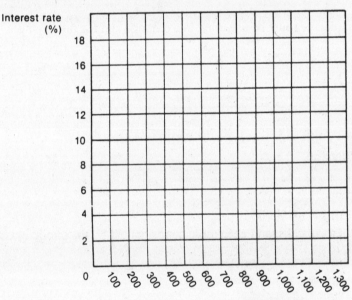

Select the best answer.

1. Money allows dissimilar goods and services to be valued according to a single common denominator—a nation's basic monetary unit, such as the dollar. Which of the following represent this function?
   a. Medium of exchange
   b. Store of value
   c. Standard of value
   d. Standard of deferred payment

2. Money is an asset. Which of the following represents this function?
   a. Medium of exchange
   b. Store of value
   c. Standard of value
   d. Standard of deferred payment

3. _____ money has value in exchange and intrinsic value in nonmoney uses.
   a. Fiat
   b. Commodity
   c. Valuable
   d. All

4. Money that, by government decree must be accepted in exchange and for the payment of debt is known as:
   a. fiat money.
   b. commodity money.
   c. demand deposits.
   d. gold.

5. One function of money that credit cards are unable to fulfill is the:
   a. medium of exchange function.
   b. store of value function.
   c. standard of value function.
   d. standard of deferred payment function.

6. The sum of currency, traveler's checks, and checkable deposits held by the public is known as:
   a. M1.
   b. M2.
   c. M3.
   d. L.

7. The sum of currency, traveler's checks, checkable deposits, and certain near monies held by the public is known as:
   a. M1.
   b. M2.
   c. M3.
   d. L.

8. _____ are assets that can easily be converted to money because they can be liquidated easily, quickly, and at little cost.
   a. Large-denomination certificates of deposit
   b. Near monies
   c. Pension funds
   d. Real estate

9. Individuals and businesses hold money because:
   a. money is necessary to carry out transactions, and it is also an asset.
   b. it is profitable to do so.
   c. it must be used to make exchanges.
   d. nothing else can be used in a commercial transaction.

10. Which of the following financial characteristics makes money attractive as an asset?
    a. Liquidity
    b. Return or yield
    c. Risk
    d. Availability

11. A/An _____ in nominal GDP shifts the money demand curve _____.
    a. decrease, rightward
    b. increase, leftward
    c. decrease, leftward
    d. increase, rightward
    e. c and d.

12. Which of the following will shift the money demand curve leftward?
    a. Payments and receipts become more synchronized.
    b. The price level declines.
    c. The level of nominal GDP decreases.
    d. All of the above.

13. The quantity of money demanded varies _____ with the nominal interest rate. Higher interest rates _____ the opportunity cost of holding money and therefore reduce the quantity of money demanded.
    a. directly, reduce
    b. inversely, increase
    c. directly, increase
    d. inversely, reduce

14. An increase in the stock of money creates a _____ of money at the current rate of interest. This in turn_____ the supply of loanable funds, which, given the demand for loanable funds, causes the market rate of interest to _____.
    a. shortage, reduces, rise
    b. shortage, reduces, fall
    c. surplus, reduces, rise
    d. surplus, increases, fall

15. A decrease in the stock of money causes interest rates to:
    a. fall.
    b. rise.
    c. not change.
    d. None of the above.

16. If the demand for money and the stock of money increased by the same amount at each interest rate, interest rates would:
    a. fall.
    b. rise.
    c. not change.
    d. None of the above.

17. If the demand for money decreases, interest rates will _____ and nominal GDP will _____.
    a. fall, fall
    b. rise, fall
    c. fall, rise
    d. rise, rise

18. If nominal GDP increases and there is greater synchronization of receipts and expenditures, what will happen to the transaction demand for money?
    a. The demand for money for transactions increases.
    b. The demand for money for transactions decreases.
    c. The demand for money for transactions does not change.
    d. The change in the transactions demand for money is indeterminate.

19. If there are expectations of higher future interest rates the:
    a. transactions demand for money increases.
    b. asset demand for money increases.
    c. asset demand for money decreases.
    d. transactions demand for money decreases.

20. If nominal GDP decreases and there are expectations of lower future interest rates, the demand for money would be expected to:
    a. decrease.
    b. increase.
    c. not change.
    d. be indeterminate.

Answer the following two questions based upon the data below.

Money Demand ($ billions)	Money Stock ($ billions)	Interest Rate
$2,000	$800	6%
1,600	800	8
1,200	800	10
800	800	12
400	800	14

21. Given the data above, what is the equilibrium rate of interest?
    a. 14%
    b. 12%
    c. 10%
    d. 8%
    e. 6%

22. Given the data above, an increase in nominal income _____ the demand for money by $400 billion at each interest rate, causing the equilibrium interest rate to _____ to _____ %.
    a. increases, increase, 14%
    b. increases, decrease, 10%
    c. decreases, decrease, 8%
    d. decreases, increase, 12%

■ THINK IT THROUGH

1. Can you think of any problems associated with the use of commodity money?

2. Why can't government bureaucrats simply make up their minds and select a single definition of money? Can you think of any reasons why there are several official definitions and why these definitions change over time?

3. Why do individuals and businesses hold money? What factors influence the desirability of holding money?

4. Suppose you are a producer of household appliances. Further assume that most appliance purchases are made on credit. You also have observed in the past that sales increase when nominal GDP increases. What would you predict for sales if you knew that the nation's central banking authorities were deliberately reducing the stock of money?

■ CHAPTER ANSWERS

The Chapter in Brief

1. Exchange 2. Value 3. Commodity 4. Not 5. Checkable 6. Large- 7. Increase 8. Opportunity cost
9. Liquid 10. Precautionary 11. Inversely 12. Increase 13. Downward sloping 14. Surplus 15. More
16. Increase 17. Increases 18. Decrease 19. Fall 20. Increases

Key Terms Review

1. Fiat money 2. Credit unions 3. Near monies 4. M3 5. Transaction demand for money 6. Money
demand curve 7. Change in money demanded 8. Commodity money 9. Mutual savings banks
10. M1 11. Time deposits 12. Demand for money 13. Money 14. Savings and loan associations
15. Bonds 16. M2 17. Commercial banks 18. Checkable deposits

Concept Review

1. a. Medium of exchange
   b. Store of value
   c. Standard of value
   d. Standard of deferred payment

2. a. M1 = currency + traveler's checks + checkable deposits held by the public.
   b. M2 = M1 + money market mutual funds + money market deposit accounts + savings
      accounts, small-denomination certificates of deposit, and certain other near monies.
   c. M3 = M2 + large-denomination certificates of deposit.
   d. Near monies = money market mutual funds + money market deposit accounts + savings
      accounts, small-denomination certificates of deposit, and certain other near monies.
   e. Commodity
   f. Fiat
   g. Money is an asset, whereas a liability or debt is incurred when credit cards are used.
      Credit cards do not satisfy the store of value function of money.

3. a. (1) Nominal GDP (2) Synchronization of receipts and payments
      (3) Interest rates
   b. (1) Interest rates (2) Expectations of inflation
      (3) Expectations of interest rates and bond prices

4. a.

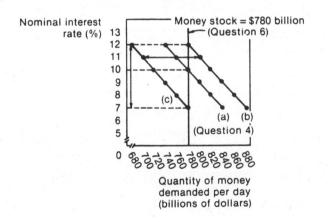

246

b.   The money demand curve is downward sloping because the nominal interest rate and the quantity of money demanded are inversely related. As interest rates rise, the opportunity cost of holding money increases, which reduces the desirability of holding noninterest-bearing or low interest-yielding assets such as money.

c.   (1) Synchronization of receipts and payments (2) Changes in real GDP (3) Changes in the price level (4) Expectations of inflation, interest rates, and bond prices

d.

(1)	(2) Rightward		e. (1)	(2) Leftward
	$780			$680
	800			700
	820			720
	840			740
	860			760
	880			780

5. a.   Left b. Left c. Left d. Left e. Right f. Right g. Left

6. a.   10% b. Increase, 12% c. Decrease, 7%

   d.   (1) Decrease (2) Increase (3) Remain unchanged

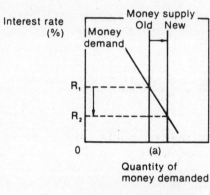

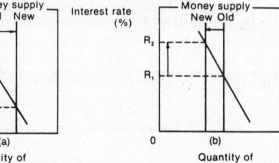

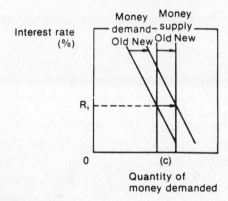

247

7. a. $MD = MT + MA = (a + c) - (b + d)R$

b. Equilibrium requires that $MD = MS$
$$M1 = (a + c) - (b + d)R$$
Solving for R gives
$$R = (a + c)/(b + d) - [1/(b + d)] \times M1$$

c. The negative sign preceding the last term in the interest rate equation shows that the stock of money, M1, is inversely related to the equilibrium interest rate. Notice that the shift terms, a and c, appear in the intercept of the interest rate equation. Any noninterest rate determinant of MT or MA that increases (a + c) will increase the interest rate. A change in one of these determinants that reduces (a + c) will reduce the interest rate. Likewise, changes in the slope of the transaction and asset money demand curves will change the interest rate.

d. $MT = 800 - 10R$ $MA = 400 - 40R$ $MD = 1200 - 50R$
$$R = 24 - (1/50)MD$$

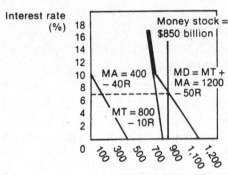

Interest rate (%)

Money stock = $850 billion

MA = 400 − 40R

MD = MT + MA = 1200 − 50R

MT = 800 − 10R

Quantity of money demanded (billions of dollars)

Mastery Test

1. c 2. b 3. b 4. a 5. b 6. a 7. b 8. b 9. a 10. a 11. e 12. d 13. b 14. d 15. b 16. c 17. c 18. d 19. b 20. a
21. b 22. a

Think it Through

1. Besides being difficult or hazardous to transport, such as was the case with gold and silver coins, commodity money often disappears from circulation when the market value of the commodity rises above the exchange value of money.

2. As new financial instruments are created such as NOW accounts and money market mutual funds, individuals in their own self-interest alter the composition of assets that are used to meet liquidity, risk, and income needs. Utility-maximizing choices lead us to use certain items to fulfill the functions of money. As long as financial innovations continue to occur and as long as the characteristics of assets change relative to one another, the money stock will continue to evolve. As a result, the central banking authorities must continually redefine money.

3. Individuals hold money (a) as an asset because it is liquid and (b) because it is an efficient way to consummate transactions. The demand for money is inversely related to the interest rate because an increase in the interest rate increases the opportunity cost of holding money and reduces the quantity of money demanded. Other factors that influence the demand for money include the synchronization of receipts and payments, the level of real GDP, the price level, and expectations of inflation, interest rates, and bond prices.

4. If the money stock decreases, it is likely that, other things being equal, interest rates will rise, making credit more costly to your customers. Total spending and GDP will decrease due to the higher rates of interest. Two factors therefore indicate that household appliance sales will fall: higher interest rates making credit more expensive, and a decline in nominal GDP.

14 THE BANKING SYSTEM

■ CHAPTER CONCEPTS

After studying your text, attending class, and completing this chapter, you should be able to:

1. Discuss the origins of banking and explain the concept of fractional reserve banking.
2. Examine bank balance sheets and show how the balance sheets are affected when the bank makes loans.
3. Show how multiple expansion of the money stock can result from an inflow of excess reserves into banks and calculate the reserve multiplier.
4. Discuss bank portfolio management practices.

■ THE CHAPTER IN BRIEF

Fill in the blanks to summarize chapter content.

In order to understand the role of money and financial institutions in the economy, it is necessary first to understand how the activities of financial institutions influence the nation's stock of money. The goldsmiths of England and the moneychangers of Italy engaged in "banking" by accepting gold for safekeeping and issuing gold receipts. In time, the receipts began to trade as a medium of exchange or money. But these early bankers discovered that (1) _Only a fraction_ (all of the, only a fraction of the) gold had to be held in reserve at any one time to honor redemption of the gold receipts. They could therefore make loans (2) _in excess_ (equal to, in excess of) the gold they had on hand. They did this by issuing additional gold receipts—they in essence created money. The fractional reserve banking that developed meant that the stock of money (3) _could be larger_ (must equal, could be larger than) the gold reserves upon which it was based.

In depository institutions today, only a fraction of the funds acquired through deposits have to be kept back as reserves. A bank's (4) _total_ (total, required) reserves consist of cash and deposits held at a regional Federal Reserve Bank. But banks and other depository institutions that issue checkable deposits are required to keep reserves equal to between 3% and 12% of various deposit liabilities. A bank will balance profit, liquidity, and risk considerations in deciding the amount of (5) _excess_ (total, excess) reserves it desires to use to acquire income-producing assets such as loans and government securities. Excess reserves are the difference between total reserves and required reserves. While a depository institution does not have to use all of its excess reserves, it (6) _cannot_ (can, cannot) make loans or purchase securities in amounts greater than the amount it has as excess reserves. When a bank uses excess reserves to make a loan, new checkable deposits are created—money is created. Even if the borrower spends the proceeds of the loan by writing a check, the funds eventually end up in the check recipient's checkable deposit account elsewhere in the banking system.

An individual bank can increase checkable deposits or the money supply to the extent of its excess reserves by (7) _making loans_ (making loans or purchasing securities, advertising bank services), but the banking system as a whole can increase the stock of money by (8) _a multiple_ (less than, a multiple of) its excess reserves. For instance, when a bank makes a loan, not only does it create new checkable deposits somewhere in the banking system, but it also passes excess reserves to other banks through the (9) _financial_ (financial, check clearing) system. Banks receiving deposits and reserves likewise make loans, increasing deposits and passing excess reserves to still other banks, which in turn do the same.

Each bank, however, has to keep some percentage of the new deposits back as required reserves, thus reducing the quantity of excess reserves available for loans and the quantity of reserves passed on to other banks. The percentage of deposit liabilities that must be held back is called the (10) _required reserve ratio_ (required reserve ratio, discount rate). This process of deposit growth continues until there are no additional excess reserves in the system. At this point banks are (11) _"loaned up"_ (deficient, "loaned up"), meaning they have no excess reserves and can no longer make loans and create money. The stock of checkable deposits (money) can potentially expand by the reciprocal of the required reserve ratio times the quantity of excess reserves. The reciprocal of the required reserve ratio is known as the (12) _reserve multiplier_ (reserve multiplier, expansion coefficient). The process works just the opposite when banks find that their total reserves are less than required reserves. To acquire reserves or reduce required reserves in order to eliminate this deficiency, banks engage in activities that (13) _increase_ (increase, reduce) the volume of checkable deposits.

Banks will often hold some excess reserves to meet both expected and unexpected deposit outflows. Because banks do not use all of their excess reserves, the money supply is (14) _smaller_ (larger, smaller) than it would be otherwise. The willingness to hold excess reserves depends, in part, on the interest rate. The interest rate is the opportunity cost of holding excess reserves. When interest rates are high, such as in the latter stages of an economic expansion, the opportunity cost of holding non-interest bearing reserves is also high, causing bankers to (15) _increase_ (reduce, increase) excess reserve balances. The money supply increases when interest rates rise. The opposite holds when interest rates are low. Banks will use a portion of their excess reserves to make overnight loans to banks in need of reserves. These loaned excess reserves are called (16) _federal funds_ (Treasury funds, federal funds).

As of the early 1990s, U.S. banks had (17) _secondary_ (primary, secondary) reserves or government securities and other liquid securities equalling about 20% of total assets. Loans accounted for (18) _2/3_ (two-thirds, one-third) of total assets. Deposits accounted for (19) _40%_ (40%, over 70%) of net worth.

■ KEY TERMS REVIEW

Write the key term from the list below next to its definition.

Key Terms

Depository institutions   Excess reserves
Bank   Default
Financial intermediaries   Check clearing
Fractional reserve banking   Reserve multiplier
Fractional reserve ratio   Prime rate
Reserves   Collateral
Required reserve ratio   Government securities
Required reserves   Secondary reserves

Definitions

1. *intermediaries* : firms that specialize in borrowing funds from savers and lending those funds to investors and others.

2. *Frational banking* : a process by which a banking system creates checkable deposits by making loans in some multiple of the reserves it actually has on hand to pay withdrawals.

3. *reserves* : balances (of a modern U.S. bank) kept on deposit with the Federal Reserve Bank in its district or as currency in its vault.

4. *default* : nonrepayment of the principal and interest on a loan.

5. *check clearing* : the process of transferring Federal Reserve deposits among banks as checks are paid.

6. *reserve multiplier* : the maximum amount of new money stock that can be created from each dollar increase in excess reserves available to the banking system.

7. *secondary reserves* : government securities held by banks.

8. *depository* : a commercial bank or thrift institution that offers checkable deposits. [*bank* written in margin]

9. *Fractional ratio* : the ratio of actual reserves to total receipts for deposits.

10. *excess reserves* : the difference between total reserves and required reserves of a bank held against deposits.

11. *securities* : interest-bearing debts of the federal government in the form of Treasury bills, Treasury notes, and Treasury bonds.

12. *Bank* : Institutions that make loans and offer checkable deposit and time deposit accounts for use by households and business firms. [*dep* written in margin]

13. *required reserves* : the dollar value of currency and deposits in Federal Reserve Banks that a bank must hold to meet current regulations.

14. *collateral* : an asset a borrower pledges to a bank in case of default.

15. *required reserve ratio* : the minimum percentage of deposits that a bank must hold in reserves to comply with regulatory requirements.

16. __*prime rate*__ : the interest rate a bank charges its most credit worthy customers for short-term loans of less than 1 year.

■ CONCEPT REVIEW

Concept 2: *Examine a bank's balance sheet; impact of making a loan on the balance sheet*

1. Identify the following as either an asset (A) or a liability (L) of a commercial bank.

    a. __L__ Certificates of deposit   A g. __L__ Reserve deposits at
A b. __L__ Cash   Federal Reserve
A c. __L__ Total reserves   h. __A__ Loans
    d. __A__ Bank building and property i. __A__ Government securities
    e. __L__ Checkable deposits   j. __L__ Borrowings
    f. __L__ Time and saving deposits

2. a. Discuss the logic of the basic accounting identity.
   b. Why must balance sheets balance at a given point in time?

3. Given a balance sheet for a commercial bank, answer parts a-d assuming a required reserve ratio on checkable deposits of 10%.

Assets		Liabilities and Net Worth	
Cash	$ 200	Checkable deposits	$ 2,000
Reserve deposits	550	Savings and time	
Loans	6,700	deposits	5,000
Securities	1,840	Borrowings	2,400
Bank building		Net worth	600
and property	710		
Total Assets	$10,000	Total Liabilities and Net Worth	$10,000

   a. Total reserves = __750__ .
   b. Required reserves = __200__ .
   c. Excess reserves = __550__ .
   d. This bank can make loans of $__550__ .

4. Reserve deposits, loans, and checkable deposits are reproduced from the balance sheet above in the balance sheet below.

Assets		Liabilities and Net Worth	
Reserve deposits	$ 550	Checkable deposits	$2,000
Loans	6,700		

   a. Indicate on the balance sheet above the impact of a loan of $550 to one of the bank's customer-depositors. Designate your entries with an (a). (Hint: For every entry there must be an offsetting entry.) Total assets have __increased__ to $__10550__ , and total liabilities have __increased__ to $__10 550__ .

b. Assume now that the customer spends the proceeds of the loan by writing a check to a merchant for $550. Assume that the merchant deposits the check in a bank in the same Federal Reserve district and the check is routed to the Fed and back to the originating bank via the check clearing process. Indicate the impact of this on the balance sheet above and designate your entries with a (b). This bank's checkable deposits have _decreased_ to $ _2000_ , but total reserves have _fallen_ to $ _200_ . Excess reserves equal $ _0_ . Total loans equal $ _7250_ .

c. Can this bank make loans in excess of its excess reserves? Why? _No_

d. As a result of this loan, the stock of money has _increased_ by $ _550_ .

Concept 3: *Multiple expansion of the money stock*

5. The following assumptions pertain to the banking system:
   i.   Commercial Bank A has $100 in excess reserves.
   ii. Required reserve ratio = 20%
   iii. Other banks are presently "loaned up."
   iv. All banks use all of their excess reserves to make loans.
   v.   Bank A makes loans to its customers that, after the check clearing process, end up as deposits in Bank B. Similarly, Bank B makes loans to its customers that end up as deposits in Bank C, and so on.

   a. Make the final entries on each bank's balance sheet assuming initially that Bank A makes a loan to the extent of its excess reserves. Trace the impact from Bank A through Bank D on the balance sheets below. (The final entries are after banks have loaned excess reserves, customers have spent the proceeds of the loans, and the checks have cleared.)

Bank A

Assets	Liabilities and Net Worth
Reserve deposits −160	Checkable deposits
Loans 100	

Bank B

Assets	Liabilities and Net Worth
Reserve deposits 20	Checkable deposits 100
Loans 80	

Bank C

Assets	Liabilities and Net Worth
Reserve deposits 16	Checkable deposits 80
Loans 64	

Bank D

Assets	Liabilities and Net Worth
Reserve deposits 12.8	Checkable deposits 64
Loans 51.2	

$$\frac{64}{.2} = 12.8$$

b. Complete the following table.

Bank	Change in Required Reserves	Change in Money Stock
A	—	—
B	20	100
C	16	80
D	12.8	64

c. The expansion of the money supply continues until the _increase in RR_ just equals the initial excess reserves of $100. At this point, excess reserves in the banking system equal $_0_. When this occurs, the money stock has increased by $_500_.

6. Find the change in the money stock for the banking system by filling in the blanks below.

	Required Reserve Ratio	Change in Excess Reserves	Change in Checkable Deposits
a.	.1	+$1 billion	10 bill.
b.	.2	0	0
c.	.25	-$500 million	-2 bill
d.	.4	+$10 billion	25 bill
e.	.5	-$5 billion	-10 bill

Insights on Issues:

7. According to Edward Kane, what is the condition of the U.S. financial system?

Select the best answer.

1. Early bankers, the goldsmiths of England and the moneychangers of Italy, accepted deposits of gold for safekeeping and in return issued gold receipts. These early bankers were similar to modern bankers in that:
   a. they created a medium of exchange.
   b. they had a fractional reserve (gold) system.
   c. they accepted deposits and made loans.
   d. gold receipts (medium of exchange) could be issued in greater volume than the gold (reserves) upon which they were based.
   e. All of the above.

2. The fractional reserve system means that:
   a. only a fraction of bank assets at any one time may be used to create money.
   b. a bank receives only a fraction of the reserves that it needs at any given time.
   c. only a fraction of a bank's liabilities must be held back as reserves to meet withdrawals at any one time.
   d. None of the above.

3. A bank's total reserves consist of:
   a. liquid assets such as private commercial paper and treasury bills.
   b. cash and treasury bills.
   c. cash only.
   d. cash and reserve deposits held at a regional Federal Reserve Bank.

4. A bank's required reserves are determined by:
   a. multiplying the required reserve ratio by certain deposit liabilities.
   b. dividing total assets by net worth.
   c. dividing the required reserve ratio into demand deposits.
   d. the U.S. Treasury.
   e. a and d.

5. The difference between total and required reserves is known as:
   a. the required reserve ratio.
   b. fractional reserves.
   c. extra reserves.
   d. excess reserves.

6. Excess reserves are important to a banker because:
   a. if they are not met, the banking regulators will shut the bank down.
   b. they represent the funds available to acquire income-producing assets such as loans and securities.
   c. they are typically deposited in special high-yielding investment accounts.
   d. they are the profits that are divided among the bank's owners.

7. An individual bank can create deposits to the extent of its:
   a. excess reserves.
   b. required reserves.
   c. total reserves.
   d. deposits.
   e. net worth.

8. A bank is "loaned up" when:
   a. deposits are no longer coming in.
   b. excess reserves are negative.
   c. excess reserves are zero.
   d. total reserves are zero.

9. The banking system can increase the stock of money by an amount _____ an increase in excess reserves.
   a. less than
   b. the same as
   c. greater than
   d. less than or equal to

10. The reserve multiplier is the:
    a. ratio of required reserves to total reserves.
    b. required reserve ratio multiplied by certain deposit liabilities.
    c. number by which the total stock of reserves changes given a change in excess reserves.
    d. number by which the total stock of money changes given a change in excess reserves.

11. The reciprocal of the required reserve ratio is the:
    a. depository institutions capital ratio.
    b. reserve multiplier.
    c. bank's required reserves.
    d. measure of excess reserves that the banker desires to use to make loans.

12. Assume that a bank in the banking system has $1,000 in total reserves and $5,000 in checkable deposits, and the required reserve ratio on checkable deposits is 10%. This bank's excess reserves equal:
    a. zero; it is loaned up.
    b. $250
    c. $500
    d. $750

13. Assume that a bank in the banking system has $2 million in reserves and checkable deposits of $9 million, and the required reserve ratio on checkable deposits is 20%. The maximum amount of loans this bank can make is:
    a. $1 million.
    b. $500,000
    c. $700,000
    d. $200,000

14. Assume that a bank in the banking system has $1 billion in reserves and checkable deposits of $6 billion, and the required reserve ratio on checkable deposits is 10%. The maximum amount by which the banking system can expand the money supply is:
    a. $4 billion.
    b. $6 billion.
    c. $8 billion.
    d. $10 billion.

15. Total reserves of the banking system of $400 billion could potentially support
    $_____ of checkable deposits assuming a required reserve ratio of 25%.
    a. $400 billion
    b. $700 billion
    c. $1200 billion
    d. $1600 billion

16. If a banking system is loaned up and the Federal Reserve engages in activities that withdraw reserves from the system:
    a. the money supply will expand.
    b. the money supply will decrease.
    c. the FDIC will intervene to replace the reserves.
    d. checkable deposits will increase.

17. As of the early 1990s, U.S. banks on average held _____ of their total assets as loans.
    a. two-thirds
    b. three-fourths
    c. one-fourth
    d. one-half
    e. one-fifth

18. Secondary reserves consist of:
    a. cash.
    b. cash and government securities.
    c. cash, reserve deposits, and government securities.
    d. government securities and other liquid securities.

Answer the following questions based upon the bank balance sheet shown below. (Assume that the required reserve ratio is 10%)

Assets		Liabilities and Net Worth	
Cash	$ 600	Checkable deposits	$ 6,000
Reserve deposits	1,650	Savings and time	
Loans	20,100	deposits	15,000
Securities	5,520	Borrowings	7,200
Bank building		Net Worth	1,800
and property	2,130		
Total Assets	$30,000	Total Liabilities	$30,000
		and Net Worth	

19. For the bank described in the balance sheet above, how much can this bank safely expand its loan portfolio?
    a. $2,250
    b. $2,000
    c. $600
    d. $1,650

20. If the manager of the bank described above regularly holds excess reserves equal to 5% of checkable deposits, how much can this bank safely expand its securities portfolio?
    a. $1,350
    b. $500
    c. $1,950
    d. $1,700

21. If the balance sheet shown above is a consolidated balance sheet for the banking system as a whole, what is the potential expansion of the money supply?
    a. $16,500
    b. $22,500
    c. $8,250
    d. $11,250

22. If the bank described above has total reserves of $300, it would likely:
    a. make additional loans.
    b. purchase securities and call in loans.
    c. sell assets or borrow.
    d. make loans and purchase securities.

23. If the balance sheet above is a consolidated balance sheet for the banking system and if total reserves are $300, the money supply will _____ by_____
    a. increase, $300
    b. decrease, $3,000
    c. decrease, $2,700
    d. increase, $600

■ THINK IT THROUGH

1. Discuss the philosophy behind fractional reserve banking. What is the implication of fractional reserve banking for the multiple expansion of the money stock in terms of the role of depository institutions?

2. Suppose you are a banker and you have difficulty predicting deposits and withdrawals. At times you unexpectedly experience large withdrawals from checkable deposits. How might this influence your decision to use excess reserves? If there are many other bankers like you in the banking system, how might the deposit expansion process be affected?

3. Why can't a bank make loans in amounts greater than the bank's excess reserves? What would happen if more loans were extended than could be supported by excess reserves?

4. Discuss the reserve multiplier and the multiple expansion of the money stock.

5. What is the significance of the Depository Institutions Deregulation and Monetary Control Act of 1980 for the money expansion process?

CHAPTER ANSWERS

The Chapter in Brief

1. Only a fraction of the 2. In excess of 3. Could be larger than 4. Total 5. Excess 6. Cannot 7. Making loans or purchasing securities 8. A multiple of 9. Check clearing 10. Required reserve ratio 11. "Loaned up" 12. Reserve multiplier 13. Reduce 14. Smaller 15. Reduce 16. Federal funds 17. Secondary 18. Two-thirds 19. Over 70%

Key Terms Review

1. Financial intermediaries 2. Fractional reserve banking 3. Reserves 4. Default 5. Check clearing 6. Reserve multiplier 7. Secondary reserves 8. Bank 9. Fractional reserve ratio 10. Excess reserves 11. Government securities 12. Depository institutions 13. Required reserves 14. Collateral 15. Required reserve ratio 16. Prime rate

Concept Review

1. a. L b. A c. A d. A e. L f. L g. A h. A i. A j. L

2. a. Assets must be exactly equal to the sum of liabilities and net worth. Assets are acquired with funds that you either own or borrow. For a depository institution, assets represent the uses of funds and deposits, and borrowings and net worth represent the sources of funds.

   b. For the accounting identity to hold, any change in assets or liabilities and net worth must have an offsetting change in the asset or liability and net worth accounts on the balance sheet. Therefore, regardless of the entries made to a balance sheet, the offsetting entries ensure that the two sides of the balance sheet always balance.

3. a. $750 b. $200 c. $550 d. $550

4. a.

Assets		Liabilities and Net Worth	
Reserve deposits	$ 550	Checkable deposits	$2,000
	(b) -550		(a) 550
Loans	6,700		(b) -550
	(a) 550		

   Increased, $10,550; increased, $10,550

   b. Decreased, $2000; fallen, $200, $0; $7,250

   c. No. If this bank makes loans in excess of its excess reserves, $550, then after borrowers spend the proceeds of the loans and the checks clear, the bank will not have enough total reserves to meet its legal reserve requirement.

   d. Increased, $550

5. a. Bank A

Assets		Liabilities and Net Worth	
Reserve deposits	-$100	Checkable deposits	
Loans	100		

   Bank B

Assets		Liabilities and Net Worth	
Reserve deposits	$20	Checkable deposits	$100
Loans	80		

Bank C

Assets		Liabilities and Net Worth	
Reserve deposits	$16	Checkable deposits	$80
Loans	64		

Bank D

Assets		Liabilities and Net Worth	
Reserve deposits	$12.8	Checkable deposits	$64
Loans	51.2		

b.

A	—	—
B	$20	$100
C	16	80
D	12.8	64

c. Increase in required reserves; $0; $500

6. a. $10 billion b. $0 c. -$2 billion d. $25 billion e.

-$10 billion

7. Although there were record bank profits in 1992, the FDIC identified over 800 banks as "troubled." Some of these were technically insolvent and as many as one-third will fail. Some of these banks were not identified earlier even though they had problems because of certain accounting practices that overstate profits and net worth. Failed banks impose losses on the FDIC and therefore indirectly on healthy banks and possibly on taxpayers. In response to these concerns, the FDIC Improvement Act of 1991 was passed to shore up bank capital.

Mastery Test

1. e 2. a 3. d 4. a 5. d 6. b 7. a 8. c 9. c 10. d 11. b 12. c 13. d 14. a 15. d 16. b 17. a 18. d 19. d 20. a 21. a 22. c 23. b

Think It Through

1. On any given day, deposit withdrawals are only a fraction of total deposits. Therefore, to meet withdrawals banks need to keep only a fraction of total assets in the form of liquid assets such as cash and reserve deposits. The upshot of this is that banks can create deposits by making loans with excess reserves and the banking system can create a money stock that is a multiple of the reserve base upon which it rests.

2. Given the uncertainty regarding the fluctuations in checkable deposit balances, it would be wise to maintain a cushion of excess reserves as a contingency against deposit outflows that might otherwise put the bank in a deficient reserve position. Of course, in doing this you sacrifice potential income, but you also reduce the risk confronting the bank. For the banking system as a whole, this implies that some portion of excess reserves is held back, thus reducing the stock of money that can be supported by a given stock of bank reserves. The reserve multiplier will also be smaller.

3. If more loans were extended than could be funded with excess reserves, a bank would not be meeting its legal reserve requirement. This is because once the proceeds of the loans are spent and the checks clear, the bank loses total reserves equal to the loans—which are greater than excess reserves. The bank would then either have to increase total reserves by borrowing or

selling other assets, or it would have to reduce checkable deposits in order to reduce required reserves.

4. The expansion process occurs because of the fractional reserve system. A portion of a bank's excess reserves is passed on to other banks in the banking system as a result of loans and cleared checks. The only thing that prevents this expansion from occurring indefinitely is that some of the excess reserves must be held back as required reserves by those banks experiencing deposit inflows. Eventually all of the initial excess reserves will be absorbed in the banking system as required reserves, leaving none as excess reserves for further expansion of deposits. The process is an infinite geometric progression that can be solved yielding the reserve multiplier, 1/required reserve ratio, as part of the solution.

5. The act allows credit unions, savings and loan associations, and mutual savings banks to compete with banks for checkable deposits and consumer and business loans. The significance of the act for the money expansion process is that banks are no longer the only institutions that can create money by making loans. Now all depository institutions having checkable deposits can create money by making loans. The act also brings all depository institutions offering checkable deposits under uniform reserve ratios administered by the Federal Reserve System.

15 THE FEDERAL RESERVE SYSTEM AND ITS INFLUENCE ON MONEY AND CREDIT

■ CHAPTER CONCEPTS

After studying your text, attending class, and completing this chapter, you should be able to:

1. Discuss the organization and structure of the Federal Reserve System.
2. Discuss the techniques used by the Fed to influence the money supply.
3. Show how the Fed's open market operations affect bank reserves, securities prices, interest rates, and the money supply.
4. Analyze the nation's money supply curve and show how desires by banks to hold excess reserves affect the quantity of money supplied.

■ THE CHAPTER IN BRIEF

Fill in the blanks to summarize chapter content.

The Federal Reserve System was established in 1913. It consists of a Board of Governors, (1) __12__ (twelve, seven) regional Federal Reserve Banks and their branch banks, the Federal Open Market Committee, and the Federal Advisory Council. The Chairman of the Board of Governors is appointed by the President to a 4-year term, whereas the other (2) __6__ (three, six) board members are appointed to 14-year terms. The Federal Reserve Banks are owned by the member banks in their respective districts. The Federal (3) __Open Market__ (Advisory, Open Market) Committee is the principal policy-making body within the Federal Reserve System. It issues directives to the account manager at the trading desk of the New York Federal Reserve Bank to achieve some level of money growth during a given time period. The account manager does this by buying and selling U.S. government securities. The Fed is to some extent independent of the legislative and administrative levels of the federal government in that it does not rely upon Congressional funding, but instead earns its own operating revenues.

The supply of money equals the monetary base times the reserve multiplier. The (4) __monetary base__ (monetary base, reserve sum) is the sum of currency in the hands of the public and total bank reserves. Total checkable deposits equal total reserves times the reserve multiplier. The Fed can influence both the monetary base (volume of reserves) and the reserve multiplier. The money expansion process is also influenced by the decisions of bankers regarding the quantity of excess reserves that are held and not used to make loans. The Fed can influence the money supply in three ways: changing the required reserve ratio, changing the (5) __discount__ (interest, discount) rate, and either buying or selling U.S. government securities.

An/A (6) __increase__ (increase, decrease) in the reserve ratio does not affect total reserves, but it does reduce excess reserves and therefore contracts the money stock. An/A (7) __decrease__ (increase, decrease) in the reserve ratio increases excess reserves and the money stock. An/A (8) __decrease__ (increase, decrease) in the discount rate relative to the yields on short-term government securities reduces both total and excess reserves in the banking system and contracts the money supply. An/A (9) __increase__ (increase, decrease) in the discount rate increases total and excess reserves and increases the money stock. Open market (10) __sales__ (purchases, sales) of securities to banks reduce reserves, the monetary base, and the money supply. Open market (11) _purchases from_ (purchases from, sales to) banks or the public will increase reserves, the monetary base, and the money stock. The most important of the three tools of monetary control is (12) _open market ops_ (open market operations, the discount rate, the required reserve ratio). Changes in the discount rate are important but often lag behind rather than cause changes in interest rates. The required reserve ratio, while very powerful, is not used as a money management tool.

Open market transactions affect the economy immediately in that the Fed buys and sells such a large volume of securities that securities prices and their yields (interest rates) are affected. A Fed purchase of securities (13) _reduces_ (increases, reduces) the outstanding supply of securities held by the public and causes securities prices to (14) _fall_ (rise, fall) and interest rates to (15) _rise_ (rise, fall). A Fed sale of securities (16) _increases_ (increases, decreases) the supply of securities held by the public, which (17) _reduces_ (increases, reduces) securities prices and (18) _increases_ (increases, decreases) interest rates. But open market transactions also affect bank excess reserves and the total stock of money. As the supply of money changes relative to the demand for money, interest rates will change. A purchase of securities (19) _decreases_ (decreases, increases) excess reserves and (20) _decreases_ (decreases, increases) the supply of money relative to the demand for money causing the interest rate to (21) _fall_ (fall, rise). A sale of securities (22) _increase_ (increases, reduces) excess reserves and the supply of money relative to the demand for money and causes the interest rate to (23) _increase_ (decrease, increase).

The supply of money is positively related to the interest rate because of the relationship between the interest rate and bankers' propensities to hold some excess reserves rather than use them for loans. Interest rates rise as the economy approaches a higher level of economic activity, but this is the time when loan demand is strong and the opportunity cost of holding noninterest-bearing assets is high. Therefore bankers (24) _reduce_ (reduce, increase) their holdings of excess reserves. Just the opposite is generally true of recessions. The demand for loans is less, interest rates are lower, and the opportunity cost of holding reserves is lower. Bankers prefer to hold (25) _more_ (less, more) excess reserves in recessions. So when interest rates are high, excess reserves held are (26) _larger_ (smaller, larger) and the stock of money is correspondingly (27) _larger_ (smaller, larger). Conversely, at lower rates of interest, excess reserves held are (28) _smaller_ (smaller, larger) and the stock of money is (29) _smaller_ (larger, smaller). This produces a/an (30) _upward_ (vertical, upward sloping) money supply curve.

KEY TERMS REVIEW

Write the key term from the list below next to its definition.

Key Terms

Board of Governors of the
 Federal Reserve System
Regional Federal Reserve banks
Monetary base
Federal Open Market Committee

Discount rate
Open market operations
Discount loans
Money supply

Definitions

1. _FOMC_ : an arm of the Federal Reserve System; affects the amount of excess reserves available to banks by instructing the Federal Reserve Bank of New York to buy or sell government securities on the open market.

2. _Monetary base_ : the sum of currency in circulation and total bank reserves outstanding at any given time.

3. _Open market op/s_ : the Federal Reserve System's purchases and sales of government securities, conducted by the Federal Open Market Committee.

4. _discount loans_ : bank borrowings from the Federal Reserve System; also called *advances*.

5. _Money Supply_ : a relationship between the quantity of money supplied in the form of currency and checkable deposits and the level of interest rates prevailing at a given point in time.

6. _Reg. Fed. Res. banks_ : perform central banking functions for banks within each of 12 Federal Reserve districts.

7. _discount rate_ : the interest rate Federal Reserve Banks charge member banks for loans.

8. _Governors_ : supervises the operation of the nation's banking system and acts as an authority to regulate the money supply; consists of seven members, each appointed by the President to serve a 14-year term.

CONCEPT REVIEW

Concepts 2 and 3: *Techniques to control the money stock*

1. Determine what happens to checkable deposits in the banking system if the Fed lowers the required reserve ratio from 20% to 19%, total reserves equal $200 billion, and banks are presently loaned up. (Hint: Total checkable deposits = reserve multiplier X total reserves.)

   a. Reserve multiplier (reserve ratio = 20%) = _5_
   b. Checkable deposits (reserve ratio = 20%) = _1000 bill_
   c. Reserve multiplier (reserve ratio = 19%) = _5.26_
   d. Checkable deposits (reserve ratio = 19%) = _1052 bill_

   $= 5 \times 200$

   $\frac{200\ 000\ 000\ 000}{5}$

   $1,000,000,000,000$

2. **a.** Complete the table.

Reserve Ratio	Reserve Multiplier	Total Reserves	Checkable Deposits
.1	10	$100 billion	$ 1000 bill
.2	5	100	500 mill
.25	4	100 reduces	400 mill

    b. An increase in the required reserve ratio _increases_ checkable deposits. A decrease in the reserve ratio _decreases_ checkable deposits.
increases

3. Below are balance sheets for the Federal Reserve and a commercial bank, Bank A. Assume that this and all other commercial banks are presently loaned up, no excess reserves are held, and the reserve ratio is 20%.

Federal Reserve

Assets	Liabilities and Net Worth
Loans to banks +10 mill	Deposits of banks 10 mill

Bank A

Assets	Liabilities and Net Worth
Reserve deposits 10 mill	Borrowings 10 mill

    a. Assume that Bank A borrows $10 million from the Fed. Make the appropriate entries in the balance sheets above.

    b. Bank A now has $ _10 mill_ in excess reserves and can extend loans equal to $ _10 mill_ .

    c. The banking system can increase checkable deposits by a maximum of $ _50 mill_ .

    d. If the Fed increases the discount rate relative to short-term interest rates (Treasury Bill rates), the volume of discounts _decreases_ , causing bank total and excess reserves to _fall_ , which causes a/an _decrease_ in checkable deposits.

    e. If the Fed decreases the discount rate relative to other short-term rates of interest, the volume of discounts _increase_ , causing bank total and excess reserves to _rise_ , which causes a/an _increase_ in checkable deposits.

4. Below are balance sheets for the Federal Reserve and Commercial Bank A. Assume that this and all other banks are loaned up, the current reserve ratio is 20%, and no excess reserves are held.

Federal Reserve

Assets	Liabilities and Net Worth
Securities 25 mill	Deposits of banks 25 mill

Bank A

Assets	Liabilities and Net Worth
Reserve deposits 25 mill	
Securities -25 mill	

    a. The Fed purchases $25 million of securities from Bank A. Make the appropriate entries on the balance sheets above.

    b. Bank A's total reserves _increase_ by $ _25 mill_ .

Bank A's required reserves _no change_ by $ _5 mill_.
Bank A's excess reserves _increase_ by $ _25 mill_.

c. Bank A can _increase_ loans by $ _25 mill_ and the banking system can _increase_ checkable deposits by $ _125 mill_.

d. If the Fed purchases securities from the public rather than a bank, would the impact on checkable deposits be any different from that which you showed in part c? _No_

e. Fed purchases of U.S. government securities _increase_ bank excess reserves and the monetary base and _increase_ the money stock.

5. Suppose the Fed sells $20 billion in U.S. government securities to banks. Assume the reserve ratio is 10% and banks are loaned up.

a. Make the appropriate entries on the balance sheets below.

Federal Reserve

Assets	Liabilities and Net Worth
Securities _−20 bill_	Deposits of banks _−20 bill_

All Banks

Assets	Liabilities and Net Worth
Reserve deposits _−20 bill_	
Securities _20 bill_	

b. Bank total reserves _decrease_ by $ _20 mill_.

c. Checkable deposits in the banking system _decrease_ by $ _200 bill_.

d. If the securities are sold to the public, total checkable deposits _decrease_ by $ _200 bill_ if the public pays for the securities with checks, but _does not fall_ if payments are made with cash.

e. Assuming no cash transactions, Fed sales of securities _decrease_ bank reserves and the monetary base and _decrease_ the money stock.

Concept 4:   *Money supply curve; equilibrium interest rate*

6. When interest rates rise, the quantity of excess reserves held and not used _decrease_, causing the supply of money to _increase_. When interest rates fall, the quantity of excess reserves held and not used _increase_ causing the supply of money to _decrease_. The relationship between the interest rate and the quantity of money supplied is a _inverse_ relationship, resulting in a _downward_ sloped money supply curve.
posit   _positive_

7. a. On the diagram below, show the effect of an increase in the stock of money.
An increase in the stock of money, given the demand for money, _decrease_ the equilibrium interest rate.

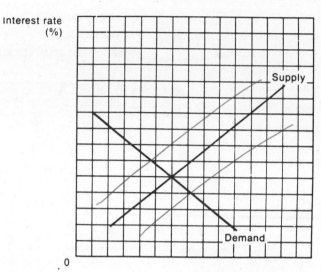

Interest rate
(%)

Supply

Demand

0

Quantity of money
supplied and demanded
(billions of dollars)

b. Show on the figure above the impact of a reduction in the supply of money. A decrease in
the stock of money, given the demand for money, _increase_ the equilibrium interest rate.

c. Indicate whether each of the following increases (+), decreases (-), or remains unchanged
(0).

Fed Policy	Change in Monetary Base	Change in Excess Reserves	Change in Checkable Deposits
1. Increase reserve ratio	0	—	—
2. Securities sales	—	—	—
3. Securities purchases	+	+	+
4. Decrease reserve ratio	0	+	+
5. Increase discount rate	—	—	—
6. Decrease discount rate	+	+	+

■ MASTERY TEST

Select the best answer.

1. The Board of Governors of the Federal Reserve System consists of how many members?

    a. 4

    b. 5

    c. 6

    d. 7

    e. 8

2. The principal policy-making body of the Federal Reserve System with regard to the regulation of the nation's money stock is the:

    a. Federal Advisory Committee.

    b. trading desk in New York.

    c. U.S. Treasury.

    d. Federal Open Market Committee.

3. The major asset of the Federal Reserve System is:

    a. bank deposits.

    b. government securities.

    c. treasury deposits.

    d. Federal Reserve notes.

    e. discounts and advances.

4. The major liability of the Federal Reserve System is:

    a. bank deposits.

    b. government securities.

    c. Treasury deposits.

    d. Federal Reserve notes.

    e. discounts and advances.

5. Which of the following is not a function of the Federal Reserve System?

    a. Regulation of the money supply

    b. Administering federal matching funds used in the banking industry

    c. Clearing checks

    d. Providing banks with currency and coin

    e. Making loans to banks

6. The sum of currency in circulation and total bank reserves equals the:

    a. total required reserves.

    b. money stock.

    c. total assets of the banking system.

    d. monetary base.

    e. money multiplier.

7. The Federal Reserve System controls the money supply primarily by controlling:
   a. the monetary base.
   b. checkable deposits.
   c. the interest rate.
   d. paper currency and coin.

8. An increase in the required reserve ratio _____ excess reserves and _____ the money stock.
   a. increases, decreases
   b. decreases, increases
   c. decreases, decreases
   d. increases, increases

9. A decrease in the discount rate _____ both total and excess reserves and _____ the money stock.
   a. increases, decreases
   b. decreases, increases
   c. decreases, decreases
   d. increases, increases

10. Sales of government securities to banks _____ total and excess reserves and _____ the money stock.
    a. increase, decrease
    b. decrease, increase
    c. decrease, decrease
    d. increase, increase

11. Federal Reserve purchases of securities _____ the money stock, and sales of securities _____ the money stock.
    a. increase, decrease
    b. increase, also increase
    c. decrease, increase
    d. decrease, also decrease

12. The most important tool for monetary control is:
    a. changing the reserve ratio.
    b. the interest rate.
    c. the discount rate.
    d. open market operations.

13. The least used tool of monetary control is:
    a. the reserve ratio policy.
    b. the interest rate.
    c. the discount rate.
    d. open market operations.
    e. the statutory ability to impose price controls.

14. An open market purchase of securities by the Fed will _____ the supply of securities and cause the price of securities to _____ and interest rates to _____.
    a. increase, increase, increase
    b. decrease, increase, decrease
    c. increase, increase, decrease
    d. decrease, decrease, increase

15. Which of the following best explains the slope of the money supply curve?
    a. Interest rates and loans are directly related.
    b. Interest rates and total bank reserves are inversely related.
    c. Interest rates and the monetary base are positively related.
    d. Interest rates vary inversely with excess reserves.

16. An increase in the supply of money, given the demand for money, will:
    a. at the prevailing interest rate cause a surplus of money, which in turn reduces the rate of interest.
    b. at the prevailing interest rate cause no change in the stock of money or the interest rate.
    c. at the prevailing interest rate cause a shortage of money, which in turn increases the rate of interest.
    d. at the prevailing interest rate cause a surplus of money, which in turn increases the rate of interest.

17. A decrease in the supply of money, given the demand for money, will _____ interest rates and _____ interest-sensitive expenditures in the economy.
    a. decrease, decrease
    b. increase, increase
    c. increase, decrease
    d. decrease, increase
    e. increase, will not change

18. Assume that an economy's reserve multiplier is 2, total reserves are $1 trillion, checkable deposits are $2 trillion, and the required reserve ratio is 20%. A decrease in the required reserve ratio to 10% has what impact on the potential amount of money growth?
    a. Potential monetary expansion increases from $1.2 to $1.6 trillion.
    b. Potential monetary contraction decreases from $800 billion to $600 billion. —
    c. Potential monetary expansion increases from $600 billion to $800 billion.
    d. The decrease in the required reserve ratio increases potential money growth from $0 to $1 trillion.

19. Which of the following is true regarding an increase in the discount rate?
    a. Bank borrowing from the Fed will fall if the discount rate rises relative to the federal funds rate and the U. S. treasury bill yield.
    b. Total reserves decrease.
    c. Excess reserves decrease.
    d. Monetary base decreases.
    e. All of the above

20. Which of the following is not true regarding open market purchases of U.S. government securities?
    a. Government security prices rise
    b. Government security yields fall
    c. Monetary base increases
    d. Money supply increases
    e. Total reserves increase, but excess reserves remain unchanged

21. Which of the following best explains why the money supply curve is upsloping?
    a. Interest rates have to increase to induce people to save.
    b. Higher interest rates increase the opportunity cost of holding excess reserves, causing bankers to reduce excess reserve holdings.
    c. Because bond prices fall as interest rates rise, fewer bonds are purchased, leaving more funds to be added to the money supply.
    d. Higher interest rates decrease the opportunity cost of making loans, causing bankers to supply more money to the money market.

22. If the Fed is concerned with producing an immediate impact on interest rates, which one of the following policies is most desirable?
    a. Required reserve ratio policy
    b. Discount rate policy
    c. Open market operations
    d. Jawboning
    e. B and d

■ THINK IT THROUGH

1. Discuss the functions of the Federal Reserve System.

2. Discuss the three tools of monetary control and how they can be used to influence equilibrium interest rates.

3. The Fed can control the rate of growth in the monetary base reasonably well over an extended period of time, but it has more difficulty achieving growth rate targets for the money supply. Can you think of any reasons why?

4. Suppose that as a manager, you are trying to decide whether to borrow short-term or long-term funds for modernization of your facilities. If you expect interest rates to rise, you will borrow by taking long-term loans at today's low interest rate. If you expect interest rates to fall, you will avoid long-term loans, preferring to borrow short-term funds until interest rates fall. What would you do if you heard that the Fed just lowered the discount rate and announced that it had been actively purchasing securities for the last several weeks?

■ ANALYZING THE NEWS

Using the skills derived from studying this chapter, analyze the economic facts that make up the following article and answer the question below.

Does the Fed control short-term interest rates?

Monetary Trends

Does The Fed Control Short-Term Interest Rates?

Because the Fed's policy actions affect expected inflation, the Fed influences interest rates *indirectly* [*Monetary Trends* (July 1995)]. It is widely believed, however, that the Fed can control short-term interest rates *directly*, without affecting inflationary expectations. There are reasons to be skeptical that this is so. One is that the Fed's ability to influence the supply of credit is relatively small.

The equilibrium level of interest rates is determined by equating the total supply of credit to the total demand for credit. Through its actions—open market operations, changes in the discount rate and changes in reserve requirements—the Fed directly affects the amount of credit channeled through banks. All other things the same, however, the direct effect of such an action on the total supply of credit is limited to the size of the action. For example, a $1 billion open market purchase increases the total supply of credit by $1 billion, no more and no less.

Changes in the adjusted monetary base, a summary measure of Federal Reserve actions, reflect the direct effect of Federal Reserve actions on the total supply of credit. The table shows changes in the 3-month T-bill rate and the proportion of the change in total credit due to Fed actions. The periods correspond to major swings in the 3-month T-bill rate.

As the table shows, the Fed supplied between 2.0 and 6.5 percent of the change in total credit during each period. Hence, the Fed's contribution to the total supply of domestic credit is relatively small.

Furthermore, there is little relationship between the behavior of interest rates and the relative contribution of the Fed to the credit market. For example, interest rates behaved quite differently during the first three periods, despite an essentially unchanged contribution of the Fed to the supply of domestic credit. Also, interest rates declined by about 600 basis points when the Fed's contribution increased from 2.1 to 4.3 percent, but then rose slightly when the Fed's contribution increased further to 6.5 percent.

This evidence alone is not sufficient to establish that the Fed has little direct influence over interest rates. It is, however, consistent with sophisticated statistical analyses that find the Fed's direct effect on short-term interest rates is small.[1]

— Daniel L. Thornton

THE DIRECT EFFECT OF FED ACTIONS ON THE SUPPLY OF CREDIT		
Period	Basis point changes in the 3-month T-bill rate	Percent of domestic credit due to Fed actions
3/85 - 10/86	-339	2.3%
10/86 - 3/88	51	2.4
3/88 - 3/89	314	2.1
3/89 - 10/92	-599	4.3
10/92 - 1/94	18	6.5
1/94 - 1/95	279	4.8
1/95 - 7/95	-34	2.0

[1]For example, see Pagan and Robertson, Federal Reserve Bank of St. Louis *Review* (May/June 1995), pp. 33-54.

Views expressed do not necessarily reflect official positions of the Federal Reserve System

Thornton, Daniel L. "Does the Fed Control Short-Term Interest Rates?" Monetary Trends. Federal Reserve Bank of St. Louis, December, 1995.

CHAPTER ANSWERS

The Chapter in Brief

1. Twelve 2. Six 3. Open Market 4. Monetary base 5. Discount 6. Increase 7. Decrease 8. Increase 9. Decrease 10. Sales 11. Purchases from 12. Open market operations 13. Reduces 14. Rise 15. Fall 16. Increases 17. Reduces 18. Increases 19. Increases 20. Increases 21. Fall 22. Reduces 23. Increase 24. Reduce 25. More 26. Smaller 27. Larger 28. Larger 29. Smaller 30. Upward sloping

Key Terms Review

1. Federal Open Market Committee 2. Monetary base 3. Open market operations 4. Discount loans 5. Money supply 6. Regional Federal Reserve Banks 7. Discount rate 8. Board of Governors of the Federal Reserve System

Concept Review

1. a. 5 b. $1,000 billion c. 5.26 d. $1,052 billion

2. a.

Reserve Multiplier	Checkable Deposits
10	$1,000 billion
5	500 million
4	400 million

b. Reduces, increases

3. a.

Federal Reserve

Assets		Liabilities and Net Worth	
Loans to banks	$10	Deposits of banks	$10

Bank A

Assets		Liabilities and Net Worth	
Reserve deposits	$10	Borrowings	$10

b. $10 million, $10 million c. $50 million d. Decreases, fall, decrease e. Increases, rise, increase

4. a.

Federal Reserve

Assets		Liabilities and Net Worth	
Securities	$25	Deposits of banks	$25

Bank A

Assets		Liabilities and Net Worth
Reserve deposits	$ 25	
Securities	-25	

b. Increases, $25 million; no change; increase, $25 million
c. Increase, $25 million, increase, $125 million
d. No e. Increase, increase

5. a.
                        Federal Reserve
    Assets   Liabilities and Net Worth
    Securities $-20   Deposits of banks $-20
                        Bank A
    Assets   Liabilities and Net Worth
    Reserve deposits $-20
    Securities   20

b. Decrease, $20 million c. Decrease, $200 million

d. Decrease, $200 million, does not fall e. Decrease, decrease

6. Decrease, increase; increase, decrease; positive, positively

7. a.

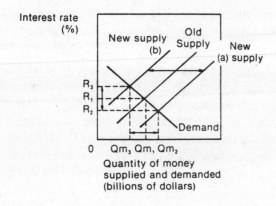

   Decrease
b. Increase
c.

	Change in Monetary Base	Change in Excess Reserves	Change in Checkable Deposits
1.	0	-	-
2.	-	-	-
3.	+	+	+
4.	0	+	+
5.	-	-	-
6.	+	+	+

Mastery Test

1. d 2. d 3. b 4. d 5. b 6. d 7. a 8. c 9. d 10. c 11. a 12. d 13. a 14. b 15. d 16. a 17. c 18. a 19. e 20. e
21. b 22. c

Think it Through

1. In addition to regulating the money supply, the Fed is responsible for maintaining the safety and solvency of the banking system, which it does through bank regulation and oversight and acting as a lender of last resort. The Fed also holds reserve deposits of member banks, supplies currency and coin to banks, clears checks, makes loans to banks, aids the Treasury in the issue of new government securities, and holds the Treasury deposits on which U.S. government checks are written.

2. The three tools of monetary control are the reserve ratio, the discount rate, and open market operations. If the Fed wants to expand the money supply, it can reduce the discount rate and the reserve ratio and purchase government securities. A policy designed to reduce the money stock might include increases in the reserve ratio and the discount rate and sales of government securities. In practice, the reserve ratio, while having a powerful impact on the supply of money, is not used as a device for regulation of the money supply. Open market operations together with support of the discount policy constitute the primary approach to monetary control.

3. The Fed has more direct control over the growth of the monetary base because of the Fed's ability to buy and sell huge quantities of government securities. In contrast, the money multiplier is determined not only by the Fed via the reserve ratio, but also by the portfolio decisions of the public such as the banking system's propensity to hold excess reserves. The growth of the money supply depends on changes in both the monetary base and the money multiplier. So while the Fed can target the growth of the monetary base reasonably well over a period of several months, it is less successful in achieving its growth targets for the money stock.

4. Both of the Fed's actions will expand the supply of money and reduce the interest rate. Because of this news, you expect interest rates to fall, which means you would be better off borrowing short-term funds and waiting until interest rates drop before you make long-term loan commitments.

Analyzing the News

Equilibrium interest rates are determined by the supply of and demand for credit. The Fed's influence on changes in the supply of credit is small. Over the last 10 years, the Fed has been responsible for only 2 to 6.5% of the changes in the supply of credit during each period shown on the table, implying a likewise small contribution to changes in interest rates. "(T)here is little relationship between the behavior of interest rates and the relative contribution of the Fed to the credit market."

PART VI

STABILIZING THE ECONOMY

■ **PART EXERCISE**

Inside Information: *Beige, Blue, and Green Books: How Monetary Authorities in the United States Compile Information to Examine Stabilization Policy Options*

In chapters 16 through 19, you will learn about monetary and fiscal policy and some options available to government and to monetary authorities for dealing with unemployment and inflation. Stabilization policy makers must have information on the economic conditions that exist in the country. Monetary authorities use the *Beige Book* to see how the economy is performing. Using the *Beige Book*, do a brief report on the performance of the national economy. Assume that the economic conditions you have described will continue through the coming year. Based upon what you have learned regarding monetary and fiscal policy, what kind of stabilization policy, if any, is desirable? Explain.

16 STABILIZATION OF THE ECONOMY THROUGH MONETARY POLICY

■ CHAPTER CONCEPTS

After studying your text, attending class, and completing this chapter, you should be able to:

1. Discuss the mechanism through which monetary policy can affect interest rates.
2. Show how an expansionary monetary policy shifts the economy's aggregate demand curve and affects macroeconomic equilibrium.
3. Show how a contractionary monetary policy shifts the economy's aggregate demand curve and affects macroeconomic equilibrium.
4. Discuss the quantity theory of money and the possible long-term effects of monetary policy on the price level.
5. Discuss the basic ideas and implications of monetarism for monetary policy.
6. Discuss monetary policy in the United States and some of the challenges the Fed faces in influencing interest rates in the modern global economy.

■ THE CHAPTER IN BRIEF

Fill in the blanks to summarize chapter content.

Monetary policy is used to influence the level of aggregate demand and macroeconomic equilibrium. The mechanism by which changes in the money supply influence aggregate demand is through changes in (1)_____ (prices, interest rates). Interest rates are (2)_____ (inversely, positively) related to the level of investment and other credit-sensitive expenditures. For instance, an increase in interest rates (3)_____ (reduces, increases) the level of investment which, in turn (4)_____ (reduces, increases) the level of aggregate demand and vice versa.

If the Fed wants to increase aggregate demand, it can engage in a/an (5)_____ (contractionary, expansionary) monetary policy. The Fed can expand the banking system's excess reserves. Excess reserves result in an increase in the stock of money, which reduces real interest rates and increases planned investment and aggregate demand. The effectiveness of such a policy depends on the willingness of the banking system to use the new excess reserves to make loans and on the sensitivity of investment and other expenditures to changes in the (6)_____ (interest rate, rate of inflation). If the increase in excess reserves is ultimately successful in increasing aggregate demand, real GDP and the price level increase if the economy is (7)_____ (above, below) potential real GDP. Expansionary monetary policy is useful as a tool for combating (8)_____ (recessionary, inflationary) GDP gaps and unemployment.

For the case of (9)_____ (recessionary, inflationary) GDP gaps, the Fed could withdraw reserves from the banking system. A decline in bank reserves will result in a/an (10)_____ (decrease, increase) in the real interest rate and a/an (11)_____ (decrease, increase) in planned investment and aggregate demand. As aggregate demand decreases, the price level and the level of real GDP will (12)_____ (rise, fall). A/An (13)_____ (contractionary, expansionary) monetary policy could be used to reduce inflation and bring the economy back to potential real GDP.

The long-run effect of monetary policy depends upon the demand for money, the growth of real GDP, and the growth of (14)_____ (the money stock, prices). If the income velocity of circulation of money, V, is defined as nominal GDP divided by the money stock, then the following identity emerges: (15)_____ (MQ = PV, MV = PQ). The stock of money times the income velocity of circulation equals the price level times real GDP. Velocity moves inversely with changes in the demand for money. But if velocity is constant and real GDP is assumed constant at its potential level, increases in the money stock result in (16)_____ (larger, proportionate) increases in the price level. This is the classical quantity theory of money. In the long run, the classical quantity theory of money implies a/an (17)_____ (vertical, upward sloping) aggregate supply curve at potential real GDP. An increase in the money stock increases aggregate demand (18)_____ (and results in an increase in both real GDP and the price level, but results in only an increase in the price level).

Monetarists and Keynesians believe that velocity is not constant, but the (19)_____ (monetarists, Keynesians) believe it is reasonably stable and changes in velocity are predictable. If changes in velocity are predictable, changes in the money supply can be used to influence nominal GDP. If the money stock is allowed to grow at the rate of growth of real GDP, then (20)_____ (some, no) inflation results. Inflation takes place when the money stock is

allowed to grow at a rate (21)_____ (in excess of, less than) the growth rate of real GDP. Monetarists recommend constant growth of the money stock at a rate (22)_____ (equal to, less than) the economy's average growth rate of real GDP as a way to prevent inflation. If the money supply increases at a rate faster than real GDP, inflation may not increase if velocity is (23)_____ (rising, falling). Velocity has not always been stable or predictable, however. In the 1980s, M1 velocity was particularly difficult to predict because of the increased volatility of interest rates.

A dilemma confronting the Fed is whether to use monetary policy to influence interest rates and aggregate demand in the short run or whether to concentrate on the long-run relationship between money growth and growth in real GDP. (24)_____ (Unfortunately, the Fed cannot, Fortunately, the Fed can) simultaneously achieve interest rate and money supply goals or targets. If real GDP or the price level increases, the demand for money will increase. In order to keep interest rates from rising, the Fed has to (25)_____ (decrease, increase) the money supply. If the goal is to keep the money supply constant in the face of an increase in money demand, then interest rates must rise. Thus controlling the interest rate means that the Fed effectively gives up control of the money stock and vice versa. This makes it (26)_____ (difficult, easy) for the Fed to achieve real GDP, employment, and inflation goals simultaneously. From the early 1940s to the mid-1970s, the Fed concentrated on controlling (27)_____ (the money stock, interest rates) as a means of stabilizing the economy. Beginning in late 1979, the Fed made an effort to concentrate on (28)_____ (the money stock, interest rates), but had to abandon the effort by mid-1982 because of the deepening recession.

In conducting monetary policy, the Fed must consider the impacts of contractionary and expansionary monetary policies on exchange rates and net exports. An expansionary policy decreases interest rates relative to foreign rates of interest. As the demand for foreign interest-yielding assets increase and the demand for lower-yielding United States assets falls, the supply of dollars to the foreign exchange market increases. This causes the international value of the dollar to (29)_____ (rise, fall), increasing net exports. The Fed could overexpand the economy and risk the possibility of inflation if these effects were not considered. Similarly, a contractionary monetary policy will raise interest rates, (30)_____ (decreasing, increasing) the international value of the dollar as the demand for dollars increases. The Fed might (31)_____ (contract, expand) the economy too much, producing an unacceptable increase in the (32) _____ (rate of inflation, unemployment rate), if it did not consider these effects.

◼ KEY TERMS REVIEW

Write the key term from the list below next to its definition.

Key Terms

Stabilization policies
Monetary policy
Expansionary monetary policy
Contractionary monetary
  policy
Monetarism

Income velocity of
  circulation of money
Equation of exchange
Classical quantity theory
  of money

Definitions

1. _____: actions taken by central banks to influence money supply or interest rates in an attempt to stabilize the economy.

2. _____: action by the Federal Reserve System to decrease the monetary base or its rate of growth.

3. _____: an identity that shows the relationship between nominal GDP, the money stock, and the income velocity of circulation of money.

4. _____: a model of the long-run functioning of the economy that maintains that over the long run, changes in the money stock result in proportional changes in the price level.

5. _____: a theory of long-term macroeconomic equilibrium, based on the equation of exchange, that assumes that shifts in velocity are reasonably predictable.

6. _____: policies undertaken by governing authorities for the purpose of maintaining full employment and a reasonably stable price level.

7. _____: action by the Federal Reserve System to increase the monetary base or its rate of growth.

8. _____: the number of times per year on average a dollar of the money stock is spent on final purchases or paid out as income.

■ CONCEPT REVIEW

Concept 1: *Monetary policy, interest rates, and aggregate demand*

1. The data below are for an economy. Using the data determine the market rate of interest, the level of planned investment, and the level of aggregate demand. (Assume that the expenditure multiplier equals 2 and the general price level is 125.)

Interest Rate	Supply of Loanable Funds	Demand for Loanable Funds	Planned Investment	Aggregate Demand
		($ billions)		
14	$125	$75	$10	$2,010
13	115	80	20	2,030
12	105	85	30	2,050
11	100	90	40	2,070
10	95	95	50	2,090
9	85	100	60	2,110
8	75	105	70	2,130

   a. Equilibrium rate of interest = _____%.

   b. Planned investment = $_____; aggregate demand = $_____.

   c. The Fed engages in an expansionary monetary policy, and the supply of loanable funds increases by $15 billion at each interest rate. The new market rate of interest is _____%, planned investment _____ to $_____, and aggregate demand _____ to $_____. The aggregate demand curve shifts to the _____.

   d. Assume that the initial supply of loanable funds is given in the table above. The Fed engages in a contractionary monetary policy such that the supply of loanable funds decreases by $20 billion at each interest rate. The new interest rate is _____%, planned investment _____ to $_____, and aggregate demand _____ to $_____. The aggregate demand curve shifts _____.

e. The figure below shows the aggregate demand curve for the economy described above. Find the point on the aggregate demand curve associated with part b. Now show what happens to the point for parts c and d. Draw new aggregate demand curves through the points parallel to ADo.

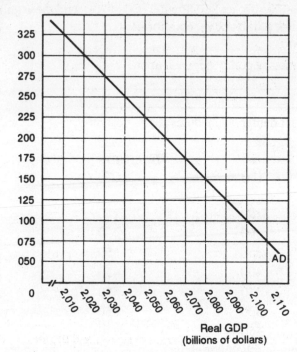

Concepts 2 and 3: *Monetary policy and macroeconomic equilibrium*

2. Below is an aggregate demand and supply model of the economy.

a. Given aggregate demand ADo, the economy is experiencing an/a _____ (inflationary, recessionary) gap. In order to eliminate the gap, the Fed could _____ the money stock. This would _____ interest rates and _____ planned investment, causing the aggregate demand curve to shift _____.

b. Given aggregate demand AD1, the economy is experiencing an/a _____ (inflation-ary, recessionary) gap. In order to eliminate the gap, the Fed could _____ the money stock. This would _____ interest rates and _____ planned investment, causing the aggregate demand curve to shift _____.

c. For part a above, equilibrium real GDP will _____ and the equilibrium price level will _____. For part b above, equilibrium real GDP will _____ and the equilibrium price level will _____.

3. The effectiveness of monetary policy depends upon:

a. _____

b. _____

4. Below are two investment demand schedules for an economy.

Interest Rate	Planned Investment (I1)	Planned Investment (I2)
(%)	($ billions)	
14	$250	$150
13	300	250
12	350	350
11	400	450
10	450	550
9	500	650
8	550	750

a. Which of the investment schedules above, I1 or I2, displays the greater sensitivity of invest-ment expenditures to changes in the interest rate? _____

b. At an interest rate of 12% the level of planned investment is the same for both I1 and I2. Assume that the aggregate demand curve shown in the figure below is associated with a level of planned investment equal to $350 billion. On the figure, show the effect of a

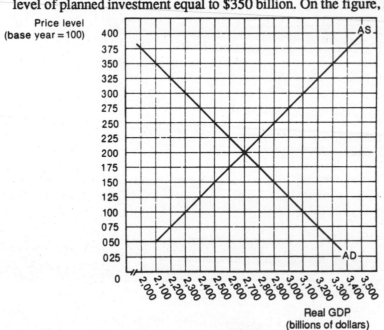

286

reduction in the interest rate from 12% to 9% on the aggregate demand curve for the case of investment schedule I1. (Assume that the aggregate demand curve shifts parallel to ADo and horizontally by an expenditure multiplier of 2.)

c.   On the figure above, show the effect of a decrease in interest rates from 12% to 9% on the aggregate demand curve for the case of investment schedule I2. (Assume that the aggregate demand curve shifts parallel to ADo.)

d.   Monetary policy is _____ effective if the investment schedule is I1 and is _____ effective if the investment schedule is I2.

Concepts 4 and 5:   *Classical quantity theory of money; long-term effects of money*

5. a.   Assume that the current level of real GDP, Q, is $2 trillion, the implicit price deflator, P, is 200, and the stock of money, M, equals $500 billion. The velocity of circulation of money equals _____.

b.   According to the classical quantity theory of money, both _____ and _____ are assumed constant. If for part a above the money stock doubles, then according to the quantity theory of money the price level, P, will _____ to _____. But if velocity falls by half its value as the stock of money doubles, the price level will

_____.

c.   Which of the two aggregate supply curves in the figure below is associated with the classical quantity theory of money and is based on the assumption of flexible wages and prices?_____ If monetary policy shifts the aggregate demand curve from ADo to AD1 along the aggregate supply curve, the price level will _____ and real GDP

_____.

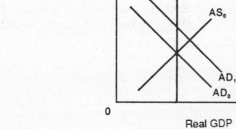

d.   The _____ believe that while velocity is not constant, it is at least predictable enough to use monetary policy to accurately influence nominal GDP.

Concept 6:   *Conflicting goals of monetary policy*

6. The figure below shows an economy's loanable funds market. Assume that the Fed wants to peg interest rates at their current level as given by the demand for loanable funds, Dlf-1. Assume that because of economic expansion, the demand for loanable funds shifts outward to Dlf-2.

a.   What must the Fed do to prevent the interest rate from changing? Show this on the figure below. This monetary policy is _____ (expansionary, contractionary) and may result in _____ (more, less) inflation.

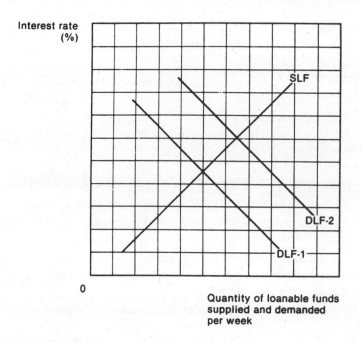

Interest rate
(%)

SLF

DLF-2

DLF-1

0

Quantity of loanable funds
supplied and demanded
per week

b. If the Fed decided to control the stock of money, interest rates would _____. Show this on the figure above.

c. The _____ (inability, ability) to simultaneously attain interest rate and money supply targets makes it _____ (easy, difficult) to reach macroeconomic goals such as full employment and stable prices.

■ MASTERY TEST

Select the best answer.

1. Policies undertaken by governing authorities for the purpose of maintaining full employment and a reasonably stable price level is the definition of which of the following?
   a. Monetary policy
   b. Stabilization policies
   c. Contractionary monetary policy
   d. Expansionary monetary policy

2. Action by the Federal Reserve System to increase the monetary base or its rate of growth is the definition for which of the following?
   a. Monetary policy
   b. Stabilization policies
   c. Contractionary monetary policy
   d. Expansionary monetary policy

3. An expansionary monetary policy _____ the monetary base, causing the real interest rate to _____ and planned investment to _____.
   a. decreases, rise, fall
   b. increases, rise, rise
   c. decreases, fall, fall
   d. increases, rise, fall
   e. increases, fall, rise

4. Which of the following is true of contractionary monetary policy?
   a. The monetary base declines.
   b. Real interest rates increase.
   c. Planned investment falls.
   d. Aggregate demand falls.
   e. All of the above.

5. If the economy is experiencing an inflationary GDP gap, _____ monetary policy could be used to _____ aggregate demand and _____ the general price level.
   a. contractionary, reduce, reduce
   b. contractionary, increase, increase
   c. contractionary, reduce, increase
   d. expansionary, reduce, reduce
   e. expansionary, increase, reduce

6. Monetary policy is more effective:
   a. the less willing bankers are to make loans.
   b. the more responsive credit-sensitive expenditures, including investment, are to changes in interest rates.
   c. the more willing bankers are to make loans with new excess reserves.
   d. A and c.
   e. B and c.

7. If the economy is experiencing a recessionary GDP gap, _____ monetary policy could be used to _____ aggregate demand and _____ real GDP.
   a. contractionary, reduce, reduce
   b. contractionary, increase, increase
   c. contractionary, reduce, increase
   d. expansionary, increase, reduce
   e. expansionary, increase, increase

8. Which of the following is not true of the income velocity of circulation of money?
   a. Velocity is defined as nominal GDP/M1.
   b. Historically, velocity has proved to be constant.
   c. Velocity is inversely related to the demand for money.
   d. Changes in velocity influence nominal GDP.

9. If the price level, P, equals 1.50, real GDP is $3000 billion, and the stock of money equals $900 billion, the velocity of circulation of money equals:
   a. 4
   b. 5
   c. 6
   d. 7
   e. 8

10. Which of the following is the equation of exchange?
    a. $MP = VQ$
    b. $MT = Q/P$
    c. $MP = QT$
    d. $MV = PQ$

11. Which of the following assumptions about the economy is central to the classical quantity theory of money?
    a. Wages and prices are rigid in the downward direction.
    b. Flexible wages and prices ensure that the economy will operate at full employment.
    c. Velocity is variable.
    d. Velocity is constant.
    e. B and d.

12. The classical quantity theory of money states that:
    a. money is a medium of exchange necessary for the efficient functioning of the economy.
    b. increases in the stock of money result in greater increases in the price level.
    c. decreases in the stock of money increase the price level.
    d. increases in the stock of money result in proportionate increases in the price level.

13. The classical quantity theory of money implies that an increase in aggregate demand will:
    a. increase only real GDP.
    b. increase output, but not nominal GDP.
    c. increase only the price level.
    d. increase the price level, but will reduce nominal GDP.

14. Evidence indicates that:
    a. velocity is unimportant.
    b. velocity is constant.
    c. velocity exhibits long-term trends.
    d. velocity can increase one year, decrease the next, and increase the following year.
    e. C and d.

15. Monetarists argue that changes in the stock of money can have predictable impacts on _____ GDP assuming that _____ is reasonably stable and predictable.
    a. real, prices
    b. real, costs
    c. nominal, velocity
    d. nominal, income

16. Which of the following groups is associated with the policy recommendation that the money stock should grow only at the rate of growth in real GDP?
    a. Monetarists
    b. Keynesians
    c. Classical quantity theorists
    d. Republicans and Democrats

17. If the Fed pegs the interest rate at its current level and the demand for money increases, what must the Fed do to prevent the interest rate from changing?
    a. Increase the interest rate on nonfinancial assets.
    b. Decrease the money stock.
    c. Decrease money demand.
    d. Increase the money stock.

18. An inflationary expansion of the economy increases the demand for money. If the Fed has a policy to peg the interest rate, what is the likely consequence of its policy response?
    a. The economy will immediately fall into a depression.
    b. Inflation will fall.
    c. Inflation will rise.
    d. Unemployment will rise and inflation will fall.

19. Which of the following is true of monetary policy?
    a. From the 1940s to the present the Fed has concentrated on attaining monetary targets.
    b. From the 1940s to the 1970s the Fed emphasized interest rate stability.
    c. From late 1979 to late 1982 the Fed pegged the interest rate.
    d. The Fed has always simultaneously targeted both interest rates and the money stock.

20. Expectations of higher bond prices have what impact on interest rates, investment, aggregate demand, real GDP and the price level? (Assume that the economy is on the upsloping portion of the aggregate supply curve)
    a. Interest rates fall, investment decreases, aggregate demand decreases, and both real GDP and the price level decrease.
    b. Interest rates fall, investment increases, aggregate demand increases, and both real GDP and the price level increase.
    c. Interest rates rise, investment decreases, aggregate demand falls, and both real GDP and the price level fall.
    d. Because the supply of money remains unchanged, all economic variables remain unchanged.

21. Suppose for an economy the expenditure multiplier is 2, a $10 billion change in the money supply changes interest rates by 1%, investment spending changes by $60 billion for each percentage-point change in the interest rate, and the economy is operating on the horizontal portion of the aggregate supply curve. Assume further that policy makers want to eliminate a recessionary gap of $240 billion. What change in the money supply would eliminate this recessionary gap?
    a. Increase the money supply $10 billion.
    b. Decrease the money supply $40 billion.
    c. Increase the money supply $20 billion.
    d. Increase the money supply $5 billion.

22. The aggregate supply curve associated with the classical quantity theory implies that an increase in the money supply will:
    a. increase both real GDP and the price level.
    b. decrease both real GDP and the interest rate.
    c. increase the price level, but will leave real GDP unchanged.
    d. be inflationary if the economy is on the horizontal portion of the aggregate supply curve.

23. If monetary policy makers are "targeting" interest rates, increases in nominal GDP:
    a. may cause additional inflation.
    b. requires increases in the money supply.
    c. will not cause inflation.
    d. requires decreases in the money supply.
    e. a and b

24. What will happen to the international value of the dollar, net exports, and real GDP if the Federal Reserve pursues an expansionary monetary policy?
    a. The value of the dollar increases, net exports and real GDP increase.
    b. The value of the dollar decreases, net exports and real GDP increase.
    c. The value of the dollar decreases, net exports and real GDP fall.
    d. The value of the dollar increases, net exports and real GDP fall.

■ THINK IT THROUGH

1. When the Fed increased the money supply after mid-1982, monetarists warned of impending inflation. Instead the U.S. economy has experienced stable inflation for several years. Can you think of any reasons why?

2. Discuss why monetary policy might be ineffective in a severe recession.

3. Explain how a policy to peg interest rates can cause the business cycle to exhibit more volatility.

■ ANALYZING THE NEWS

Using the skills derived from studying this chapter, analyze the economic facts that make up the following article and answer the questions below.

1. Does a tight money policy raise or lower interest rates in the long run?

2. What policy is recommended for reducing inflation?

ECONOMIC COMMENTARY

Federal Reserve Bank of Cleveland

A Monetary Policy Paradox

by Charles T. Carlstrom

One of the most difficult tasks faced by any central bank is explaining to the public the role that interest rates play in the conduct of monetary policy. The common understanding is that the Federal Reserve fights inflation by acting to raise short-term interest rates. But as pointed out by economist Irving Fisher many years ago, reduced inflation is associated with lower, not higher, rates of interest.

The key distinction between these two views, of course, lies in the short-run versus the long-run level of interest rates. However, the transit to the long run depends crucially on private expectations, which in turn depend on how the public perceives particular decisions in the short run.

This issue is of great practical importance. By the end of the 1970s, inflation was hovering around 13 percent. With the announcement on October 6, 1979, of the switch from interest-rate targeting to nonborrowed reserves targeting, U.S. monetary policy adopted a strong anti-inflationary stance. The new approach was successful in that inflation was cut to around 4 percent by the end of 1983. During this same period, however, the economy suffered twin recessions. Many, if not most, economists attribute the losses in jobs and output to slowly adjusting inflation expectations.

A debate is now under way about whether another monetary policy revolution is needed. The argument this time focuses on whether the Federal Reserve

should pursue price stability. Like the last battle, the new one could also prove costly unless the Fed can credibly signal its commitment to price stability and then follow that policy relentlessly.

This *Economic Commentary* explores the paradoxical link between interest rates and inflation in the short versus the long run. It may be more difficult for a central bank to achieve credibility — and hence a less costly transition to a stable price environment — without first making the monetary authorities accountable for publicly stated multiyear objectives for the price level.

■ Inflation and Monetary Policy

Years ago, Milton Friedman issued his now-famous maxim that inflation is always and everywhere a monetary phenomenon.[1] This statement is as true today as it was three decades ago. Of course, every blip in the Consumer Price Index is not caused by Federal Reserve policy. Supply shocks, such as the oil shock in the mid-1970s, can lead to short periods in which the price level rises rapidly. But continuous increases in the price level can occur only if the central bank accommodates such shocks with faster money growth.

This sounds simple enough. One can see why Friedman once called for the Fed to set the growth rate of money at 3 percent per year (the long-run growth rate of output), declare the battle over, and go home. Alas, life is not that simple. It is doubtful that a constant money growth rule would be sufficient to achieve a

Central banks wishing to pursue price stability must deal with the paradox that reducing inflation today requires raising short-term interest rates, even though price stability can ultimately be sustained only with lower, not higher, rates of interest. Without a long-term objective, such as a multi-year path for the price level, it may be extraordinarily difficult for a central bank to signal its resolve to stabilize prices.

long-run price-level target, and even when particular money growth ranges are desired, such targets are typically sought via changes in short-term interest rates.

Interest-rate operating procedures are uniformly used by the world's central banks for a variety of reasons, but many economists believe it is desirable to smooth short-term interest-rate fluctuations arising from the temporary liquidity needs of the financial sector. Since people are unable to adjust their portfolios quickly in response to various shocks to the economy, the central bank should jump in and supply the needed liquidity by adding enough reserves to smooth interest rates.

In the United States, the interest rate used to conduct monetary policy is the federal funds rate — the rate that banks charge each other for overnight loans. As with other central banks, the Federal Reserve does not directly control the money supply. Rather, it varies the supply of bank reserves to achieve its funds-rate objective. Under an interest-rate operating procedure, money growth, which determines the price level and thus the purchasing power of money, is endogenous.[2] To understand how monetary policy affects both short- and long-run price-level movements, it is necessary to understand the relationship between interest rates and money growth.

■ Money Growth and the Funds Rate: The Long and Short of It

According to conventional wisdom, interest-rate hikes are supposed to fight inflation. The mechanism by which these actions operate in the short run is straightforward: Increases in the funds rate lead to slower money growth. Slower money growth should in turn lead to lower inflation.

But what about in the long run? One of the strongest correlations in economics is the positive relationship between inflation and nominal interest rates (see figure 1). In light of this, and given that monetary policy operates via interest rates, it seems fair to ask whether the

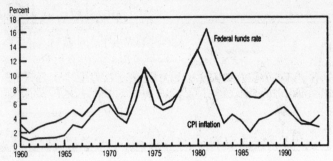

FIGURE 1 CPI INFLATION AND THE FEDERAL FUNDS RATE

SOURCES: Board of Governors of the Federal Reserve System; and U.S. Department of Labor, Bureau of Labor Statistics.

seeds of future inflation are being planted with interest-rate hikes that must ultimately be supported by excess money creation.

As pointed out by economist Irving Fisher, nominal interest rates, like the fed funds rate, contain both a real rate and an inflation premium. In general, the higher the inflation premium, the higher are nominal rates. In the long run, then, higher nominal interest rates do in fact accompany higher inflation.

Thus, we are left to contend with a paradox: Although higher federal funds rates may be associated with an anti-inflationary policy in the short run, lower inflation will ultimately be reflected in lower interest rates. The key to understanding this puzzle is the critical role played by inflation expectations.

In the near term, because inflation expectations are fixed, a higher funds rate can be supported by increasing the real (inflation-adjusted) funds rate via slower money growth. In the long run, however, the Fed has little or no effect on real economic variables — and hence on real interest rates. This means that over the long term, a high funds rate can be supported only with faster money growth and increased inflation expectations. Thus, an interest-rate hike that is not rescinded once the economy fully adjusts to it can in fact cause higher long-term inflation. Figures 2 and 3 show that although there is a weak negative relationship between changes in the

funds rate and monetary base growth over a quarterly frequency, over the long run a positive relationship exists.

The line of demarcation between the short run and the long run is not a fixed period like one day, one year, or even one decade. Rather, it is crucially related to the amount of time it takes for expectations to adjust. This adjustment period — that is, how long the "short run" lasts — is ultimately an empirical issue. However, the tight relationship between the funds rate and inflation suggests that the long-run correlations noted by Irving Fisher are apparent in the data.[3]

■ Interest Rates and Credibility

The seeds of the paradox are now sown: What should a central bank do if it wishes to reduce inflation and pursue price stability? Complicating this issue is the problematic nature of the signals that particular funds-rate decisions give about the Fed's overall objective. While increasing the funds rate may result in slower short-term money growth and hence in lower short-term inflation, it may be a poor way for a central bank to signal its resolve to pursue price stability. Eventually, a lower, not higher, funds rate will be necessary to support price stability. But failing to raise the rate may be just as unlikely to signal the Fed's resolve to cut inflation. An unchanged funds rate in the face of increasing market interest rates may fuel short-term inflation and make it difficult for the Fed to convince the public that it is serious about controlling inflation over the long term.

295

FIGURE 2 MONETARY BASE GROWTH AND CHANGES IN THE FEDERAL FUNDS RATE

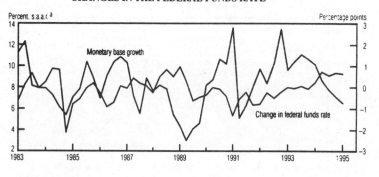

a. Seasonally adjusted annual rate.
SOURCE: Board of Governors of the Federal Reserve System.

FIGURE 3 MONETARY BASE GROWTH AND THE FEDERAL FUNDS RATE

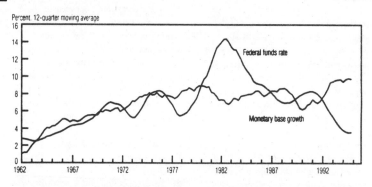

SOURCE: Board of Governors of the Federal Reserve System.

Whether increases in the funds rate can adequately signal a central bank's resolve to lower long-term inflation depends on what people expect future monetary policy to be. When the Fed raises the funds rate, do people expect that four years into the future the rate will be higher or lower than it otherwise would have been?[4] This is a hard question to answer empirically, but to believe that a higher funds rate signals lower long-term inflation is to believe that it also signals a lower long-term funds rate. If people actually expect the funds rate several years hence to be higher following a funds rate hike, the cost of achieving price stability will be unnecessarily steep. This is because

the rate hike may be successful in slowing short-term inflation, but will actually increase the market's expectations of longer-term inflation.

So how should an inflation-conscious central bank proceed? The answer obviously depends on whether one believes that increases in the fed funds rate can, in and of themselves, credibly signal a change in the long-term inflation rate. The paradox discussed in this section points out in a particularly stark manner what the market must believe about the course of future fed funds decisions if it is in fact to believe that long-term inflation expectations will fall when short-term interest rates are raised.

Even if one believes that interest-rate hikes lower long-term inflation expectations, the monetary authorities still face a difficult task. The funds rate must be raised today to fight inflation, then brought back down in the future as inflation expectations adjust. If the Fed usually decreases the funds rate before expectations have adjusted, inflation will rise, partially undoing the inflation-fighting signal sent by the initial rate hike. Yet, paradoxically, consistent failure to decrease the funds rate after expectations have adjusted can also increase inflation. After expectations have fallen into line, a high fed funds rate can be supported only via faster money growth.

■ A Possible Course for Monetary Policy
A monetary authority that wishes to pursue price stability has its job complicated enormously both by the seeming paradox that lowering interest rates in the long run may require raising them in the short run, and by the subtle but important role that near-term funds-rate decisions play in the formation of private expectations. Consequently, more fundamental changes may be required than simply adjusting the short-term funds rate. A sensible place for an inflation-conscious central bank to start is to adopt publicly announced multiyear paths for the price level.

This institutional change would likely mitigate the dilemma discussed in the previous section. The goal is to get people thinking about monetary policy in terms of objectives rather than as a series of short-term interest-rate changes. Without long-term goals, a person's best guess of the federal funds rate one year hence is likely to be dominated by the current rate. In the absence of explicit guidelines, history serves as our only teacher.

Multiyear price-level commitments would help people see short-term hikes in the funds rate in a different context. A rate increase today would necessarily be viewed as a temporary measure taken to meet tomorrow's long-term policy goals, ending the contradictory signals that people now must deal with when trying to predict future policy on the basis of current actions.

Undoubtedly, this change alone would not magically give central bankers the credibility they need to minimize the costs of disinflation. Without such a commitment, however, short-term increases in the funds rate are less likely to signal a central bank's seriousness about achieving long-term price stability. This is especially true when such hikes, if left unchanged, are consistent with higher long-term inflation. Multiyear price-level paths are therefore a potentially important first step in reducing the costs of disinflation and will likely improve any cost/benefit calculation.

■ **Footnotes**
1. See Milton Friedman, "Inflation: Causes and Consequences," in *Dollars and Deficits,* Englewood Cliffs, N.J.: Prentice-Hall, 1968, p. 39.

2. The fed funds rate target may be set in order to achieve a particular money growth objective, in which case money growth is at least partially controlled by the central bank.

3. Some argue that the positive relationship between inflation and the funds rate exists because the Federal Reserve chooses to fight inflation by raising the funds rate during inflationary periods. I believe that in all likelihood, both mechanisms are operating.

4. I arbitrarily chose four years to convey an interval in which people's expectations of the real funds rate at the end of the period are independent of whether short-term interest rates are raised today.

Charles T. Carlstrom is an economist at the Federal Reserve Bank of Cleveland.

The views stated herein are those of the author and not necessarily those of the Federal Reserve Bank of Cleveland or of the Board of Governors of the Federal Reserve System.

Carlstrom, Charles T. "A Monetary Policy Paradox." Economic Commentary. Federal Reserve Bank of Cleveland. August 15, 1995.

■ CHAPTER ANSWERS

The Chapter in Brief

1. Interest rates 2. Inversely 3. Reduces 4. Reduces 5. y 6. Interest rate 7. Below
8. Recessionary 9. Inflationary 10. Increase 11. Decrease 12. Fall 13. Contractionary 14. The
money stock 15. MV = PQ 16. Proportionate 17. Vertical 18. But results in only an increase in
the price level 19. Monetarists 20. No 21. In excess of 22. Equal to 23. Falling 24. Unfortunately, the Fed cannot 25. Increase 26. Difficult 27. Interest rates 28. The money stock 29. fall 30.
increasing 31. contract 32. unemployment rate

Key Terms Review

1. Monetary policy 2. Contractionary monetary policy 3. Equation of exchange 4. Classical quantity theory of money 5. Monetarism 6. Stabilization policies 7. Expansionary monetary policy 8.
Income velocity of circulation of money

Concept Review

1. a. 10 b. $50 billion, $2,090 billion c. 9%, increases, $60 billion, increases, $2,110 billion; right
d. 12%, decreases, $30 billion, decreases, $2,050; left

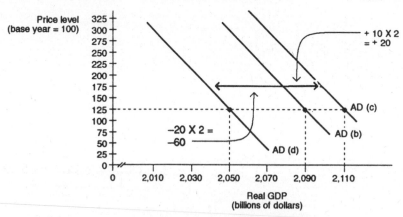

2. a.   Recessionary; increase; decrease, increase, right
  b.   Inflationary; decrease; increase, decrease, left
  c.   Increase, increase; decrease, decrease

3. a.   Willingness of bankers to make loans with the newly created excess reserves
  b.   Sensitivity of investment and other expenditures to changes in the interest rate

4. a.   I2
  b.

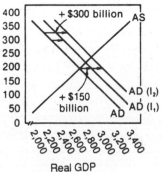

c. On figure above

d. Less, more

5. a. 8

   b. Velocity, real GDP; increase, 400; not change

   c. AS1; increase, will not change

   d. Monetarists

6. a. The Fed must increase the monetary base sufficiently to increase the stock of money equal to the increase in the demand for money. Expansionary, more

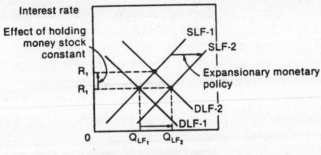

b. Rise. On figure above.

c. Inability, difficult

Mastery Test

1. b 2. d 3. e 4. e 5. a 6. e 7. e 8. b 9. b 10. d 11. e 12. d 13. c 14. e 15. c 16. a 17. d 18. c 19. b 20. b 21. c 22. c 23. e 24. b

Think it Through

1. The monetarists' warnings of inflation were based on the assumption that velocity was reasonably predictable and on the noticeable increase in the rate of growth in the money stock. According to the equation of exchange, if velocity is stable or at least predictable, increases in the money stock in excess of increases in real GDP will result in a rising price level. But velocity unexpectedly fell at times in the early to mid-1980s, offsetting the effect of increases in the money stock on nominal GDP. The deregulation of the banking industry and the introduction of financial innovations have been part of the reason for the greater volatility of velocity in the 1980s.

2. In a severe recession, bankruptcies and the consequent loan losses might cause bankers to withhold excess reserves from the loanable funds market because of the default risks associated with loans. Investment prospects would not be expected to be very bright in a recession with firms operating with substantial excess capacity. Firms will not likely borrow to expand capacity if they are operating with excess capacity. In a severe recession or depression, an increase in the monetary base may not increase the money stock enough to reduce interest rates. And if interest rates did fall, there is no assurance that firms would borrow and spend the funds. Therefore there is a chance that aggregate demand would be little affected by an expansionary monetary policy.

3. Suppose that the Fed has a policy to keep interest rates constant. In an economic expansion, the demand for money rises relative to the supply of money, putting upward pressure on market rates of interest. In order to keep interest rates from rising, the Fed has to increase the stock of money. This accelerates the expansion and may even result in worsening inflation. If the economy is declining and the demand for money is falling relative to the stock of money, the Fed must reduce the money supply in order to keep interest rates unchanged. But this results in further economic decline and unemployment. A policy to peg the interest rate over the business cycle will increase the instability of the economy.

Analyzing the News

1. Tight monetary policies raise interest rates in the short-run, slowing the economy and reducing inflation. But as shown in figure 1 in the article, the long-run relationship between interest rates (the federal funds rate) and inflation has been positive. Over time interest rates move in the same direction as inflation, not in opposite directions. The reason for this paradox has to do with inflation expectations. If contractionary monetary policies produce expectations of falling inflation, nominal interest rates will fall.

2. To reduce inflation the Fed should pursue policies that increase interest rates in the short-run. As the economy slows and inflation falls, the Fed should then reduce interest rates in line with falling inflation expectations otherwise inflation targets will not be met. The Fed can also announce multi-year inflation targets. If these announced targets are viewed as credible by the public, it is likely that tight money policies will reduce inflation expectations, inflation, and interest rates more rapidly.

17 STABILIZATION OF THE ECONOMY THROUGH FISCAL POLICY

■ CHAPTER CONCEPTS

After studying your text, attending class, and completing this chapter, you should be able to:

1. Explain how expansionary fiscal policies affect the economy and show how such policies can be used to eliminate recessionary GDP gaps.

2. Explain how contractionary fiscal policies affect the economy and show how such policies can help prevent inflation.

3. Show how built-in stabilizers automatically moderate shifts in aggregate demand.

4. Explain how supply-side fiscal policies can affect the economy in the long run and assess the effectiveness of recent supply-side policies.

■ THE CHAPTER IN BRIEF

Fill in the blanks to summarize chapter content.

The government can influence the level of aggregate demand in both the short run and the long run through the use of fiscal policy. A budget (1)_____ (surplus, deficit) exists when government purchases exceed tax revenues. Budget (2)_____ (surpluses, deficits) occur when tax revenues exceed government purchases. Budget deficits have an/a (3)_____ (expansionary, contractionary) impact on aggregate demand, whereas budget surpluses have an/a (4)_____ (expansionary, contractionary) impact.

If the economy is experiencing a recessionary GDP gap, the government can increase real GDP by pursuing an expansionary fiscal policy. Specifically, the government can (5)_____ (decrease, increase) government purchases, increase transfer payments to individuals and organizations, or (6)_____ (decrease, increase) taxes. If the economy is in the horizontal segment of the aggregate supply curve, an expansionary fiscal policy will increase real GDP (7)_____ (without igniting, and cause) inflation. The extent of fiscal stimulus can be determined by dividing the recessionary GDP gap by the multiplier.

Tax cuts have a similar effect on aggregate demand. A reduction in taxes (8)_____ (will, will not) increase aggregate demand as much as an equivalent increase in government spending because the marginal propensities to consume and import reduce the amount of new income from the tax cut available for expenditure. If government spending is financed by an equal increase in taxes, the net effect is (9)_____ (expansionary, negative) because the government spending multiplier exceeds the net tax multiplier. The most expansionary fiscal policy is an increase in government spending (10)_____ (financed with higher taxes, that increases the budget deficit).

If the economy has an inflationary GDP gap, the price level can be reduced by a contractionary fiscal policy. The government can (11)_____ (reduce, increase) its expenditures, (12)_____ (decrease, increase) transfers, or (13)_____ (decrease, increase) taxes. Real GDP falls toward its potential level as the price level falls. If, however, the government

301

expands the economy when there is an inflationary GDP gap, inflation, which is already a problem, becomes worse.

Several problems are associated with the implementation of fiscal policy. For one, it is unlikely that the political process will produce the correct economic stabilization legislation. Politicians look to the next election and recognize the political problems inherent in raising taxes or cutting programs that benefit their constituencies. While it is politically much (14)_____ (more difficult, easier) to cut taxes or increase government purchases in a recession, it is much (15)_____ (more difficult, easier) to raise taxes or cut government purchases in an inflationary period.

Economic forecasting is necessary in implementing fiscal policy. Policy makers need to know where the economy is headed in order to determine the proper amount of stimulus or contraction needed. If forecasts are in error, fiscal policy (16)_____ (will, will not) likely close the recessionary or inflationary GDP gap. Lags in fiscal policy implementation also add to the difficulty of closing recessionary and inflationary gaps. The time lags include the recognition lag, the administrative lag, and the operational lag. We do not know if we have entered an expansion or a recession until weeks or even months after the occurrence. This is the (17)_____ (operational, administrative, recognition) lag. The (18)_____ (operational, administrative, recognition) lag is the length of time it takes the government to devise a policy response. And finally, the (19)_____ (operational, administrative, recognition) lag is the length of time the policy response takes to change real GDP, the price level, and the level of unemployment. Because the lengths of these lags are not known with certainty, fiscal policy may be ill timed and as a result may not close the inflationary or recessionary GDP gap.

Fortunately, the government budget still has a stabilizing impact on the economy through its automatic stabilizers—a form of (20)_____ (discretionary, nondiscretionary) fiscal policy. These include income taxes and transfer payments. The transfers that vary over the business cycle are entitlement programs such as unemployment insurance, cash assistance welfare benefits, (21)_____ (in-kind assistance, private pension benefits), and Social Security pension payments. As the economy falls into a recession, income tax revenues decline and transfers increase automatically. This (22)_____ (increases aggregate demand more than, prevents the level of aggregate demand from falling as much as) it would have otherwise. An economic expansion increases tax revenues and reduces transfer payments, which aids in restraining aggregate demand. This (23)_____ (reduces, increases) the threat of inflation. In order to determine if discretionary fiscal policy is stimulative or contractionary, it is necessary to hold constant the effect of the automatic stabilizers. This is done with the concept of the (24)_____ (balanced budget, high-employment deficit), in which government spending and revenues are compared assuming the economy is operating over the year at the natural rate of unemployment.

In addition to demand-side effects, fiscal policies can also have supply-side effects over the long run. A cut in tax rates, it is argued, will increase the after-tax returns to work, saving, and investment. If the number of labor hours increases and the levels of saving and investment increase, the (25)_____ (aggregate supply curve will shift rightward, the aggregate demand curve will shift leftward). Evidence suggests that these effects (26)_____ (are, are not) very large, particularly in the short run. In the short run, a cut in tax rates will increase aggregate demand more than aggregate supply, implying the possibility of (27)_____ (unemployment, inflation) if the economy is on the upward-sloping portion of its aggregate supply curve. To prevent tax cuts from causing inflation and to allow sufficient time for them to have supply-side effects on the aggregate supply curve, aggregate demand will have to be restrained somewhat through reduced government spending. In addition to cuts in tax rates, legislation allowing individual retirement accounts may increase saving, and accelerated depreciation allowances and investment tax credits may (28)_____ (increase, decrease) capital formation, both of which could shift the aggregate supply curve (29)_____ (leftward, rightward).

■ KEY TERMS REVIEW

Write the key term from the list below next to its definition.

Key Terms

Fiscal policy

Government budget

Expansionary fiscal
  policy

Contractionary
  fiscal policy

Automatic stabilizers

High-employment deficit (or surplus)

Supply-side fiscal policies

Accelerated depreciation allowances

Definitions

1. _____: the use of government spending and taxing for the specific purpose of stabilizing the economy.

2. _____: features of the federal budget that automatically adjust net taxes to stabilize aggregate demand as the economy expands and contracts.

3. _____: generous deductions from pretax business income that are allowed when firms acquire new equipment or new structures.

4. _____: a policy under which the government acts to restrain aggregate demand by decreasing spending or increasing taxes, or both.

5. _____: policies that seek to influence long-run economic growth in real GDP through government subsidies and tax reductions.

6. _____: a policy under which the government acts to increase aggregate demand by increasing spending or decreasing taxes, or both.

7. _____: the budget deficit (or surplus) that would prevail if the natural rate of unemployment were achieved.

8. _____: a plan for spending funds and raising revenues through taxation, fees, and other means, and borrowing funds if necessary.

■ CONCEPT REVIEW

Concepts 1 and 2:   *Impact of the federal budget on aggregate demand; fiscal policies to close recessionary and inflationary GDP gaps*

1. Assume that the economy in the figure below is currently at its potential level of real GDP.

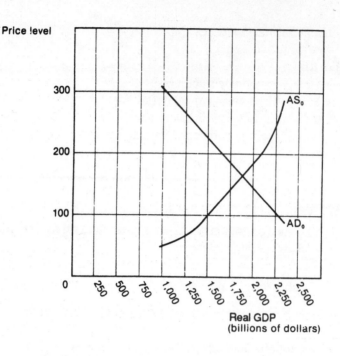

a. Identify the equilibrium price level and level of real GDP on the figure.

b. Assume a decrease in autonomous spending reduces aggregate purchases by $125 billion. If the multiplier is 2, the aggregate demand curve will shift _____ by $_____. Show the new AD curve and label it AD1.

c. The economy is now experiencing a/an _____ gap. Real GDP _____ potential GDP, and the unemployment rate _____ than the natural rate of unemployment.

d. If the government wanted to reduce unemployment by closing the recessionary gap, it would have to _____ government spending by $_____.

e. Alternatively the government could close the recessionary gap by _____ taxes and/or _____ transfer payments.

f. What would be the effect if the government pursued an expansionary fiscal policy given the initial aggregate demand curve, ADo?

304

2. Assume the economy in the figure below is presently suffering from an inflationary GDP gap.

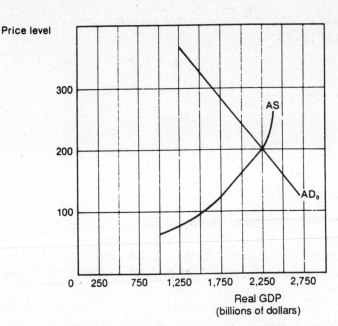

a. In order to close the inflationary gap using fiscal policy, the government could:
   (1) _____
   (2) _____
   (3) _____

b. If the economy's multiplier is 2.5 (includes price-level effects) and the decline in government spending necessary to move the economy back to its potential level of real GDP is $200 billion, potential real GDP is short of the current inflationary level of real GDP by $_____. A/An _____ in government spending of $_____ will close the inflationary gap.

c. Show on the figure above the effect of a contractionary fiscal policy. Be sure to identify the changes in the price level and real GDP.

3. List three problems associated with the implementation of fiscal policy.

   a. _____

   b. _____

   c. _____

Concept 3: *Built-in stabilizers and shifts in aggregate demand*

4. Assume that the economy represented in the figure below currently has a level of aggregate demand as shown by the AD curve, ADo.

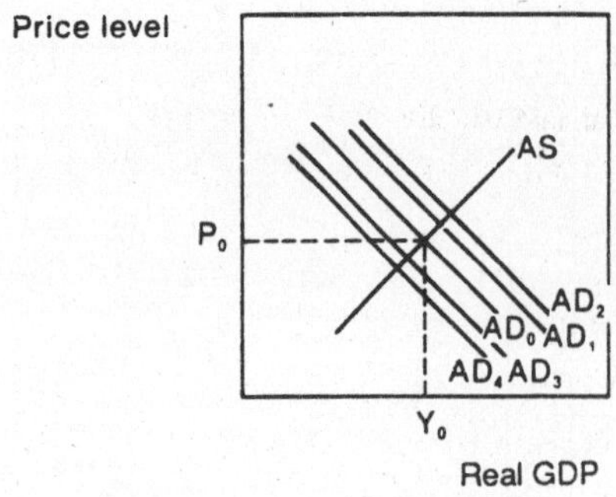

a. As an economy expands, taxes _____ and transfers _____. An increase in aggregate demand caused by a given increase in autonomous purchases is represented by AD1 and AD2 where one of the AD curves is associated with an economy having built-in stabilizers and the other is not. Which AD curve, AD1 or AD2, is consistent with the existence of built-in stabilizers? _____

b. As an economy contracts, taxes _____ and transfers _____. A given reduction in autonomous purchases shifts the aggregate demand curve leftward from ADo. AD3 and AD4 result from the same decline in autonomous spending, but one of the curves is for an economy with automatic stabilizers and the other curve is not. Which of the two aggregate demand curves, AD3 or AD4, is consistent with built-in stabilizers?_____

c. Built-in stabilizers _____ the fluctuations in aggregate demand and real GDP for given fluctuations in autonomous spending.

Concept 4: *Supply-side fiscal policy*

5. Show on the figure below the supply-side effect of a cut in tax rates. Be sure to identify the changes in real GDP and the price level.

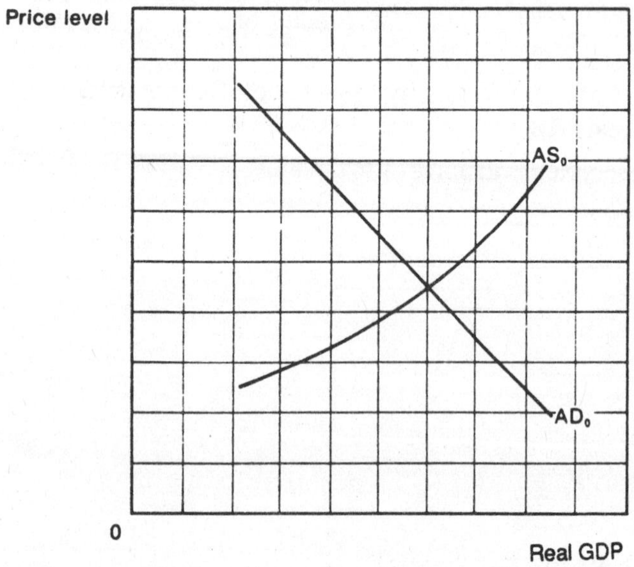

306

a. A cut in tax rates will _____ the after-tax returns to work, saving, and investment and is expected to _____ the levels of hours worked, saving, and investment.

b. If the aggregate supply curve shifts _____, the price level will fall and the level of real GDP will _____.

c. Evidence indicates that the short-run effect on the aggregate supply curve of cuts in tax rates will be _____ relative to shifts in the aggregate demand curve.

d. If the economy is at its potential level of real GDP when tax rates are reduced, the price level will likely _____ unless the government _____ government purchases.

Advanced Application: Fiscal policy and recessionary gaps

6. Given the following equations, find the change in government spending necessary to close a recessionary GDP gap of $100 billion. The recessionary gap could alternatively be closed by what change in the tax rate?

Y	=	$C + Ip + G + NE$	where A	= $300
C	=	$A + (MPC)DI$	Ip	= $400
DI	=	$Y - T$	G	= $500
T	=	tY	E	= $200
Ip	=	Io	MPC	= .9
G	=	Go	t	= .3
NE	=	$E - M$	MPI	= .15
M	=	$(MPI)Y$		

C = consumption, Y = real GDP, Ip = planned investment, G = government purchases, NE = net exports, A = autonomous consumption, DI = disposable income, MPC = marginal propensity to consume, T = net taxes, t = net tax rate, E = exports, M = imports, MPI = marginal propensity to import

Insights on Issues

7. According to Lawrence Lindsey and Allen Meltzer, how effective is fiscal policy at economic stabilization?

Select the best answer.

1. The use of government spending and taxation for the purpose of stabilizing the economy is called:
   a. budget policy.
   b. monetary policy.
   c. fiscal policy.
   d. trade policy.

2. A budget deficit exists when:
   a. tax revenue exceeds government spending.
   b. government spending equals government revenues.
   c. government spending exceeds government revenues.
   d. the public debt decreases.

3. An increase in the budget deficit _____ aggregate _____.
   a. increases, demand
   b. increases, supply
   c. decreases, demand
   d. decreases, supply

4. An increase in a budget surplus or a decrease in a budget deficit _____ aggregate demand and _____ real GDP.
   a. increases, reduces
   b. increases, decreases
   c. decreases, increases
   d. decreases, reduces

5. A recessionary GDP gap can be closed by which of the following?
   a. An increase in government spending
   b. A decrease in taxes
   c. An increase in transfer payments
   d. All of the above

6. If the marginal respending rate (MRR) is .6 and the current level of equilibrium real GDP is short of the desired level of real GDP by $250 billion, by how much will the government have to increase aggregate demand? (Assume that the economy is in the flat portion of the AS curve.)
   a. $40 billion
   b. $60 billion
   c. $80 billion
   d. $100 billion
   e. $120 billion

7. Which of the following fiscal policies is the most stimulative in the short run?
   a. Increases in government spending financed by borrowing (incurring a deficit)
   b. Increases in government spending financed by taxation
   c. Equal decreases in taxes and government spending
   d. Increases in transfers financed by taxation

8. When the price level is responsive to changes in aggregate demand, the multiplier will be _____ the multiplier presented in the text chapter.
   a. greater than
   b. less than
   c. equal to
   d. twice the size of

9. Which of the following policies should be used to close an inflationary GDP gap?
   a. Increases in government spending
   b. Tax cuts
   c. Increases in transfer payments
   d. An increase in taxes

10. Which lag in the implementation of fiscal policy is due to the length of time that it takes fiscal policy to have the desired impact on the economy?
   a. Recognition lag
   b. Administrative lag
   c. Operational lag
   d. Cyclical lag

11. Automatic stabilizers:
   a. are a form of nondiscretionary fiscal policy.
   b. include income taxes and cash assistance to the poor.
   c. include in-kind assistance and social security benefits.
   d. a and b.
   e. All of the above.

12. As the economy expands, tax revenues _____ and transfer payments _____, causing the economy to expand _____ than it would in the absence of these built-in stabilizers.
   a. fall, rise, more
   b. fall, fall, less
   c. rise, fall, more
   d. rise, fall, less
   e. rise, rise, more

13. Built-in stabilizers result in _____ fluctuations in aggregate demand for given autonomous changes in spending than as would be the case for an economy in which built-in stabilizers did not exist.
   a. greater
   b. more severe
   c. smaller
   d. the same

14. Which of the following budget concepts measures the policy stance of discretionary fiscal policy—that is, whether it is expansionary or contractionary?
    a. Balanced budget
    b. Budget deficit
    c. Potential output budget
    d. High-employment deficit (or surplus)

15. A reduction in tax rates _____ the after-tax returns to work, saving, and investment, which in the long run may _____ aggregate supply.
    a. reduces, increase
    b. reduces, decrease
    c. increases, decrease
    d. increases, increase

16. Proponents of supply-side fiscal policies argue that a cut in tax rates will:
    a. increase the number of hours worked.
    b. increase the level of saving.
    c. increase the level of investment.
    d. increase potential real GDP.
    e. All of the above.

17. Evidence indicates that a cut in tax rates in the short run will likely increase _____ more than _____, causing the price level to _____ unless government reduces _____.
    a. aggregate demand, aggregate supply, rise, government spending
    b. aggregate supply, aggregate demand, fall, transfers to the poor
    c. aggregate supply, aggregate demand, rise, tax rates
    d. aggregate demand, aggregate supply, fall, its borrowing
    e. None of the above

18. Assume that the economy is currently operating below potential real GDP along the upsloping portion of the aggregate supply curve. If the economy has a budget surplus and legislation is passed, increasing the surplus, what will happen to real GDP and the price level?
    a. Real GDP will increase and the price level will fall.
    b. Real GDP and the price level will fall.
    c. Real GDP and the price level will rise.
    d. Real GDP will fall and the price level will rise.

19. Assume that the economy is on the horizontal portion of the aggregate supply curve and $300 billion below potential real GDP. The economy's expenditure multiplier with price-level effects is 2 and without price-level effects is 3. What change in government spending is necessary to close the recessionary gap?
    a. Increase government spending by $150 billion
    b. Decrease government spending by $150 billion
    c. Increase government spending by $100 billion
    d. Increase government spending by $300 billion

Answer the following three questions based upon the data below. (All data are in billions of dollars

Real GDP	Government Spending	Tax Revenue
$2,000	$1,000	$ 800
3,000	1,000	900
4,000	1,000	1,000
5,000	1,000	1,100
6,000	1,000	1,200

20. At what level of real GDP is the budget balanced?
   a. $2,000 billion
   b. $3,000 billion
   c. $4,000 billion
   d. $5,000 billion
   e. $6,000 billion

21. Assume that the economy's actual real GDP is $4,000 billion, but potential real GDP is $5,000 billion. Which of the following is true regarding the high-employment budget?
   a. At a level of real GDP of $4,000 billion, the high-employment budget is in balance.
   b. At a level of real GDP of $5,000 billion, the high-employment budget has a surplus of $100 billion.
   c. At a level of real GDP of $5,000 billion, the high-employment deficit is $100 billion.
   d. At a level of real GDP of $4,000 billion, the high-employment deficit equals the actual budget deficit.

22. If government spending is increased by $100 billion at each level of real GDP and the economy is currently at potential real GDP with a balanced budget, which of the following statements is correct?
   a. The actual budget will be balanced at a level of real GDP of $5,000 billion, but the high-employment budget will have a deficit of $100 billion.
   b. The high-employment budget will be balanced at a level of real GDP of $4,000 billion, but the actual budget will have a deficit of $100 billion.
   c. The actual and high-employment budgets will be balanced at a level of real GDP of $5,000.
   d. The actual and high-employment budgets will both have deficits of $100.

■ THINK IT THROUGH

1. If the current unemployment rate exceeds the natural rate of unemployment and the current government budget is in balance, the high-employment budget is in (balance/deficit/surplus). What are the effects on the economy?

2. Conflicts such as World War II and the Vietnam War created domestic economic expansion. Explain. How does this relate to the ease or difficulty of implementing fiscal policy?

3. Discuss the case for and against supply-side fiscal policies.

CHAPTER ANSWERS

The Chapter in Brief

1.Deficit 2. Surpluses 3. Expansionary 4. Contractionary 5. Increase 6. Decrease 7. Without igniting 8. Will not 9. Expansionary 10. That increases the budget deficit 11. Reduce 12. Decrease 13. Increase 14. Easier 15. More difficult 16. Will not 17. Recognition 18. Administrative 19. Operational 20. Nondiscretionary 21. In-kind assistance 22. Prevents the level of aggregate demand from falling as much as 23. Reduces 24. High-employment deficit 25. Aggregate supply will shift rightward 26. Are not 27. Inflation 28. Increase 29. Rightward

Key Terms Review

1. Fiscal policy 2. Automatic stabilizers 3. Accelerated depreciation allowances 4. Contractionary fiscal policy 5. Supply-side fiscal policies 6. Expansionary fiscal policies 7. High-employment deficit (or surplus) 8. Government budget

Concept Review

1. a.

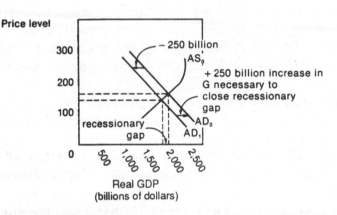

b. Leftward, $250 billion
c. Recessionary GDP gap, falls below, is higher
d. Increase, $125 billion
e. Reduce, increase
f. Real GDP would exceed potential real GDP and the unemployment rate would fall below its natural rate, putting upward pressure on the price level.

2. a. (1) Increase taxes (2) Reduce transfer payments (3) Reduce government spending
   b. $500 billion; decrease, $200 billion
   c.

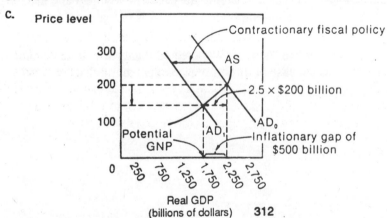

3. a. Political problems b. Forecasting problems c. Timing problems
4. a. Increase, decrease; AD1
   b. Decrease, increase; AD3
   c. Moderate
5.

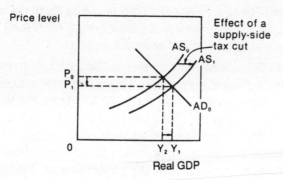

a. Increase, increase b. Rightward, Increase c. Very small d. Rise, reduces
6. This particular model is analyzed in the appendix that presents a complete Keynesian model. For the equations and values given, the multiplier is 1.923. Thus if the policy goal is to expand real GDP by $100 billion, divide this amount by the multiplier to determine the necessary change in government spending. ($100 billion/1.923 = $52 billion.) Government spending must be increased by $52 billion in order to increase equilibrium real GDP by $100 billion and close the recessionary GDP gap.

Alternatively, the recessionary gap can be closed by a reduction in the tax rate. The first step is to find the tax rate multiplier (change in real GDP/change in the tax rate). Dividing the tax rate multiplier into the recessionary gap of $100 billion will give the necessary change in tax rates. For those students familiar with calculus, the tax rate multiplier can be found by solving the system of equations for the equilibrium level of real GDP, Y, and taking the partial derivative of Y with respect to the tax rate, t. The tax rate multiplier is as follows:

$$\text{Tax rate multiplier} = -[MPC(Y)]/[1 - MPC + (MPC)t + MPI]$$

For the values given, the tax rate multiplier equals -4659.75. Dividing this into $100 billion gives -.021. The tax rate must be reduced from 30% to 27.9% in order to close the recessionary gap.

7. Lawrence Lindsey says that fiscal policy is not "...well-adapted to fine tuning the economy." Because of long lags, fiscal policy can be ill-timed. He suggests taking a long view, making sure that the tax system results in the least amount of economic inefficiency and government spending passes the benefit-cost test. Allen Meltzer agrees that fiscal policy cannot successfully fine tune the economy and suggests that the problem is forecasting. Both Lindsey and Meltzer suggest the focus should be on a monetary policy of low and stable inflation.

313

1. c 2. c 3. a 4. d 5. d 6. d 7. a 8. b 9. d 10. c 11. e 12. d 13. c 14. d 15. d 16. e 17. a 18. b 19. c 20. c 21. b 22. a

Think it Through

1. If the current government budget is in balance but the economy is operating below potential real GDP, the high-employment budget would be in surplus. Thus discretionary fiscal policy would be contractionary if the economy expanded to its potential level of real GDP. Fiscal policy would act as a "drag" on the economy as it approached potential real GDP.

2. During wars, U.S. government spending has far exceeded tax revenues. The increases in the deficit during the war years created domestic economic expansion. This is powerful evidence of the ability of government budget deficits to expand the economy in the short run. But it also points to a difficulty in the implementation of fiscal policy. National defense and security, economic stabilization, and other goals of society compete with one another. Economic stabilization may require certain budget changes, whereas the provision of national defense may require completely different budget changes. Nevertheless, any budget change that alters a deficit or surplus will have short-run macroeconomic effects that may or may not be desirable with regard to economic stabilization.

3. During periods of stagflation, the traditional discretionary fiscal policy of aggregate demand management is unlikely to reduce inflation and unemployment simultaneously. If fiscal policy could shift the economy's aggregate supply curve rightward in the short run, real output would increase and both the unemployment rate and price level (or rate of inflation) would fall. The argument for supply-side fiscal policies is that not only would the price level and unemployment fall, but the potential level of real GDP would increase, allowing higher future living standards. All of this is based upon the belief that a cut in tax rates will have large impacts on hours worked, saving, and investment, thus shifting the aggregate supply curve rightward. Few economists would dispute the argument that tax rate cuts increase to some extent hours worked, saving, and investment. But the empirical evidence suggests that the short-run impacts of a cut in tax rates will primarily affect the aggregate demand curve rather than the aggregate supply curve. If the economy is already suffering from inflation and tax rates are cut, there will be greater rather than less pressure for prices to rise.

18 THE FEDERAL BUDGET DEFICIT AND THE NATIONAL DEBT

■ CHAPTER CONCEPTS

After studying your text, attending class, and completing this chapter, you should be able to:

1. Discuss the federal budget deficit, methods of financing it, and how its possible impact on interest rates can influence private investment, economic growth, international trade, and macroeconomic equilibrium.
2. Discuss the impact of the national debt on the well-being of current and future generations.
3. Discuss some of the problems involved in measuring the federal budget deficit.
4. Discuss the concept of Ricardian equivalence of tax and deficit finance.

■ THE CHAPTER IN BRIEF

Fill in the blanks to summarize chapter content.

Until the 1930s, it was believed that it was necessary to balance the budget annually. Government outlays for the year had to be financed by an equal amount of government revenue. An annually balanced budget, (1)_____ (stabilizes rather than destabilizes, destabilizes rather than stabilizes) the business cycle. In recessions, tax revenue falls and transfer payments rise, producing a federal budget deficit where federal government outlays exceed government receipts. In order to balance the budget, (2)_____ (revenues, government outlays) must be increased or (3)_____ (revenues, government outlays) reduced. But this is contractionary and will make the recession worse. In expansions, federal government surpluses may arise where taxes and other government revenues rise above government outlays. But a balanced-budget policy requires decreases in taxes or increases in government outlays, both of which are (4)_____ (expansionary, contractionary) in an economic expansion.

Deficits can be financed in two ways if taxes are not increased. The deficit can be (5)_____ (financed by selling government securities to the public, monetized), which ultimately results in an increase in the money supply. Or the deficit can be (6)_____ (financed by selling government securities to the public, monetized). In the latter case, because the Fed does not intervene and buy an equivalent quantity of securities, the money supply does not increase. Deficits are expansionary, and the method of financing deficits may add to or retard that expansionary effect. With monetization, the increase in the money stock is (7)_____ (contractionary, expansionary). The aggregate demand curve will shift farther (8)_____ (leftward, rightward) when deficits are financed by monetization. When the government sells securities to the public, the demand for loanable funds increases, causing interest rates to (9)_____(rise, fall). This causes some (10)_____ (crowding out, crowding in) meaning that rising interest rates reduce the level of private borrowing below the level that would have prevailed if the government had not borrowed to finance budget deficits. Empirical evidence suggests that on average the crowding-out effect from government deficits is (11)_____ (large, small). On net, the expansionary effect of the deficit is still positive, (12)_____ (and larger than, but not as large as) the case of monetization. Both methods of financing are (13)_____ (more, less) expansionary, however, than increasing taxes to cover the deficit.

Deficits may also have an impact on international trade. If the financing of deficits results in higher U.S. interest rates relative to foreign rates of interest, foreigners will seek to (14)_____ (purchase, sell) the relatively higher-yielding U.S. financial assets such as U.S. government securities. But they first have to convert their foreign currencies into dollars in order to make the purchases. This increases the (15)_____ (supply of, demand for) dollars, causing the dollar's price to rise relative to those of foreign currencies. This in turn causes the relative prices of U.S. goods to (16)_____ (fall, rise) in foreign countries and the relative prices of imported goods in the United States to fall. Exports fall and imports rise, resulting in an/a (17)_____ (increase, decline) in aggregate demand. Deficits also affect international trade because deficits are expansionary and increases in the nation's disposable income cause imports to (18)_____ (fall, rise) relative to exports, causing net exports and aggregate demand to fall.

If crowding out is significant to the extent that interest rates are higher and investment spending is lower, U.S. businesses may not engage in enough development of new technology to remain competitive in world markets. A lower rate of capital growth (19)_____ (reduces, increases) the rate of growth of the economy and reduces future potential standards of living. But the government's use of resources is (20)_____ (always unproductive, not unproductive). The government subsidizes research and new technologies and encourages investment through government tax policies.

A deficit (21)_____ (reduces, adds to) the national debt, whereas a budget surplus (22)_____ (reduces, adds to) the national debt. The (23)_____ (net federal debt, national debt) is the dollar amount that the federal government owes to its creditors at a given point in time. The (24)_____ (net federal debt, national debt) is the credit extended to the federal government by those other than the Fed and government agencies. The national debt as a percentage of GDP fell from 89% in 1950 to 33% in 1980 (25)_____ (and has continued to fall to under 23%, but has risen since then to almost 50%). In 1994, most of the net public debt, 79%, was (26)_____ (externally, internally) held by U.S. individuals, businesses, and state and local governments. The remainder of the net public debt, 21%, is (27)_____ (externally, internally) held by foreigners. This inflow of foreign saving acts to (28)_____ (offset to some extent, worsen) the crowding-out effect.

Two major burdens are associated with a large public debt. First, future generations will have to pay more taxes to pay interest on the debt. These additional taxes otherwise would have been used to provide additional government goods and services. Second, assuming a large crowding-out effect, a decline in investment (29)_____ (will not, will) impair the growth rate of the economy.

The rate of economic growth influences the size of the federal budget deficit. A (30) _____ (higher, lower) rate of economic growth causes tax receipts to rise and transfer payments to fall. And since tax collections increase at a rate faster than inflation, real tax revenues (31)_____ (decrease, increase). Deficits are also influenced by inflation and interest rates. Inflation causes tax receipts to increase faster than outlays, causing a decline in the deficit. Higher interest rates (32)_____ (reduce, increase) the deficit.

The federal budget deficit can be measured using the unified budget deficit or the NIPA budget deficit. The (33)_____ (NIPA, unified) budget deficit is the best measure of the impact of the federal budget deficit on the volume of saving. The (34) _____ (NIPA, unified) budget deficit is the best measure of the government's total borrowing needs for the year and includes all government expenditures and revenues, both "on" and "off" budget.

Inflation affects the real value of the national debt. For instance, during periods of inflation and high interest rates, the real value of the national debt (35)_____ (rises, falls). The actual deficit overstates the real value of the deficit. This constitutes a transfer of purchasing power from the government's creditors to the government. During periods of low and stable inflation and low interest rates, the real value of the national debt is higher, in effect transferring purchasing power from the government to the holders of government securities. Here the actual deficit (36)_____ (understates, overstates) the real value of the deficit.

It is argued that deficits have a negative impact on the economy by influencing saving and real interest rates. But according to (37)_____ (Ricardian equivalence, the life cycle hypothesis), forward-looking individuals will save enough in the present in anticipation of higher future taxes to offset increases in government borrowing resulting from the deficit. As a result, the supply of and demand for loanable funds increase by the same amount, leaving interest rates unchanged. The evidence, however, is mixed regarding the impact of deficits on interest rates.

■ KEY TERMS REVIEW

Write the key term from the list below next to its definition.

Key Terms

Crowding-out effect	Internal debt
National debt	External debt
Net federal debt	Ricardian equivalence

Definitions

1. _____: the portion of the national debt owed to citizens of other nations.

2. _____: the dollar amount that the federal government owes to its creditors at a given point in time.

3. _____: prevails when an increase in government borrowing to finance a deficit causes a sufficient increase in private saving to keep the real interest rate fixed.

4. _____: the portion of the national debt owed to those other than the Fed and government agencies.

5. _____: the portion of the national debt owed to the nation's own citizens.

6. _____: the reduction in private investment purchases caused by higher interest rates that result from borrowing by the government to cover its budget deficit.

■ CONCEPT REVIEW

Concept 1: *Annually balanced budget, deficits, interest rates, crowding out, and international trade*

1. Assume that the economy shown in the figure below is at its potential level of real GDP and the federal budget policy is to balance the budget.

a. Suppose the level of aggregate demand falls from ADo to AD1. As real GDP _____, tax revenues _____ and transfer payments _____, causing the budget to be in _____.

b. Because of the balanced-budget policy, the government must _____ or _____, both of which shift the AD curve _____. Show this graphically on the figure above and identify the change in equilibrium real GDP.

c. Assume that the economy is once again at its potential level of real GDP and aggregate demand increases to AD2. As real GDP _____, tax revenues _____ and transfers _____, causing the budget to be in _____.

d. In order to balance the budget, the government must _____ or _____, both of which shift the AD curve _____. Show this graphically on the figure above and identify the change in equilibrium real GDP.

e. Given initial changes in aggregate demand, a balanced-budget policy results in _____ (larger, smaller) fluctuations in real GDP.

2. The figure below shows a loanable funds market for an economy.

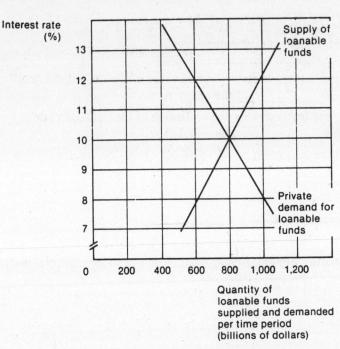

a. Suppose the government enters the loanable funds market to borrow $200 billion at the prevailing rate of interest to finance the deficit. Government borrowing _____ the demand for loanable funds by $200 billion at every interest rate. Show this on the figure above and identify the change in the interest rate. Interest rates _____ to _____%, causing investment spending and other credit-sensitive expenditures to _____ by $_____.

b. As investment spending _____, the economy's future rate of growth will be _____.

c. If the economy is in a deep recession, it is likely that investment spending is _____ to changes in interest rates. In a deep recession, crowding out is _____.

3. If deficits increase U.S. interest rates relative to foreign rates of interest:
   a. Foreign demand for U.S. dollars _____ (increases, decreases).
   b. The price of the U.S. dollar _____ (rises, falls) relative to the prices of foreign currencies.
   c. U.S. goods and services become _____ (more, less) price competitive abroad.
   d. Exports _____ (rise, fall) and imports _____ (rise, fall).
   e. Net exports and aggregate demand _____ (increase, decrease).
   f. Equilibrium real GDP _____ (increases, decreases).

Concepts 2 and 3:   *Burden of the national debt, measuring and reducing the deficit*

4. List and describe the two major burdens of the national debt.

    a. _____

    b. _____

5. a. During periods of high inflation and interest rates, the real value of the net federal debt _____. The actual deficit _____ the real deficit.

    b. During periods of low inflation and interest rates, the real value of the net federal debt _____. The actual deficit _____ the real deficit.

6. List three ways government can reduce the deficit.

    a. _____

    b. _____

    c. _____

Insights on Issues

7. Briefly discuss Robert Eisner's views regarding the costs associated with a large federal budget deficit.

■ MASTERY TEST

Select the best answer.

1. In 1994, the federal budget deficit was $_____.
   a. $100 billion
   b. $100 million
   c. $202 million
   d. $203 billion

2. Which of the following prevails when federal government receipts for a year exceed government outlays?
   a. High-employment budget
   b. Balanced budget
   c. Federal budget deficit
   d. Federal government surplus

3. What was true of budget policy prior to the 1930s?
   a. The budget should be balanced annually.
   b. Recessions produced deficits, requiring a contractionary budget response.
   c. Expansions produced surpluses, requiring an expansionary budget response.
   d. The budget actually destabilized the economy.
   e. All of the above.

4. Of the ways listed below for financing or eliminating a deficit, which policy is the least expansionary?
   a. Tax financing
   b. Sale of government securities to the public
   c. Monetization
   d. None of the above

5. Of the ways listed below for financing or eliminating a deficit, which policy is the most expansionary?
   a. Tax financing
   b. Sale of government securities to the public
   c. Monetization
   d. Privatization

6. A deficit financed by monetization results in an aggregate demand curve:
   a. that lies to the left of the ad curve when deficits are financed by taxes.
   b. that lies to the left of the ad curve when deficits are financed by selling government securities to the public.
   c. that does not shift.
   d. that lies to the right of the AD curve when deficits are financed by selling government securities to the public.

7. If a deficit results in _____ interest rates and _____ private investment, there is said to be _____ .
   a. higher, less, crowding out
   b. higher, less, monetization
   c. lower, more, crowding in
   d. lower, less, crowding out
   e. b and c

8. Empirical studies suggest that the impact of federal budget deficits on interest rates:
   a. is very large.
   b. is large and has caused our international trade problems.
   c. is mixed.
   d. rises and falls with fluctuations in real GDP.

9. If the budget deficit causes _____ U.S. interest rates relative to foreign interest rates, imports will _____ and exports will _____.
   a. lower, rise, rise
   b. higher, rise, fall
   c. higher, rise, rise
   d. higher, fall, fall
   e. lower, fall, fall

10. An increase in the budget deficit will eventually _____ the nation's disposable income, which _____ imports and _____ aggregate demand below what it would be in the absence of international trade.
    a. decrease, decreases, increases
    b. increase, decreases, decreases
    c. decrease, increases, decreases
    d. increase, increases, decreases
    e. decrease, decreases, decreases

11. Which of the following terms represents the credit extended to the federal government by those other than the Fed and government agencies?
    a. All private securities holders
    b. Government debt
    c. National debt
    d. Net federal debt

12. Which of the following terms is defined as the dollar amount that the federal government owes to its creditors at a given point in time?
    a. All private securities holders
    b. Government deficit
    c. National debt
    d. Net federal debt

13. Most of the national debt is _____ held, which means that when the debt is repaid there is _____ in aggregate demand.
    a. internally, a significant reduction
    b. internally, no change
    c. externally, no change
    d. externally, a significant reduction
    e. internally, an increase

14. The externally held debt was what percentage of the total net public debt in 1994?
    a. 12%
    b. 50%
    c. 80%
    d. 21%

15. During periods of high inflation and high interest rates, the actual deficit _____ the real deficit, resulting in a gain to _____ at the expense of _____.
    a. overstates, the government's creditors, the government
    b. overstates, the government, the government's creditors
    c. understates, the government, the government's creditors
    d. understates, the government's creditors, the government

16. Which of the following is true regarding monetization of the deficit?
    a. Monetization is the most expansionary way to finance the deficit in the short-run.
    b. Monetization results in a larger increase in the interest rate than if securities are sold to the public.
    c. With monetization, newly-issued government securities are purchased by the public while the Fed simultaneously sells an equivalent amount of previously-issued securities.
    d. All of the above

17. Which of the following ways to finance government spending results in the highest interest rate?
    a. Tax increases
    b. Monetization
    c. Security sales to the public
    d. Increases in the money supply

18. You have been asked to advise the government regarding the type of deficit financing that would least likely impair business investment spending in the short-run. Which of the following would you recommend?
    a. Tax increases
    b. Monetization
    c. Security sales to the public
    d. Decreases in the money supply

19. Which of the following describes the effects of an increase in the budget deficit on international trade?
    a. If the deficit is financed by monetization, interest rates in the United States rise relative to foreign interest rates, causing the international value of the dollar to fall and net exports to rise.
    b. If the deficit is financed by monetization, leaving domestic interest rates unchanged, the international value of the dollar and the level of net exports also remain unchanged.
    c. If the deficit is financed by selling bonds to the public, leaving interest rates unchanged, the international value of the dollar rises and causes net exports to fall.
    d. An increase in the budget deficit always causes the international value of the dollar and net exports to fall.

20. You have been asked by government to recommend a method for financing the budget deficit which would least-likely worsen the trade deficit. Which of the following will you recommend?
    a. Decrease the money supply
    b. Monetization
    c. Sales of government securities to the public
    d. Purchases of government securities from foreigners

■ THINK IT THROUGH

1. If the economy is at its potential level of real GDP and the government budget deficit increases, which method of deficit financing would you favor and why? Would it be better to raise taxes or borrow?

2. "A balanced-budget amendment is necessary to keep lawmakers fiscally responsible and to stabilize the economy." Do you agree? Explain.

3. Discuss the implications for the relationship between the budget deficit and international trade given studies that suggest that government deficits do not have large crowding-out effects.

◼ CHAPTER ANSWERS

The Chapter in Brief

1.Destabilizes rather than stabilizes 2. Revenues 3.Government outlays 4. Expansionary 5.
Monetized 6. Financed by selling government securities to the public 7. Expansionary 8.
Rightward 9. Rise 10. Crowding out 11. Small 12. But not as large as 13. More 14. Purchase 15.
Demand for 16. Rise 17. Decline 18. Rise 19. Reduces 20. Not unproductive 21. Adds to 22.
Reduces 23. National debt 24. Net federal debt 25. But has risen since then to almost 50% 26. In-
ternally 27. Externally 28. Offset to some extent 29. Will 30. Higher 31. Increase 32. Increase
33. NIPA 34. Unified 35. Falls 36. Understates 37. Ricardian equivalence

Key Terms Review

1. External debt 2. National debt 3. Ricardian equivalence 4. Net federal debt 5. Internal debt
6. Crowding-out effect

Concept Review

1. a.   Falls, fall, rise, deficit
   b.   Increase taxes, reduce government outlays, leftward
   c.   Increases, rise, fall, surplus
   d.   Reduce taxes, increase government outlays, rightward
   e.   Larger

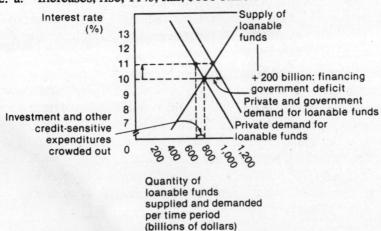

2. a.   Increases, rise, 11%, fall, $100 billion

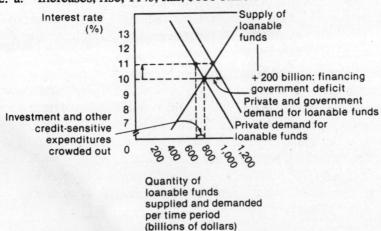

b. Falls, reduced

c. Unresponsive, very small or nonexistent

3. a. Increases b. Rises c. Less d. Fall, rise e. Decrease f. Decreases

4. a. Future generations will have to pay more interest on the debt instead of receiving government goods and services in return for those taxes. If the percentage of the net federal debt externally held increases, the payment of interest results in an outflow of purchasing power from the United States, resulting in a lower level of aggregate demand than otherwise would be the case.

   b. If the crowding-out effect is substantial, a growing federal debt will decrease private investment and reduce the growth rate of the private capital stock. This slows the growth of worker productivity and real GDP and results in lower living standards than would have been the case if investment spending had not been crowded out. The inflow of foreign saving resulting from the externally held debt, however, serves to moderate the crowding-out effect.

5. a. Falls; overstates b. increases; understates

6. a. Increase taxes, charges and fees b. Reduce government outlays c. Sale of public assets

7. Robert Eisner believes that the cost of the federal budget deficit has been exaggerated. Critics focus on the presumed crowding out of private investment, but they ignore the positive effects of increased public investment. Because the economy has been at less than full employment, deficits have not crowded out investment, but have increased consumption and, therefore, induced some saving and investment. As a result, deficits have "crowded in" rather than "crowded out" investment.

Mastery Test

1. d 2. d 3. e 4. a 5. c 6. d 7. a 8. c 9. b 10. d 11. d 12. c 13. b 14. d 15. b 16. a 17. c 18. b 19. b 20. b

Think it Through

1. If a deficit must be incurred at the level of potential real GDP, then the least expansionary form of financing should be used to prevent excessive overheating of the economy. A deficit will produce an inflationary GDP gap, but it can be minimized by selling U.S. government securities to the public rather than monetizing the deficit. At least the sale of securities to the public will not add fuel to the fire by expanding the money stock. With monetization, in contrast, the money stock increases, resulting in a larger inflationary gap. At potential real GDP, it would be preferable to finance government outlays with tax increases. On net, there would still be an expansionary effect producing an inflationary gap, but the gap would be smaller than if the expenditures were financed by borrowing.

2. Regarding fiscal responsibility, a balanced budget does not necessarily mean a cap on spending or taxes. Higher taxes allow higher spending, but if lawmakers want to spend sums in excess of current revenues they can simply increase taxes. With regard to stabilization of the economy, a balanced-budget policy would destabilize rather than stabilize the economy. A decline in real GDP produces a recessionary gap and results in a deficit, which must be eliminated by increasing taxes or cutting government outlays, both of which make the recession worse. An increase in real GDP beyond potential real GDP produces an inflationary gap, which results in a budget surplus. The surplus can be eliminated by increasing government outlays or cutting taxes, both

of which make inflation worse. A balanced-budget rule would not allow the policy flexibility needed for dealing with recessions and inflationary periods.

3. Large budget deficits have been blamed for worsening the U.S. balance of trade. The argument is that rising budget deficits caused U.S. interest rates to rise relative to those prevailing abroad. Foreigners increased their demand for U.S. dollars so that they could purchase U.S. financial assets such as government securities. The increase in the price of the dollar relative to the prices of foreign currencies reduced the price competitiveness of U.S. goods abroad and resulted in a reduction in net exports. This prevented aggregate demand and equilibrium real GDP from attaining a higher level. If empirical evidence shows that the impact of deficits on interest rates is small, then the high interest rates that were in part causing the deterioration of net exports must be due to factors other than federal budget deficits. The point is that theoretical cause-and-effect relationships may or may not have important quantitative impacts on the economy even though it is commonly believed by the public that those relationships are significant.

19 ISSUES IN STABILIZATION POLICY: INFLATION VERSUS UNEMPLOYMENT AND RATIONAL EXPECTATIONS

■ CHAPTER CONCEPTS

After studying your text, attending class, and completing this chapter, you should be able to:

1. Discuss the historical tradeoff between annual inflation and unemployment in modern economics through the use of the Phillips curve.

2. Show how shifts in aggregate supply can affect the tradeoff between the goals of reducing inflation and reducing unemployment.

3. Understand how rational expectations of changes in the price level can affect the behavior of workers and investors and influence macroeconomic equilibrium.

4. Understand some of the difficulties of implementing stabilization policies and compare the views of major schools of thought on such policies.

■ THE CHAPTER IN BRIEF

Fill in the blanks to summarize chapter content.

In the 1950s, A.W. Phillips investigated the relationship between the unemployment rate and the rate of change in wages for Great Britain. He discovered what appeared to be a very stable (1)_____ (direct, inverse) relationship between the unemployment rate and wage inflation. As the unemployment rate fell, the rate of wage inflation increased and vice versa. The Phillips curve was consistent with models of the economy that emphasized changes in aggregate (2)_____ (demand, supply) as the source of fluctuations in real GDP and the price level. Using data for the (3)_____ (1970s, 1960s), a stable Phillips curve (expressed as a relationship between the unemployment rate and the rate of change in prices) seemed to explain the unemployment-inflation experience of the United States. Policy makers believed that it was possible to choose the desired unemployment rate-inflation rate along the Phillips curve by using demand-management policies. The Phillips curve analysis assumes that the aggregate supply curve shifts rightward in an/a (4)_____ (erratic, predictable) manner. Further, it does not consider the role of inflation expectations.

In the 1970s and 1980s the Phillips curve for the United States has (5)_____ (not remained stable but has shifted due to, remained stable in part because of) supply-side shocks and changes in inflation expectations. For instance, the oil-price shocks of the early 1970s caused the aggregate supply curve to shift (6)_____ (leftward, rightward) more than the aggregate demand curve shifted (7)_____ (leftward, rightward) resulting in a rising price level at a time when the economy was experiencing increases in the rate of unemployment. Between 1978 and 1980, as unemployment rose from 6% to 7%, the rate of inflation rose from 8% to over 13% per year. These events directly (8)_____ (support, counter) the belief that the Phillips curve is stable over the long run. Over short periods, such as 1986 and 1987 or 1990 and 1991, the Phillips curve tradeoff between inflation and the unemployment rate was present, but over the long run the Phillips curve shifts. Supply-side shocks that increase input prices increase the rate of inflation for given unemployment rates and shift the Phillips curve (9)_____ (downward, upward). Supply-side shocks that reduce input prices, such as the decline in oil prices in 1986, shift the Phillips curve (10)_____ (downward, upward).

There are two major competing theories of how we form expectations. One theory holds that we form expectations adaptively. Our expectations are dependent solely on past observations of the variable to be forecast. The other major theory, the theory of (11)_____ (aggregate expected demand, rational expectations), holds that individuals use all information, past and present, including relevant economic models, in their forecasts of economic variables. This theory assumes that the expected value of the forecast variable equals the actual future value of that variable. This doesn't mean that individuals forecast correctly all the time; rather it means that forecasting errors will not be systematically high or low in the long run.

If an increase in aggregate demand is anticipated, it is argued that rational individuals will use this information in forming inflation expectations. If labor, for instance, expects higher inflation as a result of an anticipated increase in aggregate demand, they will press for higher wages as a way of maintaining the real value or purchasing power of their wage income. If wages and other input prices rise at exactly the same rate as prices, real wages and real input prices will not change, (12)_____ (causing, and there is no reason for) employers to alter their current rates of employment and production. Thus the rational expectations theory holds that anticipated changes in aggregate demand, which include changes caused by fiscal and monetary policy, will be (13)_____ (completely, partially) offset by input suppliers as they react to anticipated changes in inflation. The aggregate supply curve shifts leftward by (14)_____ (the same amount as, less than) the aggregate demand curve shifts rightward. The price level increases, but real GDP and employment remain unchanged.

Increases in inflation expectations cause the Phillips curve to shift (15)_____ (downward, upward). If inflation expectations rise, labor and other input suppliers will renegotiate contracts, thus increasing unit production costs and causing firms to raise prices. Inflation rises at given levels of unemployment. The (16)_____ (Keynesian model, accelerationist hypothesis) argues that attempts by policy makers to reduce the rate of unemployment below the natural rate with expansionary fiscal or monetary policy will work only in the (17)_____ (long run, short run). In the (18)_____ (long run, short run), input suppliers will increase their inflation expectations and press for higher input prices when they discover that inflation is higher than expected. This causes the unemployment rate to return to its natural level, resulting in a vertical long-run Phillips curve.

Counter cyclical policy requires that policy makers first determine if macroeconomic problems are the result of demand-side or supply-side shocks. If they are due to demand-side shocks, the first problem of stabilization efforts is (19)_____ (to implement policy, forecasting shifts in aggregate demand). Second, the government must respond quickly to offset the undesired change in aggregate demand. Third, the extent to which monetary and fiscal policy should be used depends upon the predicted impacts of changes in the money supply or the government deficit. The ability of policy to offset an undesired change in aggregate demand depends to some extent on whether the policy change is anticipated or unanticipated. Policy will likely be (20)_____ (more, less) effective if it is unanticipated.

Some economists argue that policy makers often make errors that result in economic instability. They argue that policy exacerbates business cycle fluctuations and should not be used. They suggest that policy makers (21)_____ (use a policy rule such as a constant rate of money growth, always balance the budget) rather than use discretionary fiscal and monetary policy. Another view holds that stabilization policy has nevertheless (22)_____ (reduced, increased) the severity of economic fluctuations since the end of World War II. (23)_____ (Fiscal, Incomes) policies such as jawboning, wage-price guidelines, and wage-price controls have been used in addition to monetary and fiscal policy to control inflation. Wage-price controls are (24)_____ (frequently, rarely) used in peacetime because they distort the price system and contribute to the variability of inflation.

There are several competing views on stabilization policy. (25) _____ (Keynesian, Classical) economists argue that discretionary changes in aggregate demand are unnecessary because flexible wages and prices will quickly restore GDP to its potential level. Monetary policy, however, can limit inflation by allowing the money supply to grow at a rate equal to the rate of growth in potential real GDP. The (26) _____ (classicists, Keynesians) also view fiscal policy as having no impact on real interest rates, capital formation, or real GDP in the long run. (27) _____ (Monetarists, Keynesians) are proponents of both fiscal and monetary policy. In a very severe recession, monetary policy may be ineffective, requiring exclusive reliance on expansionary fiscal policy. The (28) _____ (monetarists, Keynesians) warn that fiscal policy only changes the composition of government and private goods and will likely cause inflation if expansionary policy is accommodated by increases in the money supply. The (29) _____ (Keynesians, monetarists) note that inflation can be controlled if the rate of growth in the money supply is equal to the rate of growth in potential real GDP. They also advocate the need to increase incentives to save and work by keeping marginal tax rates low and reducing the growth of government programs. Finally, the new classical economists, (30) _____ (monetarists and Keynesians; supply-siders and rational expectationists), view expansionary policy as resulting in inflation and a change in the mix of government and private goods. They promote fiscal policies that increase saving and work incentives and a monetary policy that keeps the rate of growth in the money supply equal to the rate of growth in potential real GDP.

■ KEY TERMS REVIEW

Write the key term from the list below next to its definition.

Key Terms

Phillips curve
Disinflation
Rational expectations
Accelerationist hypothesis

Policy rule
Incomes policies
Wage-price guidelines
Wage-price controls

Definitions

1. _____: argues that attempts by policy makers to reduce the unemployment rate below the natural rate can succeed only in the short run.

2. _____: a preannounced government rule that will inform the public of future economic stabilization policies.

3. _____: refers to use by individuals of all available information, including any relevant economic models, in their forecasts of economic variables.

4. _____: policies that seek to curb inflation by directly influencing both prices and wages without reducing aggregate demand through the use of monetary or fiscal policy.

5. _____: a sharp reduction in the annual rate of inflation.

6. _____: rules established by government authorities that result in control of prices, wages, and their rate of increase.

7. _____: a curve showing the hypothesized inverse relationship between annual unemployment and annual inflation in a nation.

8. _____: standards established by government authorities that seek to keep wage and price increases within certain bounds over a period.

■ CONCEPT REVIEW

Concept 2: *Shifts in the aggregate supply curve and the inflation-unemployment tradeoff*

1. The figure below shows an economy at its potential real GDP of $3,000 billion with a natural unemployment rate of 6%. The price level is 100, and the rate of inflation is zero.

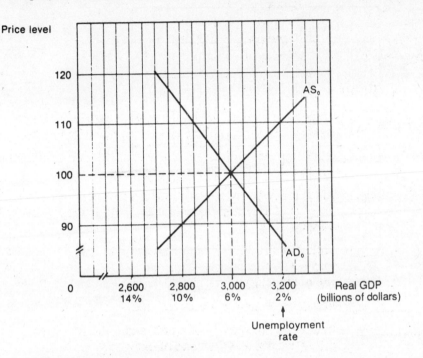

a. Assume that autonomous increases in aggregate demand shift the AD curve by $100 billion at every price level. The aggregate demand curve shifts _____. Show this on the figure above and label the new AD curve AD1.

b. Now assume that in addition to the increase in aggregate demand, a supply-side shock increases input prices, shifting the AS curve by $250 billion at every price level. The aggregate supply curve shifts _____. Show this on the figure above and label the new AS curve AS1.

c. The price level has _____ from 100 to _____, resulting in a _____ % change in the price level. Real GDP _____ from $3,000 billion to $_____, and the unemployment rate _____ from 6% to _____ %.

d. On the figure below, find the point representing the initial rate of inflation, 0%, and initial rate of unemployment, 6% and label that point A. Now find the coordinate that represents the new rate of change in the price level and the new rate of unemployment from part c and label that point B.

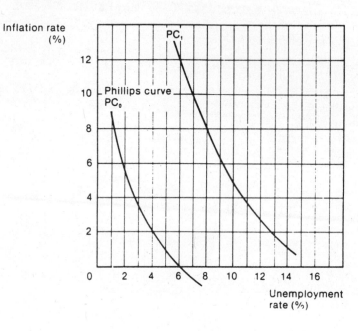

e. The Phillips curve shown in the figure above has shifted _____ from PC1 to _____. The inflation-unemployment tradeoff has _____ (worsened, improved). Adverse supply-side shocks that increase input prices shift the Phillips curve _____.

2. Given the level of aggregate demand, a favorable supply-side shock that decreases input prices will shift the aggregate _____ curve _____ and will shift the Phillips curve _____. The unemployment-inflation tradeoff _____ (worsens, improves).

334

Concept 3: *Rational expectations, the AD-AS model, and implications for stabilization policy*

3. Suppose the economy shown in the figure below, like that in the first figure, is at potential real GDP where the natural rate of unemployment is attained with a zero rate of inflation.

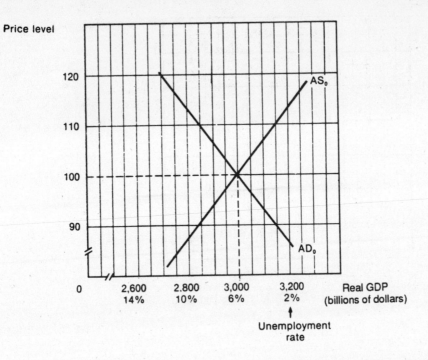

a. Assume that an increase in the money supply that shifts the aggregate demand curve rightward by $150 billion at every price level is fully anticipated by the public. Show the new AD curve and label the curve AD1. According to rational expectations theory, if the increase in aggregate demand is fully anticipated, input suppliers push for _____ input prices, causing the AS curve to shift _____ by $_____ billion. Show the new AS curve in the figure above and label it AS1. After the shifts in the AD and AS curves, the price level _____ from 100 to _____, resulting in a _____% change in the price level. Real GDP and the rate of unemployment _____.

b. In the figure below, plot the initial rate of change in the price level and unemployment rate. Now plot the new rate of change in the price level and unemployment rate found in part a. Draw a line connecting the two points.

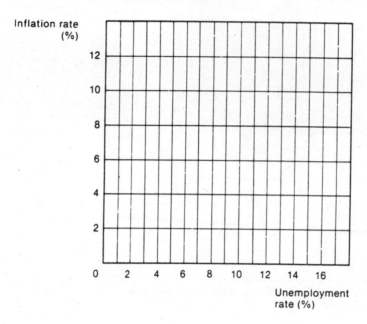

c. The proponents of the rational expectations theory view the Phillips curve as _____(downward sloping, vertical). Anticipated increases in aggregate demand _____ real GDP and the unemployment rate, although the rate of inflation _____.

d. According to the rational expectations theory, if changes in the federal budget deficit or the money supply are completely anticipated, fiscal and monetary policy are _____ (effective, ineffective) in altering real GDP and the rate of unemployment.

4. List two criticisms of the rational expectations theory.

a. _____

b. _____

Concept 4:   *Accelerationist hypothesis and stabilization policy*

5. The economy shown in the figure below is currently operating at its potential level of real GDP with an inflation rate equal to zero.

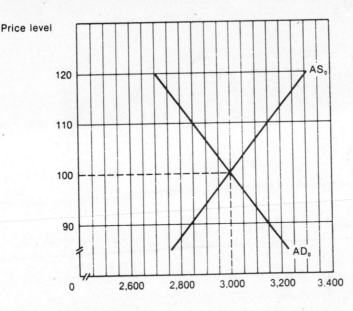

a. Suppose policy makers want to reduce the unemployment rate below the natural rate of unemployment to 3% by using expansionary fiscal policy. Equilibrium real GDP must rise to $3150 billion in order to reduce the unemployment rate to 3%. Show the new aggregate demand curve in the figure above and label the AD curve AD1.

b. The price level rises from 100 to _____, producing a _____% change in the price level. Workers and other input suppliers will eventually revise their expected rates of inflation from 0% to _____. As this happens, wages and other input prices _____, causing the aggregate _____ curve to shift _____ until real GDP equals $_____.   Show the new aggregate supply curve and label the AS curve AS1.

c. If government once again expands the economy in an effort to reduce the unemployment rate below the natural rate, real GDP will _____, the rate of unemployment will _____, and the price level will _____. The effects on real GDP and the unemployment rate _____ in the long run as input suppliers react to the realization that actual inflation exceeds expected inflation. The price level is_____ in the long run.

d. According to the accelerationist hypothesis, fiscal and monetary policy are able to affect real GDP and the unemployment rate in the _____, but not in the _____.

337

■ MASTERY TEST

Select the best answer.

1. In the 1950s, A.W. Phillips investigated the relationship between:
   a. wage and price inflation.
   b. output and price changes.
   c. the unemployment rate and the rate of change in wages.
   d. the unemployment rate and the rate of change in prices.

2. The U.S. Phillips curve in the 1960s:
   a. shifted erratically.
   b. appeared to be stable.
   c. shifted consistently upward.
   d. shifted downward during the first half of the decade.

3. The Phillips curve tradeoff implies:
   a. that if the curve is stable, society must accept increases in inflation in exchange for decreases in unemployment.
   b. that if the curve is unstable, society must accept increases in inflation in exchange for decreases in unemployment.
   c. that if the curve is stable, society must accept increases in inflation in exchange for increases in unemployment.
   d. that if the curve is unstable, society must accept falling unemployment when inflation falls.

4. Which of the following can cause the Phillips curve to shift?
   a. An increase in inflation expectations
   b. A decrease in inflation expectations
   c. An adverse supply-side shock increasing input prices
   d. A favorable supply-side shock decreasing input prices
   e. All of the above

5. The oil-price shock of 1973 had the effect of shifting the aggregate supply curve _____ by _____ than the aggregate demand curve shifted _____. The outcome was stagflation.
   a. rightward, less, leftward
   b. rightward, less, rightward
   c. leftward, less, leftward
   d. leftward, less, rightward
   e. leftward, more, rightward

6. The U.S. Phillips curve in the 1970s:
   a. was stable.
   b. shifted upward due to supply-side shocks and rising inflation expectations.
   c. shifted downward due to supply-side shocks.
   d. shifted downward in the first half of the decade and upward in the second half.

7. In the 1980s, the Phillips curve shifted _____ in part because of _____ and _____.
   a. downward, declines in oil prices, falling inflation expectations
   b. upward, increases in oil prices, rising inflation expectations
   c. downward, rising wages, falling prices
   d. upward, falling wages, rising prices
   e.   None of the above

8. Which of the following terms represents a sharp reduction in the rate of inflation?
   a. Crawling inflation
   b. Deflation
   c. Hyperinflation
   d. Disinflation
   e. B and d

9. Which of the following theories of expectations holds that individuals form expectations by looking only to past values of the variable to be forecast?
   a. Rational expectations theory
   b. Certainty equivalent theory
   c. Expected value analysis
   d. Adaptive expectations theory

10. Which of the following theories of expectations holds that individuals use all information available in forming expectations?
   a. Rational expectations theory
   b. Certainty equivalent theory
   c. Expected value analysis
   d. Adaptive expectations theory

11. Rational expectations theory implies that anticipated changes in aggregate demand:
   a. affect real gnp and the price level only in the long run.
   b. will be completely offset by the actions of input suppliers as they react to their inflation expectations.
   c. will always affect real but not nominal gnp.
   d. will result in economic expansion over the long run.
   e. a and d.

12. Which of the following theories holds that efforts by policy makers to reduce the unemployment rate below the natural rate of unemployment will be successful only in the short run?
   a. Adaptive expectations theory
   b. Rational expectations theory
   c. New classical-RE model
   d. Accelerationist hypothesis

13. An increase in inflation expectations causes input suppliers to push for _____ input prices, which _____ unit production costs and prices. This results in a/an _____ shift in the Phillips curve.
   a. higher, increase, downward
   b. lower, decrease, downward
   c. lower, increase, upward
   d. higher, increase, upward
   e. lower, decrease, upward

14. The first problem of stabilization policy is to:
   a. predict the impact of changes in the money stock or the government deficit on the economy.
   b. quickly implement countercyclical policies.
   c. predict shifts in aggregate demand.
   d. follow a policy rule.

15. The second problem of stabilization policy is to:
   a. predict the impact of changes in the money stock or the government deficit on the economy.
   b. quickly implement countercyclical policies.
   c. predict shifts in aggregate demand.
   d. follow a policy rule.

16. The third problem of stabilization policy is to:
   a. predict the impact of changes in the money stock or the government deficits on the economy.
   b. quickly implement countercyclical policies.
   c. predict shifts in aggregate demand.
   d. follow a policy rule.

17. Incomes policies have proved _____ in reducing wage and price inflation over the long run and as a result are used _____ during peacetime.
   a. successful, frequently
   b. unsuccessful, often
   c. successful, infrequently
   d. unsuccessful, only rarely

18. Which of the following are examples of incomes policies?
   a. Jawboning
   b. Wage-price guidelines
   c. Wage-price controls
   d. Tax cuts
   e. A, b, and c

19. An increase in aggregate demand:
    a. shifts the phillips curve upward in the short run.
    b. shifts the phillips curve downward in the short run.
    c. results in a move up a fixed phillips curve in the short run.
    d. does not shift the Phillips curve nor does it result in a movement along the curve in the short run.

20. Which of the following will shift the Phillips curve upward in the long run?
    a. An increase in the price of an important raw material
    b. A decrease in the price of oil
    c. Falling inflation expectations
    d. Rising inflation expectations
    e. A and d

21. Which of the following will shift the Phillips curve downward in the long run?
    a. An increase in the price of an important raw material
    b. An increase in the price of oil
    c. Falling inflation expectations
    d. Rising inflation expectations
    e. A and c

22. You are an advisor to the President of the United States. You report to the President that the impact of an increase in the money supply is to increase inflation in the short and long run, but real GDP is unchanged. Which of the following theories is primarily responsible for your view?
    a. Keynesian macroeconomic theory
    b. Theory of rational expectations
    c. Accelerationist hypothesis
    d. Theory of adaptive expectations

23. You are a corporate economist and have recently reported to your chief executive that an increase in the money supply will increase both real GDP and the price level in the short run, but will increase only the price level in the long run. Which of the following theories is primarily responsible for your view?
    a. Keynesian macroeconomic theory
    b. Theory of rational expectations
    c. Accelerationist hypothesis
    d. Ricardian Equivalence

THINK IT THROUGH

1. "At times during the 1970s and 1980s in the United States, the rate of inflation and the rate of unemployment moved in the same direction. This is evidence that the Phillips curve does not exist and policy makers need not pay any attention to the tradeoff it implies." Analyze this statement.

2. Identify the implication of rational expectations theory regarding the ability of monetary and fiscal policy to affect real GDP and the rate of unemployment. This policy implication depends upon several important assumptions: (a) individuals form expectations rationally, (b) wages and prices are flexible, and (c) all markets are competitive markets that constantly clear—are in equilibrium. How might this policy implication change if wages and prices are in fact slow to adjust?

3. Use the accelerationist hypothesis to describe an inflationary process that begins with demand-pull inflation and is followed by cost-push inflation to be followed again by demand-pull inflation and so on. In other words, how can the accelerationist hypothesis be used to explain a wage-price spiral?

CHAPTER ANSWERS

The Chapter in Brief

1. Inverse 2. Demand 3. 1960s 4. Predictable 5. Not remained stable, but has shifted due to
6. Leftward 7. Rightward 8. Counter 9. Upward 10. Downward 11. Rational expectations 12.
And there is no reason for 13. Completely 14. The same amount as 15. Upward
16. Accelerationist hypothesis 17. Short run 18. Long run 19. Forecasting shifts in aggregate
demand 20. More 21. Use a policy rule such as a constant rate of money growth 22. Reduced 23.
Incomes 24. Rarely 25. Classical 26. Classicists 27. Keynesians 28. Monetarists 29. Monetarists
30. Supply-siders and rational expectationists

Key Terms Review

1. Accelerationist hypothesis 2. Policy rule 3. Rational expectations 4. Incomes policies
5. Disinflation 6. Wage-price controls 7. Phillips curve 8. Wage-price guidelines

Concept Review

1. a. Rightward

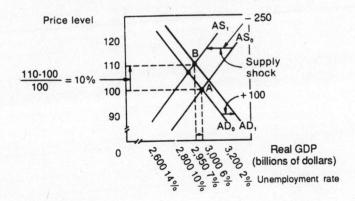

b. Leftward
c. Increased, 110, 10%; falls, $2,950 billion, rises, 7%
d.

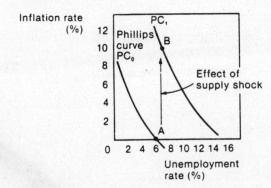

343

e. Upward, PC1; worsened; upward

2. Supply, rightward, downward; improves

3. a.

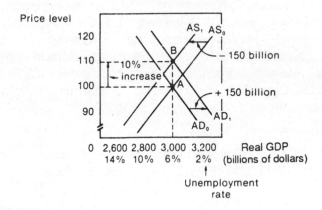

Higher, leftward, $150 billion; rises, 110, 10%; remain unchanged

b.

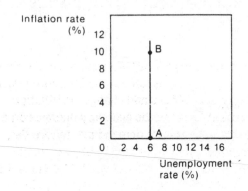

c. Vertical; do not change the level of; increases
d. Ineffective

4. a. Individuals do not have access to all information, nor do they make use of all available information.

b. Wages and other input prices are slow to adjust due to the existence of annual and multi-year contracts.

5. a.

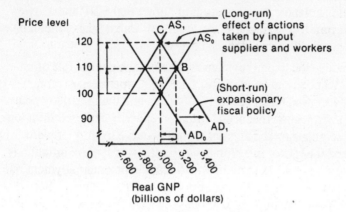

Price level

Real GNP
(billions of dollars)

b. 110, 10%; 10%; rise, supply, leftward, $3,000 billion
c. Increase, decrease, rise; vanish, higher
d. Short run, long run

Mastery Test

1. c 2. b 3. a 4. e 5. e 6. b 7. a 8. d 9. d 10. a 11. b 12. d 13. d 14. c 15. b 16. a 17. d 18. e 19. c 20. e 21. c 22. b 23. c

Think It Through

1. The Phillips curve and the tradeoff it implies between the rate of inflation and the unemployment rate does indeed exist in the short run when the economy is not buffeted by supply-side shocks and changes in inflation expectations. Supply-side shocks and changes in inflation expectations shift the Phillips curve. But at a given point in time the economy operates on a Phillips curve that is not necessarily stable. Increases in aggregate demand that reduce the unemployment rate below the natural rate will cause inflation unless the Phillips curve is shifting, in which case inflation may increase or decrease as the unemployment rate falls. For instance, if an increase in aggregate demand is accompanied by a favorable supply-side shock that shifts the aggregate supply curve rightward more than the aggregate demand curve shifts rightward, the unemployment rate falls while the price level falls. The Phillips curve is shifting downward at the same time that the unemployment rate is falling. Policy makers need to be aware that the inflation-unemployment tradeoff will likely present itself in the short run, although it is likely to shift over the long run and therefore is not a reliable guide to the long-run tradeoff.

2. Rational expectations theory holds that monetary and fiscal policy changes will be anticipated by the public. For example, an anticipated increase in the money stock will produce expectations of rising inflation, which will cause workers and other input suppliers to push for higher input prices. This increases unit production costs, causing firms to increase prices at given levels of output. The aggregate supply curve shifts leftward as the aggregate demand curve shifts rightward. There is no change in real variables such as real GDP and the unemployment rate, only increases in the price level. Thus it is argued that anticipated monetary or fiscal policy will not be effective in altering real GDP or unemployment rates and should not be used. If, however, wages and other input prices are slow to adjust as they certainly are due to the ex-

345

istence of multi-period contracts, leftward shifts in the aggregate supply curve will lag behind the rightward shift in the aggregate demand curve, resulting in higher real GDP and a lower rate of unemployment in the short run. It is argued that the length of time it takes for complete adjustment may well be quite long, resulting in a "long" short run.

3. Suppose policy makers want to reduce the unemployment rate below the natural rate of unemployment. If the economy is at its potential level of real GDP and expansionary monetary or fiscal policy is used, demand-pull inflation results as real GDP rises and the unemployment rate falls. In time, input suppliers will realize that actual inflation exceeds expected inflation and will push for higher input prices, causing the aggregate supply curve to shift leftward. Now the unemployment rate is rising and the rate of inflation is worsening—cost-push inflation is occurring. But suppose policy makers persist in their efforts to reduce the unemployment rate and once again use expansionary policy. This causes inflation to worsen still further but reduces the unemployment rate below the natural rate. As was the case previously, workers and other input suppliers will eventually realize that actual inflation is outpacing expected inflation, which will cause them to press for higher input prices. Again the aggregate supply curve shifts leftward, returning the unemployment rate to its natural level, but at still higher rates of inflation. Activist demand-management policy that tries to keep the rate of unemployment below the natural rate of unemployment will only succeed in creating a wage-price spiral in the long run.

PART VII

INTERNATIONAL
ECONOMIC ISSUES

■ **PART EXERCISE**

Inside Information: *Where to Go to Get Information on United States International Trade and Economic Conditions in Foreign Nations*

In Part VII, you will learn about international trade issues. Use *United States Trade* and detail the volume and type of exports and imports for the year. What happened to net exports during the year? Assume that the change in net exports resulted from changes in foreign exchange markets. Based on what you have learned about foreign exchange markets, provide a plausible explanation for the change in net exports.

20 INTERNATIONAL TRADE

■ CHAPTER CONCEPTS

After studying your text, attending class, and completing this chapter, you should be able to:

1. Understand the underlying basis for international trade, the principle of comparative advantage and the gains in well-being possible from free trade with foreign nations.

2. Show how productivity changes in specific industries can affect their comparative advantage in international trade.

3. Discuss protectionism and analyze the impact on the economy of tariffs, import quotas, and other trade restrictions.

■ THE CHAPTER IN BRIEF

Fill in the blanks to summarize chapter content.

In 1994, the United States exported over $700 billion in goods and services and imported $800 billion, resulting in a trade deficit of $100 billion.

Nations engage in international trade because it is mutually beneficial for all trading nations to do so; otherwise they would not trade. Some nations may have a/an (1)_____ (comparative, absolute) advantage in producing goods, meaning that with a given complement of resources, one nation can produce more of an item than another nation with the same quantity of resources. But the presence of an absolute advantage in the production of an item does not indicate whether a nation should specialize in and export that good or whether the good should be imported. A country should specialize in and export those goods for which it has an/a (2)_____ (absolute, comparative) advantage and import those goods for which other countries have a comparative advantage. A nation has a comparative advantage in the production of a good relative to another nation if it produces the good at (3)_____ (lower, higher) opportunity cost than its trading partner.

Nations that trade on the basis of comparative advantage (4)_____ (gain at the expense of their rivals, mutually gain from trade). On an international scale, resources are used more efficiently as nations produce output based upon comparative advantages. World output, income, and living standards are (5)_____ (higher, lower) as a result of specialization and trade than would be the case in the absence of trade. All trading partners gain, although not equally. The distribution of the gains from trade is determined by the (6)_____ (foreign exchange rate, terms of trade)—the rate at which goods can be traded or exchanged for one another on international markets. A nation will be induced to trade goods for which it has a comparative advantage for import goods if it can obtain the imported goods at prices below the domestic opportunity cost of production. The real terms of trade are determined by (7)_____ (government, world demand and supply). For trade incentives to exist, the terms of trade must be (8)_____ (below, above) the opportunity cost of producing each additional unit of the good a nation desires to import. When countries specialize in and export those goods for which they have a comparative advantage and import goods for which other nations have a comparative advantage, the consumption possibilities curve of each nation lies (9)_____ (outside, inside) the production possibilities curve.

Changes in productivity can affect a nation's competitiveness in international markets. If a nation experiences slower technological growth or lower levels of investment in human and physical capital relative to those of its trading partners, in time it may lose its (10)_____ (absolute, comparative) advantage in those industries where international competitiveness requires improvements in productivity. The nation that invests more heavily in things that enhance productivity will eventually (11)_____ (gain, lose) a comparative advantage relative to the lagging nation and will capture a share of the international market that it previously did not have. Slow productivity growth (growth in output per labor hour) in the United States in the 1980s has been cited as a reason for the decline in the competitiveness of some U.S. export industries. The primary cause of the low productivity growth is believed to be the low rate of annual (12)_____ (government, investment) spending as a percentage of domestic production relative to other nations, particularly Japan. Increased government regulation and (13)_____ (falling wages, higher energy prices) have also been cited as factors contributing to the productivity decline of the 1970s.

As comparative advantage changes, nations losing the comparative advantage in a good no longer export that good. Industry sales and output fall, causing some workers with specialized skills to become unemployed and other suppliers of specialized inputs to experience a decline in income. Both the owners of the declining industry and its input suppliers are harmed. But this has to be balanced against the widespread gains to society when a nation produces on the basis of comparative advantage. Changes in comparative advantage are painful in the short run, but nations are better off in the long run by specializing in and exporting those goods for which they have a comparative advantage and trading for those goods for which they do not.

Several arguments, however, have been advanced for protecting domestic industries. It is argued that some industries may need to be protected from international competition to maintain production capacity (14)_____ (vital to national security, necessary to be self-sufficient). Protecting (15)_____ (large and established industries, new and emerging "infant" industries) from the rigors of international competition is considered a way of allowing an industry to grow in a sheltered environment until it attains sufficient economies of scale to compete internationally. Industries experiencing changes in comparative advantage can be spared some of the short run costs to specialized input suppliers and owners by receiving some protection from foreign rivals. Some industries are protected from what is viewed as unfair competition by foreign governments that subsidize their export industries. Arguments against free trade derive from changes in the (16)_____ (distribution of income that occur, efficiency with which goods are produced) as some industries fail and lose their comparative advantage.

Two methods of import protection are import tariffs and import quotas. A (17)_____ (quota, tariff) is a tax on an imported good. The intention is to reduce imports and increase the sales of domestic products. A tariff (18)_____ (raises, lowers) the price of the imported good to the consumer, (19)_____ (increases, reduces) the net price to the foreign producer, and generates tax revenue for the government. A/An (20)_____ (tariff, import quota) is a limit on the quantity of foreign goods that can be sold in a nation's domestic market. Like the tariff, an import quota (21)_____ (increases, reduces) the quantity of imported goods sold and (22)_____ (raises, lowers) the price to the consumer, but unlike a tariff, the import quota also (23)_____ (lowers, raises) the price received by the foreign producer. If the demand for the imported good is inelastic, the foreign producer (24)_____ (is always worse off, may be better off) operating with a quota. Further, quotas raise no revenue for government. But protectionism invites retaliation from trading partners. If a nation's trading partners also impose import tariffs and quotas, all of the trading nations (25)_____ (lose, gain) because the level of international trade is lower and consumers in each country are paying higher prices than necessary.

■ KEY TERMS REVIEW

Write the key term from the list below next to its definition.

Key Terms

Specialization
Mutual gains from
   international trade
Absolute advantage
Comparative advantage

Consumption possibilities
   curve
Tariff
Import quota
Real terms of trade

Definitions

1. _____ : shows combinations of two goods a nation can consume given its resources, technology, and international trade.

2. _____ : the actual market exchange rate of one good for another in international trade.

3. _____ : a tax on imported goods.

4. _____ : a nation has a comparative advantage over a trading partner in the production of an item if it produces that item at lower opportunity cost per unit than its partner does.

5. _____ : a limit on the quantity of foreign goods that can be sold in a nation's domestic markets.

6. _____ : a nation has an absolute advantage over other nations in the production of an item if it can produce more of the item over a certain period with a given amount of resources than the other nations can.

7. _____ : on average, citizens in all trading nations gain from exchanging goods in international markets.

8. _____ : use of labor and other resources in a nation to produce the goods and services for which those resources are best adapted.

■ CONCEPT REVIEW

Concept 1: *Absolute vs. comparative advantage, terms of trade, gains from trade*

1. The domestic production possibilities of two nations, nation A and nation B, for two goods, cases of wine and boxes of cheese, are shown below.

	Production Possibilities	
	Nation A	*Nation B*
Wine (cases)	1 million	600,000
Cheese (boxes)	500,000	400,000

a. Plot the production possibilities curve for each nation in a and b in the figure below.

a.

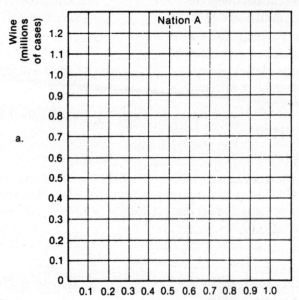

b.

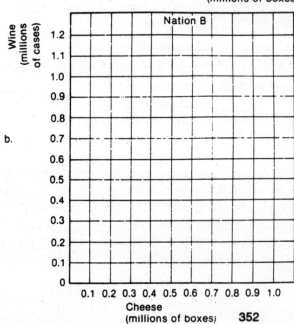

352

b. Assuming each nation has the same quantity of resources, 1000 workers, and both nations produce only wine, the number of cases of wine per worker in nation A of _____ cases _____ the number of cases of wine per worker of _____ cases in nation B. Similarly, if both nations produce only cheese, the number of boxes of cheese per worker in nation A of _____ boxes _____ the number of boxes of cheese per worker in nation B of _____ boxes. Nation A has a/an _____ advantage in the production of both wine and cheese. Nation A's production possibilities curve _____ nation B's production possibilities curve.

c. In nation A, the opportunity cost of producing a case of wine is _____ boxes of cheese and the opportunity cost of producing a box of cheese is _____ cases of wine. The slope of nation A's production possibilities curve is _____, which means that the opportunity cost of producing an additional box of cheese is _____ cases of wine.

d. In nation B, the opportunity cost of producing a case of wine is _____ boxes of cheese and the opportunity cost of producing a box of cheese is _____ cases of wine. The slope of nation B's production possibilities curve is _____, which means that the opportunity cost of producing an additional box of cheese is _____ cases of wine.

2. Regarding the problem above, nation A has a comparative advantage in the production of _____, whereas nation B has a comparative advantage in the production of _____. Nation A should specialize in and export _____ and should import _____. Nation B should specialize in and export _____ and should import _____. For nation A to be induced to trade for _____, it must give up less _____ than that implied by its domestic opportunity cost of _____. For nation B to be induced to trade for _____, it must give up less _____ than that implied by its domestic opportunity cost of _____. Trade will be mutually beneficial to both nations if 1 box of cheese trades for between _____ and _____ cases of wine. Alternatively, trade will result if 1 case of wine trades for between _____ and _____ boxes of cheese.

3. a. Assume that the terms of trade for cheese are set at 1 box of cheese = 12/7 cases of wine. What are the terms of trade for a case of wine?
   1 box of cheese = 1 and 5/7 (or 12/7) cases of wine
   1 case of wine   = _____ boxes of cheese

   b. Given the terms of trade, in a and b in the figure above plot the consumption possibilities curve for each nation.

   c. If nation A specializes in wine and keeps 800,000 cases for its domestic consumption and trades 200,000 cases to nation B, how many boxes of cheese can it get in return? _____ boxes Given nation A's domestic opportunity cost of cheese of _____ cases of wine, it can domestically produce only _____ boxes of cheese by sacrificing 200,000 cases of wine. Trade results in a gain of _____ boxes of cheese over what was possible in the absence of trade.

   d. If nation B trades cheese for 200,000 cases of nation A's wine, how much cheese will it have to trade? _____ boxes of cheese. Given B's domestic opportunity cost of wine of _____ boxes of cheese, it can domestically produce 200,000 cases of wine only by sacrificing _____ boxes of cheese, but it only has to give up _____ boxes of cheese through international trade to acquire the same quantity of wine. Trade results in a gain of _____ boxes of cheese over what was possible in the absence of trade.

Concept 3:   *Protectionism, tariffs, and quotas*

4. List four arguments in favor of protectionism.

   a. _____

   b. _____

   c. _____

   d. _____

5. In a and b in the figure below are shown the domestic and import markets for shoes.

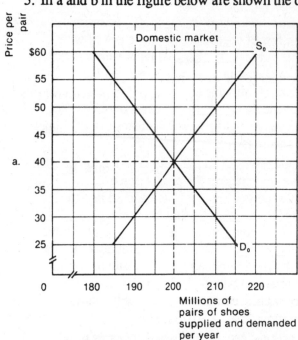

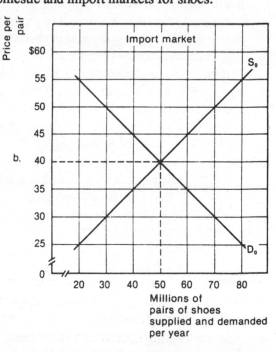

a.   Suppose that domestic shoe manufacturers and their input suppliers are able to win an import tariff of $10 per pair of imported shoes. Show the new import supply curve in b above. The $10 tariff causes the price to the consumer to _____ to $_____ and the net price to foreign shoe manufacturers to _____ to $_____. Sales of imported shoes _____ to _____ million pairs. The tariff has raised tax revenue of $_____. Show these effects in b.

b.   In a, assume that the decline in import sales causes an increase in domestic shoe demand by an equal amount at each price level. The domestic demand for shoes shifts _____ by _____ million pairs of shoes. Domestic shoe prices _____ to $_____ and sales _____ to _____ million pairs.

c.   In effect, the tariff redistributes income from _____ and _____ to the owners and input suppliers of the protected domestic shoe industry.

d.   If an import quota had been used instead to achieve the lower level of import sales that you found in part a above, the price of imported shoes paid by the consumer and received by the foreign producer _____ to $_____. The domestic market price of shoes _____ to $_____, and sales _____ to _____ million pairs of shoes. In this case, the government receives _____ tax revenue and the foreign producer may experience a/an _____ in total revenue if the demand for imported shoes is sufficiently inelastic. Show the case of an import quota in b in the figure above.

■ MASTERY TEST

Select the best answer.

1. If a nation has a/an _____ in the production of an item, it can produce more of the item with a given quantity of resources than can other nations.
   a. special advantage
   b. comparative advantage
   c. absolute advantage
   d. mutual gain

2. A nation's comparative advantage is determined by:
   a. the total cost of production.
   b. the quantity of resources required to produce a unit of output.
   c. the opportunity cost of producing an item relative to a trading partner's opportunity cost of producing the same item.
   d. specialization in the production of all goods.

3. If nations trade on the basis of comparative advantage, a nation should specialize in and _____ those goods for which it has a comparative advantage and should _____ those goods for which other nations have a comparative advantage.
   a. export, import
   b. import, export
   c. export, export
   d. import, import

4. If nations trade on the basis of comparative advantage:
   a. a nation can gain only at the expense of trading partners.
   b. exporting nations gain and importing nations lose.
   c. importing nations gain and exporting nations lose.
   d. all trading partners mutually gain.

5. A nation will be induced to trade for imported goods if the nation can give up _____ goods through international trade for the imported item than implied by its domestic _____ cost of production.
   a. more, total
   b. more, opportunity
   c. fewer, variable
   d. fewer, opportunity

6. Which of the following refers to the rate at which goods are exchanged for one another in international markets?
   a. Exchange rate
   b. Terms of trade
   c. Specialization
   d. Opportunity cost
   e. None of the above

7. If nations trade on the basis of _____ advantage, the consumption possibilities curve lies _____ the production possibilities curve.
   a. absolute, inside
   b. a unique, parallel to
   c. comparative, parallel to
   d. comparative, outside

8. When a nation's productivity growth lags behind that of its trading partners, in time it may:
   a. lose its comparative advantage in some industries.
   b. gain a comparative advantage as a result of the lag in productivity growth.
   c. diversify with "infant" industries.
   d. experience a reduction in the opportunity cost of producing the good.

9. Lagging productivity growth of a nation relative to its trading partners:
   a. results in a loss of comparative advantage in some industries.
   b. results in an increase in the opportunity cost of producing some goods relative to that of foreign rivals.
   c. results in a loss of income to the owners and specialized input suppliers in the industries experiencing lagging productivity growth.
   d. All of the above.

10. Which of the following have been cited as reasons for the slow productivity growth in the United States in the 1970s?
    a. Average annual net investment of 6% of domestic production
    b. Increased government regulation to improve working conditions and the environment
    c. Rising energy prices
    d. All of the above
    e. None of the above

11. Which of the following is not an argument in favor of protectionism?
    a. National security
    b. Reducing structural unemployment
    c. Protecting infant industries
    d. Protecting U.S. industries against subsidized foreign producers
    e. Goal of self-sufficiency

12. Which of the following is a tax on an imported good?
    a. Income tax
    b. Import quota
    c. Rationing tax
    d. Tariff

13. A tariff does which of the following?
    a. Increases the price of the imported good to the consumer
    b. Decreases the net price received by the foreign producer
    c. Increases the price of the domestic good
    d. Redistributes income from domestic consumers and foreign producers to the protected industry
    e. All of the above

14. Which of the following places a limit on the quantity of a foreign good that can be imported into a domestic market?
    a. Import capacity limit
    b. Import quota
    c. Export quota
    d. Tariff

15. An import quota does which of the following?
    a. Increases the price of the imported good to the consumer
    b. Increases the price received by the foreign producer
    c. Increases the price of the domestic good
    d. Redistributes income from domestic consumers to the protected domestic exporter
    e. All of the above

Answer the following questions based upon the data below.

Production Possibilities

	Good X	Good Y
Country A	100	50
Country B	200	150

16. Which of the following statements is true?
    a. Country A has an absolute advantage in the production of both goods X and Y.
    b. Country B has an absolute advantage in the production of good X, but not good Y.
    c. Country B has an absolute advantage in the production of good Y, but not good X.
    d. Country A has a comparative advantage in the production of good Y.
    e. None of the above

17. Which of the following statements is true?
    a. Country A has a comparative advantage in the production of good X.
    b. Country B has a comparative advantage in the production of good Y.
    c. Country B should specialize in and export good X.
    d. Country A should specialize in and export good Y.
    e. A and b

18. If countries A and B trade on the basis of comparative advantage, which of the following terms of trade would result in mutually-gainful trades?
    a. $1X = (3/2) Y$
    b. $1Y = (3/2) X$
    c. $1X = (1) Y$
    d. $1Y = (2/3) X$

19. Assume that country B specializes in the production of good Y. Country B keeps 100Y for domestic consumption and trades 50Y for good X. If the terms of trade are 1X = (2/3) Y, what are the gains to nation B from trade?

   a. 8 1/3X

   b. 15Y

   c. 75X

   d. 66 2/3X

■ THINK IT THROUGH

1. "In international trade, one nation's trade surplus (exports in excess of imports) must be another nation's trade deficit (imports in excess of exports). Therefore the mercantilists must have been correct in stating that a nation should encourage exports and discourage imports." Evaluate this statement.

2. The United States has lost its international competitiveness in some basic industries, particularly those that produce standardized goods with large economies of scale. Can you think of any reasons why?

3. If a nation employs protectionist measures such as tariffs or quotas and trading partners retaliate in kind, discuss some likely consequences.

■ ANALYZING THE NEWS

Using the skills derived from studying this chapter, analyze the economic facts that make up the following article and answer the questions below.

1. What were the U.S. merchandise trade and services balances for 1994?

2. Does the merchandise trade deficit reflect domestic economic strength or weakness?

National Economic Trends

Does the Merchandise Trade Deficit Hurt Growth?

In 1994, the U.S. merchandise trade deficit reached an all-time high, with imports exceeding exports by $166.3 billion. Such trade imbalances are frequently cited as a cause for concern about the prospects for economic growth. One often hears analyses that bemoan the decline of U.S. competitiveness, the prospect of losing jobs to competitors overseas, or the detrimental shortfall of saving relative to investment implied by large, persistent trade deficits. When the underlying determinants and composition of the widening U.S. merchandise trade deficit are examined in greater detail, however, such pessimism seems unwarranted.

In considering the deficit's importance to the U.S. economy, one should bear in mind that merchandise represents only part of the nation's volume of trade. Although broader measures of the U.S. external deficit have also increased in recent years, they have remained below their 1987 record levels. In fact, the United States has experienced a growing surplus in services trade, which has risen from $7.6 billion in 1987 to $58.2 billion in 1994.

The primary reason for the recent widening of the U.S. trade deficit is the strong economic performance of this nation relative to our major trading partners. Rapid economic growth in the United States has fueled demand for goods and services including imports, while relatively sluggish growth overseas has dampened world demand for U.S. exports. Rather than indicating a lack of competitiveness, this cyclical factor reflects the robust economic growth recently experienced in the United States.

The composition of recent increases in U.S. imports is also significant. Fundamentally, a trade deficit represents a shortfall of domestic savings; when a country imports more than it exports, the difference must be made up by borrowing from abroad. Just as is true for an individual household, borrowing to increase current consumption can lead to future financial difficulties. But borrowing for investment purposes — in order to enhance future productivity — may be a sound strategy.

As the chart below illustrates, the recent rise in the U.S. trade deficit has coincided with an increase in the share of merchandise imports represented by capital goods. Since 1990, in fact, real capital goods imports have accounted for nearly 60 percent of the growth in real merchandise imports. This increase is consistent with the overall strength of investment spending during the current economic expansion and indicates that the U.S. economy is operating in an environment flush with profitable investment opportunities. This strength in investment spending bodes well for future growth in productivity and output.

— Michael R. Pakko

Capital Goods Import Share*

Ratio

* Ratio of capital goods imports (excluding automotive) to total merchandise imports, both measured in 1987 dollars.

Views expressed do not necessarily reflect official positions of the Federal Reserve System.

Pakko, Michael R. "Does the Merchandise Trade Deficit Hurt Growth?" National Economic Trends. Federal Reserve Bank of St. Louis, March, 1995.

CHAPTER ANSWERS

The Chapter in Brief

1. Absolute 2. Comparative 3. Lower 4. Mutually gain from trade 5. Higher 6. Terms of trade 7. World demand and supply 8. Below 9. Outside 10. Comparative 11. Gain 12. Investment 13. Higher energy prices 14. Vital to national security 15. New and emerging "infant" industries 16. Distribution of income that occur 17. Tariff 18. Raises 19. Reduces 20. Import quota 21. Reduces 22. Raises 23. Raises 24. May be better off 25. Lose

Key Terms Review

1. Consumption possibilities curve 2. Real terms of trade 3. Tariff 4. Comparative advantage 5. Import quota 6. Absolute advantage 7. Mutual gains from international trade 8. Specialization

Concept Review

1. a.

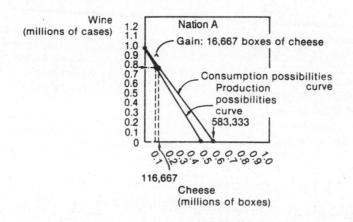

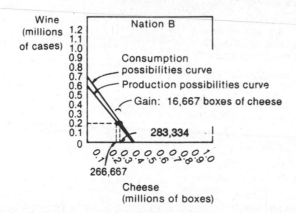

   b.   1,000, exceeds, 600; 500, exceeds, 400; absolute; lies farther from the origin than
   c.   1/2, 2; -2, 2
   d.   2/3, 1.5; -1.5, 1.5

2. Wine, cheese; wine, cheese; cheese, wine; cheese, wine, 2 cases of wine; wine, cheese, 2/3 boxes of cheese; 1.5, 2; 1/2, 2/3

3. a.   7/12 box of cheese

b. Shown on figure above
c. 116,667; 2, 100,000; 16,667
d. 116,667; 2/3, 133,333; 116,667; 16,667

4. a. National security
   b. Protect infant industries
   c. Reduce structural unemployment
   d. Protect U.S. industries against subsidized foreign producers

5. a. Rise, $45, fall, $35; fall, 40; $400 million

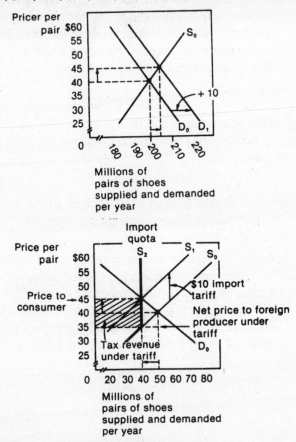

b. Rightward, 10; increase, $45, rise, 205
c. Consumers, foreign producers
d. Increase, $45; increases, $45, rise, 205; no, increase

Mastery Test

1. c 2. c 3. a 4. d 5. d 6. b 7. d 8. a 9. d 10. d 11. e 12. d 13. e 14. b 15. e 16. e 17. e 18. b 19. a

Think It Through

1. A nation's wealth is not defined in terms of the foreign currency (or gold during the mercantilist era) earned from trade surpluses, but by the total goods consumed by the nation in part as a result of international trade. A nation may run a trade deficit yet still consume more goods than if the nation engaged in no international trade. It is true that a trade deficit means a lower

level of domestic aggregate demand and level of real GDP, but that level of real GDP may be higher than it would have been if the nation did not produce and trade on the basis of comparative advantage.

2. The United States has experienced lagging productivity growth in several of its heavy industries—those that produce standardized goods and whose firms realize substantial economies of scale. Other nations have had more rapid productivity growth in some of these industries, taking away the comparative advantage once enjoyed by the U.S. industries. New techniques of production were being introduced abroad at a time during which many U.S. plants were aging and becoming obsolete. U.S. firms were not investing enough in new plant and equipment and technology to maintain their relatively lower opportunity cost of production. Several foreign nations that have captured the comparative advantage from the United States have done so by investing a greater percentage of their domestic production in physical capital and technology. They also have an advantage in having a relatively less costly labor force.

3. If all trading nations are engaging in protectionist measures, all lose in that the volume of international trade will be lower, the level of world output and living standards will be lower, and household real incomes will be lower because the prices of imported and domestic goods will be higher than in the absence of trade restrictions.

Analyzing the News

1. The merchandise trade deficit reached an all-time high of $166.3 billion in 1994. The balance of trade in services, however, was a $58.2 billion <u>surplus</u>, rising from a surplus of $7.6 billion in 1987.

2. The "recent widening" of the trade deficit is a sign of economic strength, not weakness. Strong U.S. economic growth relative to that of our trading partners has caused increases in the demand for imports. Slow growth abroad, in contrast, has reduced the demand for U.S. exports. If the U.S. imports more than it exports, the difference has to be financed by borrowing from abroad. Borrowing may actually increase domestic productivity if capital goods are imported. As shown in the figure, the share of imports made up by capital has steadily increased through the 1990s.

362

21 THE ECONOMICS OF FOREIGN EXCHANGE AND THE BALANCE OF INTERNATIONAL TRADE

■ CHAPTER CONCEPTS

After studying your text, attending class, and completing this chapter, you should be able to:

1. Understand how international transactions between the United States and the rest of the world involve the exchange of dollars for units of foreign currency.

2. Use supply and demand analysis to show how exchange rates of one currency into another are established in foreign exchange markets and explain the causes of currency appreciation and depreciation. Discuss the evolution of the current international monetary system and understand how a balance of trade deficit in the United States in a given year implies an increase in net foreign acquisition of U.S. financial and other assets in that year.

■ THE CHAPTER IN BRIEF

Fill in the blanks to summarize chapter content.

International trade requires the exchange of currencies. The (1)_____ (foreign exchange rate is, terms of trade are) the price of one nation's monetary unit in terms of the monetary unit of another nation. The (2)_____ (stock market, foreign exchange market) is a market in which currencies are exchanged. Here the forces of supply and demand determine the rate at which any two currencies are exchanged. For example, a U.S. importer wants to purchase foreign goods with dollars but foreign exporters want to be paid in their own currencies. An exchange of currency must take place. For a fee, the importer can use dollars to purchase a bank draft denominated in foreign currency from a U.S. bank. This constitutes (3)_____ (a demand for, an increase in the supply of) the foreign currency.

Equilibrium in the foreign exchange market occurs where the supply of and demand for a currency are equal—where the supply and demand curves for a currency intersect. If the price of a currency (expressed in terms of units of another currency) is higher than the equilibrium exchange rate, a (4)_____ (shortage, surplus) of the currency will cause a decline in the exchange rate. If the exchange rate is below the equilibrium exchange rate, a (5)_____ (shortage, surplus) of the currency results in an increase in the exchange rate. Influences that shift the demand or supply curves will alter the exchange rate between two currencies. Several factors can affect the equilibrium exchange rate of the U.S. dollar: (a) foreign demand for U.S. exports, (b) U.S. demand for imports, (c) real interest rates in the United States relative to those in foreign nations, (d) profitability of direct investment in U.S. businesses and real estate relative to profitability of similar investments in foreign nations, (e) expectations of an increase in the price of the dollar in terms of foreign currency, and (f) the price level (6)_____ (established by the Bretton Woods agreement; in the United States) relative to the price levels in foreign nations.

If real interest rates in the United States rise relative to interest rates in Great Britain, for instance, the British will increase their (7)_____ (supply of, demand for) U.S. dollars in the foreign exchange markets in order to purchase higher-yielding U.S. financial assets. As the demand for dollars rises relative to the supply of dollars, the exchange rate of the dollar (8)_____ (falls, rises). The dollar will be exchanged for more British pounds than previously. Conversely, the British pound will be exchanged for (9)_____ (more, fewer) U.S. dollars. The dollar (10)_____ (depreciates, appreciates) and the pound (11)_____ (depreciates, appreciates). British goods valued in dollars fall in price, and U.S. goods valued in British pounds increase in price. As a result, U.S. goods exported to Great Britain become (12)_____ (more, less) price competitive with British domestic output. Likewise, in the United States, British imported goods become (13)_____ (more, less) expensive relative to U.S. domestic output.

The (14)_____(nominal, real) exchange rate is the price of a unit of one nation's currency in terms of a unit of a foreign currency. The (15) _____ (nominal, real) exchange rate is the sacrifice of goods and services produced in their own countries that foreign buyers must make when they use their own currency to purchase a unit or the currency of another nation. If the real interest rate increases, the real exchange rate of the dollar (16) _____ (decreases, increases), reducing the attractiveness of U.S. exports to foreigners. Net exports fall, causing aggregate demand to decrease. Aggregate supply, however, increases because of the decline in the cost of imported inputs. According to the aggregate supply and demand model presented in a previous chapter, real GDP and the price level will fall. Just the opposite is expected if the real exchange rate (17) _____ (falls, rises). Empirical evidence indicates that it may take as long as 2 years before changes in real exchange rate significantly influence import prices.

The foreign exchange market described above is a free market often referred to as a (18)_____ (fixed, floating or flexible) exchange rate market. Prior to the 1930s, however, exchange rates were fixed within narrow limits. This was accomplished by the gold standard, under which currencies were convertible into (19)_____ (gold, the U.S. dollar) at fixed rates. This meant that each currency had (20)_____ (several exchange rates, a unique exchange rate) relative to every other currency. Exchange rates remained fixed as long as the gold price of each currency remained (21)_____ (flexible, unchanged). Nations concerned with domestic macroeconomic problems would often devalue their currency rather than allow an outflow of gold that would reduce the nation's money stock. Devaluation alters exchange rates, however. This system was replaced in 1944 by the (22)_____ (managed float, Bretton Woods system) in which the values of foreign currencies were tied to the U.S. dollar rather than to gold. The United States abandoned its role as the guarantor of exchange rate stability when it chose to suspend convertibility of the dollar into gold in (23)_____ (1971, 1961). In 1973, the United States and other nations abandoned the fixed exchange rate system in favor of the (24)_____ (modified gold standard, flexible exchange rate system). Today the foreign exchange market is characterized as a managed float rather than a freely floating or flexible exchange rate system. The Federal Reserve System and foreign central banks intervene in the market to effect desirable changes in exchange rates.

The balance of payments for a nation shows the net exchange of the nation's currency for foreign currencies from all transactions between that nation and foreign nations in a given year. In the United States the balance of payments consists of the current account and the capital account. The (25)_____ (capital, current) account shows the effect of the volume of goods and services traded on international markets, including changes in investment income and other miscellaneous transactions. The balance (26)_____ (on the current account, of trade) represents the difference between the value of merchandise exports and imports. The balance (27)_____ (on the current account, of trade) is more comprehensive in that it measures U.S. net exports for the year, including transactions involving services, investment income, and transfers. As recently as 1981, the United States had a surplus in its current account balance but had a large merchandise trade deficit.

In 1994, the current account (28)_____ (deficit, surplus) was $151 billion. When the current account is in deficit, the United States must sell assets or borrow to finance the deficit. These transactions are shown in the (29)_____ (capital, current) account. As foreigners purchase U.S. financial and real assets at a rate greater than U.S. citizens purchase those assets abroad, the net inflow of dollars just offsets the current account deficit.

■ KEY TERMS REVIEW

Write the key term from the list below next to its definition.

Key Terms

Foreign exchange rate
Foreign exchange market
Foreign exchange
Currency appreciation
Currency depreciation
Purchasing power parity
Gold standard
Balance on current account
  of the balance of
  payments

Bretton Woods system
International Monetary
Fund (IMF)
Special drawing right (SDR)
International balance of
  payments
Balance of trade
Managed float
Real exchange rate
Nominal exchange rate

Definition

1. _____: the price of a unit of one nation's currency in terms of a unit of a foreign currency.

2. _____: the price of one nation's monetary unit in terms of the monetary unit of another nation.

3. _____: the sacrifice of goods and services produced in their own countries that foreign buyers must make when they use their own currency to purchase a unit of the currency of another nation.

4. _____: a market in which buyers and sellers of bank deposits denominated in the monetary units of many nations exchange their funds.

5. _____: an international monetary system that required that currencies be converted into gold at a fixed price.

6. _____: the money of one nation held by citizens of another nation either as currency or as deposits in banks.

7. _____: describes the current international monetary system, under which central banks affect supply of and demand for currencies in ways that influence equilibrium in foreign exchange markets.

8. _____: occurs when there is an increase in the number of units of one nation's currency that must be given up to purchase each unit of another nation's currency.

9. _____: established under the Bretton Woods agreement; set rules for the international monetary system to make loans to nations that lack international reserves of dollars.

10. _____: occurs when there is a decrease in the number of units of one nation's currency that must be given up to purchase each unit of another nation's currency.

11. _____: an international monetary system developed in 1944 and based on fixed exchange rates, with the value of foreign currencies tied to the U.S. dollar.

12. _____: a principle that states that the exchange rate between any two currencies tends to adjust to reflect changes in the price levels in the two nations.

13. _____: a paper substitute for gold that is created by the International Monetary Fund and is distributed to member nations to use as international reserves.

14. _____: a statement showing the net exchange rate of a nation's currency for foreign currencies from all transactions between that nation and foreign nations in a given year.

15. _____: the difference between the value of merchandise exported by a nation's firms and the nation's imports of foreign-produced goods.

16. _____: measures U.S. net exports for the year, including transactions involving services, investment income, and transfers.

■ CONCEPT REVIEW

Concept 2: *Foreign exchange rates, foreign exchange markets, and international balance of payments*

1. The figure below represents a foreign exchange market for the U.S. dollar and the Canadian dollar.

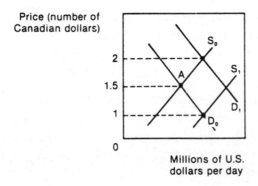

Price (number of Canadian dollars)

Millions of U.S. dollars per day

a. Given demand curve Do and supply curve So, the equilibrium exchange rate between the Canadian and U.S. dollar is 1 U.S. dollar = _____ Canadian dollars or alternatively, 1 Canadian dollar = _____ U.S. dollars.

b. A U.S. good valued at $1000 in U.S. dollars would cost _____ Canadian dollars. A Canadian good valued at 100 Canadian dollars would cost _____ U.S. dollars.

2. List six factors that influence the exchange rate of the dollar.

a. _____

b. _____

c. _____

d. _____

e. _____

f. _____

3. Referring to the figure above, suppose real interest rates in the United States rise relative to interest rates abroad, causing the demand for dollars to increase to D1.

a. What are the new exchange rates?

(1) 1 U.S. dollar = _____ Canadian dollars

(2) 1 Canadian dollar = _____ U.S. dollars

b. The U.S. dollar has _____, and the Canadian dollar has _____.

c. A U.S. good valued at 1000 U.S. dollars now costs _____ Canadian dollars. A Canadian good valued at 100 Canadian dollars now costs _____ U.S. dollars.

d. U.S. goods become _____ price competitive in Canada, and Canadian goods become _____ price competitive in the United States.

4. Referring to the figure above, given the initial demand curve, Do, assume that U.S. firms increase their imports from Canada, causing the supply of U.S. dollars to shift to S1.

a. What are the new exchange rates?

(1) 1 U.S. dollar = _____ Canadian dollars

(2) 1 Canadian dollar = _____ U.S. dollar

b. The U.S. dollar has _____, and the Canadian dollar has _____.

c. A U.S. good valued at 1000 U.S. dollars now costs _____ Canadian dollars. A Canadian good valued at 100 Canadian dollars now costs _____ U.S. dollars.

d. U.S. goods become _____ price competitive in Canada, and Canadian goods become _____ price competitive in the United States.

5. Identify which of the following represent a *capital account* and which represent a *current account* transaction in the balance of payments and state whether the transaction results in an *inflow* or *outflow* of U.S. dollars.

a. U.S. exports of services increase.

b. Foreigners purchase U.S. Treasury bills.

c. Automobile imports into the United States increase.

d. Transfers to foreigners increase.

e. U.S. firms purchase factories abroad.

f. Rich oil sheiks purchase Texas ranch land.

g. Hitachi receives income from its U.S. plants.

h. Foreigners increase imports of U.S. merchandise goods.

i. U.S. citizens purchase stock in foreign enterprises.

	Capital or Current Account?	*Inflow or Outflow?*
a.	_____	_____
b.	_____	_____
c.	_____	_____
d.	_____	_____
e.	_____	_____
f.	_____	_____
g.	_____	_____
h.	_____	_____
i.	_____	_____

■ MASTERY TEST

Select the best answer.

1. A market in which buyers and sellers of bank deposits denominated in the monetary units of many nations exchange their funds is known as the:
   a. loanable funds market.
   b. money market.
   c. capital market.
   d. foreign exchange market.

2. If the price of a dollar in terms of units of a foreign currency is above the equilibrium exchange rate, a _____ exists, which will put _____ pressure on the equilibrium exchange rate of the dollar.
   a. shortage, downward
   b. shortage, upward
   c. surplus, downward
   d. surplus, upward

3. If a $10,000 U.S.-made automobile is sold in France and the exchange rate between the dollar and the franc is $1 = 8 francs, the U.S. automobile sold in France will cost _____ francs.
   a. 20,000
   b. 40,000
   c. 60,000
   d. 80,000
   e. 100,000

4. The exchange rate between the dollar and the franc is $1 = 8 francs, and the price of a bottle of imported French wine is $5. If the exchange rate changes to $1 = 4 francs, the dollar price of the French wine _____ to $_____.
   a. falls, $2.50
   b. rises, $10
   c. rises, $20
   d. does not change

5. An increase in foreign demand for U.S. exports will _____ demand for the dollar, causing the dollar to _____.
   a. decrease, appreciate
   b. increase, depreciate
   c. increase, appreciate
   d. decrease, depreciate

6. An increase in U.S. demand for imports will _____ the _____ U.S. dollars, causing the dollar to _____.
   a. increase, demand for, appreciate
   b. increase, supply of, appreciate
   c. decrease, supply of, depreciate
   d. decrease, demand for, appreciate
   e. increase, supply of, depreciate

7. If real interest rates in the United States rise relative to interest rates abroad, the _____ dollars will _____, causing the dollar to _____.
   a. demand for, increase, appreciate
   b. demand for, increase, depreciate
   c. supply of, decrease, depreciate
   d. supply of, increase, appreciate

8. If the rate of inflation in the United States rises relative to the rate of inflation in foreign nations, U.S. exports _____ and imports _____, causing the demand for dollars to _____ and the supply of dollars to _____.
   a. increase, decrease, rise, fall
   b. decrease, increase, fall, rise
   c. increase, increase, fall, fall
   d. decrease, decrease, rise, rise

9. The price of a unit of one nation's currency in terms of a unit of a foreign currency is called:
   a. the nominal exchange rate.
   b. the real exchange rate.
   c. foreign exchange.
   d. purchasing power parity.
   e. None of the above.

10. Empirical evidence suggests that:
    a. import prices respond very quickly to changes in exchange rates.
    b. net exports respond within a year to changes in the exchange rate of the dollar.
    c. import prices are slow to respond to changes in exchange rates, taking up to 2 years to be affected.
    d. there is an immediate link between exchange rates and import prices.

11. The Bretton Woods agreement:
    a. represented a new international monetary system.
    b. tied the value of foreign currencies not to gold but to the dollar.
    c. was established in 1944.
    d. also established the International Monetary Fund.
    e. All of the above.

12. The present international monetary system is best described as a:
    a. fixed exchange rate system.
    b. purchasing power parity system.
    c. flexible exchange rate system.
    d. managed float.

13. Which of the following summarizes the transactions involving the international exchange of goods and services, investment income, and other miscellaneous transactions?
    a. Balance of trade
    b. Statistical discrepancy
    c. Current account
    d. Capital account

14. Which of the following is the difference between the value of merchandise exported and merchandise imported?
    a. Balance of trade
    b. Balance on the current account
    c. Budget balance
    d. Balance of payments

15. Which of the following measures net exports for the year, including transactions involving services, investment income, and transfers?
    a. Balance of trade
    b. Balance on the current account
    c. Budget balance
    d. Balance of payments

16. When the current account is in deficit, the capital account must:
    a. be balanced.
    b. be zero.
    c. not add to the deficit.
    d. have an equal and offsetting surplus.

Answer the following three questions based upon the data below.

(Millions of dollars per day)

French Francs (per dollar)	*Quantity of Dollars Demanded*	*Quantity of Dollars Supplied*
9	10	50
7	20	40
5	30	30
3	40	20
1	50	10

17. Which of the following is the equilibrium exchange rate between the dollar and the franc?
    a. 1 franc = 1 dollar
    b. 1 franc = 20 cents
    c. 1 franc = 14 cents
    d. 1 dollar = 5 francs
    e. B and d

18. If the quantity of dollars supplied increases by 20 million dollars at each exchange rate, what happens to the equilibrium exchange rate?
    a. The dollar appreciates to 1 franc = 7 dollars
    b. The dollar depreciates to 1 dollar = 3 francs
    c. The franc depreciates to 1 franc = 33 1/3 cents
    d. The exchange rate remains unchanged at 1 dollar = 7 francs

19. An increase in the demand for American goods by the French _____ the demand for dollars by 20 million dollars at each exchange rate and causes the international value of the dollar to _____ to _____.
    a. increases, appreciate, 1 dollar = 7 francs
    b. increases, depreciate, 1 dollar = 3 francs
    c. decreases, appreciate, 1 dollar = 5 francs
    d. decreases, depreciate, 1 dollar = 3 francs

20. If the rate of inflation increases more in France than in the United States, the franc will likely:
    a. appreciate.
    b. depreciate.
    c. remain unchanged.
    d. depreciate until the dollar becomes stronger.

21. Assume that the balance of payments current account is in deficit. Which of the following will likely occur if domestic interest rates rise relative to foreign interest rates?
    a. The demand for dollars by foreigners will increase.
    b. The dollar will appreciate.
    c. Net exports will fall.
    d. The current account deficit will increase.
    e. All of the above

■ THINK IT THROUGH

1. How can the Fed, through domestic monetary policy, cause the U.S. dollar to depreciate?

2. How can the Fed, through direct intervention in foreign exchange markets, cause the U.S. dollar to depreciate?

CHAPTER ANSWERS

The Chapter in Brief

1. Foreign exchange rate is 2. Foreign exchange market 3. A demand for 4. Surplus
5. Shortage 6. In the United States 7. Demand for 8. Rises 9. Fewer 10. Appreciates
11. Depreciates 12. Less 13. Less 14. nominal 15. real 16. increases 17. falls 18. Floating or
flexible 19. Gold 20. A unique exchange rate 21. Unchanged 22. Bretton Woods system 23.
1971 24. Flexible exchange rate system 25. Current 26. Of trade 27. On the current
account 28. Deficit 29. Capital

Key Terms Review

1. Nominal exchange rate 2. Foreign exchange rate 3. Real exchange rate 4. Foreign exchange
market 5. Gold standard 6. Foreign exchange 7. Managed float 8. Currency appreciation
9. International Monetary Fund (IMF) 10. Currency depreciation 11. Bretton Woods system
12. Purchasing power parity 13. Special drawing right (SDR) 14. International balance of payments
15. Balance of trade 16. Balance on the current account of the balance of payments

Concept Review

1. a. 1.5, 2/3
   b. 1,500, $66.67
2. a. Foreign demand for U.S. exports
   b. U.S. demand for imports
   c. Real interest rates in the United States relative to those in foreign nations
   d. Profitability of direct investment in U.S. businesses and real estate relative to profitability
       of similar investments in foreign nations
   e. Expectations of an increase in the price of the dollar in terms of foreign currency
   f. The price level in the United States relative to the price levels in foreign nations
3. a. 2, 1/2
   b. Appreciated, depreciated
   c. 2,000; 50
   d. Less, more
4. a. 1, 1
   b. Depreciated, appreciated
   c. 1,000; 100
   d. More, less
5. a. Current, inflow
   b. Capital, inflow
   c. Current, outflow
   d. Current, outflow
   e. Capital, outflow
   f. Capital, inflow
   g. Current, outflow
   h. Current, inflow
   i. Capital, outflow

Mastery Test

1. d 2. c 3. d 4. b 5. c 6. e 7. a 8. b 9. a 10. c 11. e 12. d 13. c 14. a 15. b 16. d 17. e 18. b 19. a 20. b 21. e

Think It Through

1. If the Fed pursues an expansionary monetary policy that reduces the real rate of interest in the United States relative to interest rates abroad, Americans will increase their demand for foreign currencies by supplying more dollars to the international foreign exchange markets in order to purchase higher-yielding foreign financial assets. The increase in the supply of dollars relative to demand will cause the dollar to depreciate. The expansionary monetary policy will also increase the nation's income, causing imports to increase. In order to increase imports, Americans must supply dollars to acquire foreign exchange to purchase the foreign goods. This too will cause the dollar to depreciate. If the expansionary monetary policy is also inflationary such that the rate of inflation in the United States rises relative to foreign rates of inflation, U.S. exports will fall and imports will rise. This will cause foreign demand for the dollar to fall and the supply of dollars to increase, also resulting in depreciation of the dollar.

2. If the Fed wished to depreciate the dollar, it could purchase foreign currencies with its dollar holdings, causing the demand for foreign currencies to rise and the supply of dollars to increase. This in turn would cause the dollar to depreciate relative to the foreign currencies purchased by the Fed.